NUT**SHELLS**

Tort

YOU'VE GOT IT CRACKED

Nutcases – your essential revision and starter guides

- Provides you with in-depth case analysis of the facts, principles and decision of the most important cases in an area of law

- Incorporates colour to help distinguish cases and legislation and aid ease of use

- Presents the text in bite-size chunks and includes bullets where appropriate to aid navigation, assimilation and retention of information

- Breaks the subject down into key topics to enable you to easily identify and concentrate on particular topics

- Opens each chapter with a short introduction to outline the key concepts covered and condense complex and important information

- Highlights Court of Appeal and House of Lords cases to enable you to easily identify the relative significance of the cases examined

- Includes boxed "think points" at the end of each chapter providing further case analysis

- Fully indexed by individual cases and topics

Available from all good booksellers

NUT**SHELLS**

Tort

NINTH EDITION

by
VERA BERMINGHAM
Director of Studies,
Kingston Law School

SWEET & MAXWELL      THOMSON REUTERS

First Edition – 1987
Second Edition – 1990
Third Edition – 1993
Fourth Edition – 1996
Fifth Edition – 1999
Reprinted 2000
Sixth Edition – 2002
Reprinted 2003
Seventh Edition – 2005
Eight Edition – 2008
Ninth Edition – 2011

Published in 2011 by Sweet & Maxwell, 100 Avenue Road, London NW3 3PF
Part of Thomson Reuters (Professional) UK Limited
(Registered in England & Wales, Company No 1679046.
Registered Office and address for service:
Aldgate House, 33 Aldgate High Street, London EC3N 1DL)

*For further information on our products and services, visit
www.sweetandmaxwell.co.uk

Typeset by YHT
Printed in Great Britain by Krips

No natural forests were destroyed to make this product;
only farmed timber was used and re-planted

A CIP catalogue record for this book is available from the British Library.

ISBN 978-0-41404-483-8

Thomson Reuters and the Thomson Reuters logo are trademarks of Thomson Reuters.
Sweet & Maxwell ® is a registered trademark of Thomson Reuters (Professional) UK
Limited

Crown copyright material is reproduced with the permission of the Controller
of HMSO and the Queen's Printer for Scotland.

Contents

CONTENTS

Using this Book

Welcome to our new look NUTSHELLS revision series. We have revamped and improved the existing design and layout and added new features, according to student feedback.

NEW DETAILED TABLE OF CONTENTS
for easy navigation.

REDESIGNED TABLES OF CASES AND LEGISLATION for easy reference.

NEW CHAPTER INTRODUCTIONS to outline
the key concepts covered and condense
complex and important information.

Other Statutory R...

NATIONAL MINIMUM WAGE AC1

The National Minimum Wage Act 19
minimum hourly rate of pay for all
State to determine and amer
are set: one

**DEFINITION CHECKPOINTS AND
EXPLANATION OF KEY CASES**
to highlight important information.

the HL reversed the
not customary and did need

DEFINITION CHECKPOINT
Procession
The **Public Order Act 1986**, s.16 de.
sion in a public place. This is not ov
nition can be found in the case of *Flo*
at 502, where Lord Goddard C.J. sta
body of persons: it is a body, of pe

DEFINITION CHECKPOINT
Assembly
The **Public Order Act 1986**
mbly of two or

KEY CASE

CARMICHAEL V NATIONAL POW
Mrs Carmichael worked as a gu
required" basis, showing group
tion. She worked some hours m
wore a company uniform, was s
vehicle, and enjoyed many of th
question for the court to determ
"umbrella" or "global" emplov
which she worked and the ir

Held: (HL) During th
her dut

DIAGRAMS, FLOWCHARTS AND OTHER DIAGRAMMATIC REPRESENTATION to clarify and condense complex and important information and break up the text.

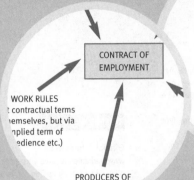

Figure 1 Court and Tribunal System

House of Lords ━ ━ ━

COURT OF APPEAL
(CIVIL DIVISION)

EMPLOYMENT APPEAL
TRIBUNAL

CONTRACT OF
EMPLOYMENT

WORK RULES
t contractual terms
iemselves, but via
nplied term of
edience etc.)

PRODUCERS OF
COLLECTIVE

END OF CHAPTER REVISION CHECKLISTS outlining what you should now know and understand.

Chapter Checklist

You should now know and unders:

- the three heads of claim for
- issues regarding the choice o
- the role of the independent e:
- what is meant by "pay".

QUESTION AND AN'

END OF CHAPTER QUESTION AND ANSWER SECTION with advice on relating knowledge to examination performance, how to approach the question, how to structure the answer, the pitfalls (and how to avoid them!) and how to get the best marks.

QUESTION AND ANSWER

The Question

David and Emily are employed as machi worked for them for one and a half yea

Emily discovers that David earns £9.0′ paid £8.50 per hour. She also disc employed by a subsidiary of XCo ir

HANDY HINTS AND USEFUL WEBSITES
– revision and examination tips and
advice relating to the subject features
at the end of the book, along with a list of useful websites.

HANDY HINTS

Examination questions in employme
either essay questions or problem ques
format and in what is required of the ex
of question in turn.

Students usually prefer one type
normally opting for the problem ques
examinations are usually set in a wa
least one of each style of question

Very few, if any, questions
ows about a topic, and it
make a p

USEFUL WEBSITES

Official Information
www.parliament.uk—very user-friendly.
www.direct.gov.uk—portal for governm
www.opsi.gov.uk—Office of Public Secto
and statutory instruments available
www.dca.gov.uk—Department for Con
www.dca.gov.uk/peoples-rights/hum
Unit at the Department for Con
www.homeoffice.gov.uk/police
the **Police and Criminal**

NEW COLOUR CODING throughout to
help distinguish cases and legislation
from the narrative. At the first mention,
cases are highlighted in colour and
italicised and legislation is highlighted
in colour and emboldened.

w has d
are an ethnic group (*Seia*
ypsies are an ethnic group (*CRE*
Rastafarians are not an ethnic group
ment [1993] I.R.L.R. 284)
(d) Jehovah's Witnesses are not an ethnic o
Norwich City College case 1502237/97)
(e) RRA covers the Welsh (*Gwynedd CC v Jone*
(f) Both the Scots and the English are covere
"national origins" but not by "ethnic or
Board v Power [1997], *Boyce v British Ai*

It should be noted that Sikhs, Jews, Je
ians are also protected on
Equality (Religion or

Table of Cases

Table of Statutes

Trespass to the Person

INTRODUCTION

Trespass to the person may take one of three forms: assault, battery and false imprisonment. Trespass will lie for any direct and immediate inter-ference with the person of the claimant and is actionable without proof of damage. As to the distinction between direct and indirect interference, the classic illustration is that given in *Reynolds v Clarke* (1725) of a man who throws a log into the highway. If the log hits someone, that, it was said, would be a trespass, but if it merely obstructs the highway and someone later trips over it, that would be indirect and the plaintiff would have to sue in case (now the tort of negligence) and prove damage.

As a result of modern developments, an action in trespass now requires deliberate, not negligent harm and attention focuses upon the nature of the defendant's conduct. In *Fowler v Lanning* (HC, 1959) it was held that in an action of unintentional trespass to the person, the plaintiff had the burden of proving negligence. This was approved in *Letang v Cooper* (CA, 1965) where Lord Denning M.R. went so far as to suggest that where the interference is negligent, as opposed to intentional, the proper cause of action is negligence and not trespass. Support for this view is to be found in *Wilson v Pringle* (CA, 1986).

BATTERY

A battery may be defined as the direct and intentional application of physical force to the person of another without lawful justification. It is the act of making physical contact which must be intentional and there is certainly no requirement of an intention to cause injury. If A, intending to strike B, misses and hits C by mistake, it has long been a principle of the criminal law that A commits an offence (known as the doctrine of transferred intent). The same principle applies to a civil action—in *Bici v Ministry of Defence* (2004), transferred intent applied in the case of a peace-keeping soldier in Kosovo who shot an unintended victim.

Figure 1: Trespass to the person: the present position

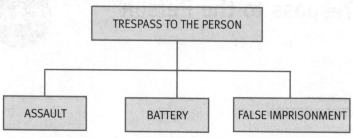

TRESPASS TO THE PERSON

ASSAULT   BATTERY   FALSE IMPRISONMENT

THE PRESENT POSITION
(a) An intentional act, if sufficiently direct, may be actionable in
    trespass without proof of damage. Negligence may be
    equally appropriate where the act causes unintended but
    foreseeable harm.
(b) An unintentional act which causes foreseeable harm may be
    actionable in negligence.
(c) An intention to cause harm, though not sufficiently direct to
    constitute a trespass, may be actionable under the principle
    in *Wilkinson v Downton* (HC, 1897; see later in this
    Chapter).

DEFINITION CHECKPOINT

What constitutes "force" for the purposes of battery?
Any physical contact, however trivial, may constitute "force" for the
purposes of the tort notwithstanding the absence of bodily harm,
subject to the proviso that the ordinary and sometimes inevitable
physical contacts of everyday existence (e.g. jostling in a crowded
place or touching a person for the purpose of engaging his attention)
are not actionable. This qualification has been explained on the ground
either that the plaintiff impliedly consents to such contact or, according
to *Collins v Wilcock* (HC, 1984), that cases of this nature are to be
treated as "falling within a general exception embracing all physical
contact which is generally regarded as acceptable in the ordinary
conduct of daily life".

It was further held in *Wilson v Pringle* (CA, 1986) that the act must be
"hostile" but, although this accords with the dictum in *Cole v Turner* (1704)
that the least touching of another "in anger" is a battery, no clear indication
was given as to the meaning of "hostile", save to say that it was not
necessarily to be equated with ill-will or malevolence, the existence or
otherwise of which was a question of fact.

What is "hostile" intent?

In *F v West Berkshire Health Authority* (HL, 1989) Lord Goff doubted whether hostility was a requirement in battery and said that to hold otherwise would be difficult to reconcile with the principle that any touching of another's body is, in the absence of lawful excuse, a battery. Thus, he said, a prank which misfires, an over-friendly slap on the back, or surgical treatment in the mistaken belief that the plaintiff has consented, are prima facie actionable. However, he pointed out that physical conduct (such as jostling in a crowded street) which is generally accepted in the ordinary conduct of everyday life would not constitute a battery.

Apart from the more obvious examples of striking another with a fist or weapon, battery may take many forms. Thus, to spit in a person's face or to throw water over them, or to seize something from their hand, may be actionable wrongs. The defendant's act must be a positive one, voluntarily done; merely to obstruct the claimant's passage by standing still is not sufficient (*Innes v Wylie* (1844)), just as there is no battery if the act is done in a state of complete automatism. However, in *Fagan v Metropolitan Police Commissioner* (HC, 1969) the defendant was held liable for criminal assault in respect of what appeared, on the face of it, to be a mere omission to act. The accused in that case accidentally drove his car on to the foot of a police officer and then deliberately delayed in removing the vehicle. One judge dissented on the ground that at the time of driving onto the officer's foot the defendant had no *mens rea*, and that after forming an intention to allow the car to remain there he did no positive act. The reasoning of the majority was that, where the defendant's act is a continuing one, the *mens rea* need not be present at the inception of that act but could, at some later time, be superimposed upon it.

ASSAULT

An assault may be defined as an act which directly and intentionally causes the claimant reasonably to apprehend a battery is about to be inflicted by the defendant. Although the term "assault" is popularly used to include a battery, a person may be liable for an assault even though no battery is committed, for all that is required is the reasonable apprehension by the claimant of immediate violence. For example, to shake one's fist in another's face, or to aim a blow which is intercepted, is an assault, but the claimant must reasonably believe that the defendant has the means of carrying the threat into effect, so that there is no assault where the claimant is in such a position as to be inaccessible to physical force.

DEFINITION CHECKPOINT

Fear of an "immediate" battery

The defendant's fear of an immediate battery must be reasonable. In *Thomas v National Union of Mineworkers* (HC, 1985) there was no assault when picketing miners made violent gestures to working colleagues who were being transported across the picket line under police escort because there was no danger of an immediate battery.

Just as there may be an assault without a battery, so there may be a battery without assault, as where the plaintiff is struck from behind, or whilst asleep, by an unseen aggressor. Even if the defendant is for some reason unable to carry out the threat or equally has no intention of so doing, there seems to be no logical reason why he should not be guilty of an assault, provided that his act induces in the claimant a reasonable apprehension that force is about to be inflicted upon him. A commonly cited illustration of this problem is that of pointing an unloaded gun at the claimant. In the civil case of *Blake v Barnard* (1840) it appears to have been held that this would not constitute an assault, although the decision has been explained on the ground that the plaintiff, having averred that a loaded gun was pointed at him, then sought a verdict on the basis that it was unloaded. In the criminal case of *R v St George* (1840) the court was clearly of the view that it would be a common law assault to point an unloaded gun at the plaintiff (unless he knows it to be unloaded), and this would seem to be correct in principle.

As with battery there must be a positive act by the defendant, so that passive obstruction unaccompanied by any threatening move or gesture cannot amount to an assault (*Innes v Wylie* (1844)). Words which accompany a threatening act may negate what would otherwise be an assault where they clearly indicate no intention to carry out the threat (*Tuberville v Savage* (1669)). A conditional threat accompanied by gestures may constitute an assault, at least where the defendant has no authority to require compliance with the condition (*Read v Coker* (1853)).

FALSE IMPRISONMENT

This may be defined as an act which directly and intentionally places a total restraint upon the claimant's freedom of movement without lawful justification. The term "false" means wrongful and "imprisonment" signifies that the claimant has been deprived of their right to go where they will. Thus, a person may be imprisoned in their own home, in a motor car, or even in a public street, as long as their movements have been constrained by the defendant's will. Such constraint may be evidenced by the use of actual physical force amounting to an assault and battery, or simply by the reasonable apprehension of such force. However, whilst the wrong of false imprisonment is often that of assault also, it is not necessarily so. For example, to lock a person in a room into which she or he has freely and voluntarily wandered is a false imprisonment but clearly not assault, although it is not clear whether a mere negligent lack of awareness of the claimant's presence in the room would suffice for the purposes of the tort.

The act of imprisonment

It has been seen that there need be no imprisonment in the ordinary sense of the word. An unlawful arrest is in itself a false imprisonment, as is the continued detention of one who, though originally in lawful custody, has acquired a right to be discharged. On the other hand, an arrest which is initially unlawful on the ground that no reason was given for the arrest may subsequently become lawful as from the time a reason is given (*Lewis v Chief Constable of South Wales* (CA, 1991)). The deprivation of the claimant's liberty must, however, be complete, and a mere partial interference with their freedom of movement is not an imprisonment.

KEY CASE

THE RESTRAINT MUST BE TOTAL

In *Bird v Jones* (1845), as part of a boat race the defendants wrongfully closed off part of a public footpath over Hammersmith Bridge. The plaintiff (Bird) climbed into the enclosure but was refused permission to proceed and was told that he might make a detour by crossing to the other side of the bridge. Because there was another route which Bird could have taken there was held to be no false imprisonment. Provided the restraint is total, how large the area of confinement can be must depend on the circumstances of the case.

An imprisonment usually involves some positive act, and there is generally no duty to assist another to obtain their liberty. In *Herd v Weardale Steel, Coke & Coal Co* (HL, 1915) the plaintiff miner refused to do certain work in the mine which he believed to be dangerous and demanded that the defendants take him to the surface. The defendants refused for some 20 minutes to do so and, in an action for false imprisonment, it was held that the defendants' omission to accede to the plaintiff's demands did not amount to an imprisonment. The plaintiff had voluntarily accepted a restriction upon his liberty by initially going into the mine, and it was he who was in breach of contract by refusing to complete the shift.

DEFINITION CHECKPOINT

No liability for a mere failure to act

In *Iqbal v Prison Officers Association* (2010), the claimant did not succeed in false imprisonment because a mere failure of the prison officers to work at the prison involved no positive action on their part. Here, a sudden unannounced strike in breach of contract by prison officers meant that prisoners spent an extra six hours of their day locked in their cell. Following *Herd* the Court of Appeal held that since the strike was a mere failure to act there was no liability and, as a general principle, a defendant was not to be held liable in tort for the result of his inaction unless there was a specific duty to act, arising out of the particular relationship between the claimant and defendant.

It may be that the defendants could have been liable had they been in breach of their own contractual duty. To similar effect is *Robinson v Balmain New Ferry Co Ltd* (PC, 1910) where the plaintiff, having paid a penny to enter the defendants' wharf to catch a ferry, discovered that he had just missed one and wished to leave. He was directed to the exit turnstile where he refused to pay a further penny which, as was clearly stated on a notice-board, was chargeable upon leaving. It was held that there was no false imprisonment because the plaintiff had entered the wharf upon the terms of a definite contract by which the parties contemplated that he would take the ferry, and, since there was no agreement as to the terms on which he might go back, the defendants were not obliged to make the exit from their premises gratuitous but were entitled to impose a reasonable condition for the privilege.

There are numerous instances in which a person may voluntarily accept a degree of restraint upon their freedom of movement, but the above cases do not necessarily support the proposition that that person cannot thereafter revoke their consent and demand that the restraint be terminated, even though that would put them in breach of contract. Whether the defendant is obliged to comply with the demand will presumably depend, in particular, upon the degree of inconvenience caused in so doing.

A question which has recently been considered by the courts is whether a prisoner can be said to retain a degree of residual liberty such as to enable an action in false imprisonment to be maintained against the prison governor if he or she is further unlawfully restrained (e.g. by segregation from other prisoners in breach of the Prison Rules). The question received a negative answer in *Hague v Deputy Governor of Parkhurst Prison and Weldon v Home Office* (HL, 1991). Similarly, a remand prisoner detained after expiry of the statutorily prescribed time limit cannot sue the prison governor for false imprisonment, since only an order of the court can terminate the period of custody (*Olotu v Home Office* (CA, 1997)). Furthermore, no action for false imprisonment lies where the detention is carried out under an order of the court. In *Quinland v Governor of Swaleside Prison* (2003) the judge made an arithmetical error in calculating the claimant's sentence but his appeal against his sentence was not heard until after his release. The governor was not liable for false imprisonment because until the court order was set aside it justified the claimant's detention. Nevertheless, if the governor has authority to release the prisoner without an order of the court to terminate the period of custody, there may be liability.

KEY CASE

INTENTION TO RESTRICT MOVEMENT IS REQUIRED BUT IT IS NOT NECESSARY FOR THE DEFENDANT TO HAVE INTENDED TO ACT UNLAWFULLY
In *R. v Governor of Brockhill Prison, Ex p. Evans* (HL, 2001), the prison governor was held liable in false imprisonment to a prisoner kept in prison for 59 days longer than she should have been because of the miscalculation of the date for her release. Although the error arose because of a subsequent judicial reinterpretation of the law and the governor had not been at fault, because it is a tort of strict liability, the prisoner was entitled to compensation for false imprisonment.

The plaintiff's knowledge
In *Meering v Grahame-White Aviation Co Ltd* (CA, 1919) it was held to be immaterial that the plaintiff was unaware of the fact of his detention, though this conflicted with the earlier decision in *Herring v Boyle* (1834). In *Murray v Ministry of Defence* (HL, 1988) the House of Lords approved Meering, but expressed the view that a plaintiff who did not know of the detention would normally receive only nominal damages.

Means of escape
If a reasonable means of escape is available to the claimant there may be no false imprisonment. An escape route will very likely be unreasonable if it exposes the claimant to a risk of injury. If the claimant is unaware that such a route exists, the question is probably whether a reasonable man would have realised that there was an available outlet.

INTENTIONAL PHYSICAL HARM

Where the defendant wilfully does an act, or makes a statement, which is calculated to cause, and actually does cause, physical harm to the claimant, he is liable in tort.

KEY CASE

LIABILITY FOR PSYCHIATRIC INJURY (WITHOUT PHYSICAL FORCE) AS THE RESULT OF "INTENTIONAL" CONDUCT

In *Wilkinson v Downton* (HC, 1897), conduct which could amount to a battery was extended to include situations where no contact or physical force is used. In this case the defendant was held liable for falsely telling the plaintiff, by way of a perverted practical joke, that her husband had met with a serious accident, in consequence of which she suffered physical illness through nervous shock.

Wilkinson v Downton was approved in *Janvier v Sweeney* (CA, 1919) which also concerned a false statement causing shock, and both cases were relied upon in *Khorasandjian v Bush* (CA, 1993) as authority for the grant of an injunction where the defendant's campaign of harassment by means, inter alia, of threatening telephone calls was likely to injure the plaintiff's health, even though at the time of the action no damage had in fact been caused. In *Hunter v Canary Wharf Ltd* (1997) the House of Lords was prepared to preserve the rule in Wilkinson v Downton as a general cause of action but it anticipated that claimants alleging harassment ought to rely on new statutory provisions contained in the Protection from Harassment Act 1997 rather than the common law.

KEY CASES

CONDUCT "CALCULATED TO CAUSE HARM"

The meaning of "calculated to cause harm" has been considered in two cases which emphasise the need to show that, under the principle in *Wilkinson v Downton*, there must be both actual harm and an intent to cause damage.

- In *Wong v Parkside Health NHS Trust* (CA 2003), a campaign of rudeness and unfriendliness by colleagues was not regarded as the intentional infliction of harm, and in refusing to develop a general tort of harassment from the rule in *Wilkinson v Downton* the Court of Appeal held that there was no tort of intentional harassment which gave a remedy for anything less than physical damage or a recognisable psychiatric injury.

- In *Wainwright v Home Office* (HL, 2003), a mother and son visiting a family member in prison, who were strip-searched in a manner which breached the Prison Service Rules, claimed for breach of privacy and the intentional infliction of harm. The court said that even if there was an intention to cause harm, *Wilkinson v Downton* was not authority for the proposition that damages for distress falling short of psychiatric injury were recoverable. In this case, even if damages were recoverable, the prison officers' deviation from the procedure laid down for strip-searches showed no evidence of intention to cause distress or increase the humiliation necessarily involved but was merely the result of "sloppiness".

Although the above decisions restrict the principle in *Wilkinson v Downton*, the Protection from Harassment Act 1997 might provide a remedy for intentional harassment where a claimant has been the victim of a "course of conduct". For example, there may be a remedy under the Act where the intentional harassment is perpetrated by a fellow employee; see *Majrowski v Guy's and St Thomas's NHS Trust* (below).

Figure 2: Damages in Trespass

DAMAGES IN TRESPASS

All forms of trespass are actionable per se without proof of damage but:
- nominal damages only may be awarded where no actual loss is suffered
- aggravated damages may be awarded where, for example, an assault or battery takes place in humiliating or undignified circumstances
- in an appropriate case, exemplary or punitive damages may be awarded.

DEFENCES

The following defences are available in an action of intentional trespass to the person:

Consent

If the claimant expressly or impliedly consents to an act which would, but for that consent, amount to the commission of a tort, the defendant is not liable. Thus, the claimant may give their consent to physical contact within the rules of a lawful sport or to the performance of a surgical operation.

Although consent is not a defence to a criminal assault occasioning actual harm, Lord Denning M.R. in *Murphy v Culhane* (CA, 1977) suggested that a person could, in an appropriate case, either be taken to have "assumed the risk" or be defeated by ex turpi causa (see Ch.5). This might be so where, for example, the claimant was the aggressor and "got more than he bargained for". This view is further supported by *Barnes v Nayer* (CA, 1986), but it cannot apply where the defendant's response to the provocation is a "savage blow out of all proportion to the occasion" (*Lane v Holloway* (CA, 1968)).

In the context of medical treatment the principles applicable to the defence continue to evolve. Treatment without consent is prima facie a battery, and an adult of full mental capacity has an absolute right to choose whether or not to consent to treatment (*Airedale NHS Trust v Bland* (HL, 1993); *Re MB (Medical Treatment)* (CA, 1997)). This right to self-determination was in issue in *Secretary of State for the Home Department v Robb* (HC, 1995) where, following *Airedale*, a declaration was granted that prison officials and nursing staff responsible for the care of a prisoner of sound mind who went on hunger strike could lawfully abide by his refusal to receive nutrition, for so long as he retained the mental capacity to do so. In reaching this decision the court declined to follow *Leigh v Gladstone* (HC, 1909), which had held the forcible feeding of a suffragette justified on the ground of necessity.

DEFINITION CHECKPOINT

Interpretation of the right to life guaranteed by Art.2 of the European Convention on Human Rights

The right to life guaranteed by Art.2 could not be interpreted as conferring a right to die. In *Pretty v United Kingdom* (2346/02) 2002, the appellant was mentally alert but terminally ill with an incurable degenerative illness and physically incapable of committing suicide without help. Her husband, who was prepared to help her to do this, was refused immunity against prosecution by the DPP. She appealed against this refusal and attempted to enforce her rights under Art.2 of the European Convention on Human Rights which guarantees the right to life and requested legal permission "to decide how and when I die". In a unanimous decision it was held that the right to life was never intended to convey the right to be killed by someone else and that such an interpretation could not be given to Art.2 of the Convention.

Where an adult patient is not in a fit state to give or withhold consent, a practitioner may nevertheless administer treatment in an emergency, in which case the practitioner may rely on the defence of necessity (see below). Otherwise, if the practitioner reasonably considers it to be in the best interests of the patient to administer treatment, the guidance of the court in the form of a declaration that the proposed treatment would not be unlawful should be sought.

A minor of 16 or 17 may consent to treatment without parental approval (Family Law Reform Act 1969, s.8) as may a minor below that age, provided that he or she has sufficient intelligence and understanding to know precisely what is involved (*Gillick v West Norfolk & Wisbech Area Health Authority* (HL, 1986)). It seems, however, that no minor of whatever age can refuse medical treatment to which a parent has validly consented, and that the court can, in all cases involving minors, override the wishes of the patient in the exercise of its inherent wardship jurisdiction (*Re W* (CA, 1992)).

Consent must be freely given and will therefore be vitiated if obtained by duress. It may also be invalid if obtained by fraud or misrepresentation, but only if the claimant is thereby mistaken as to the essential nature of the act (but see *Appleton v Garrett* (HC, 1996)). A mistake merely as to the consequences of the act does not affect consent, so that a patient need only be informed in broad terms of the nature of any proposed treatment (*Chatterton v Gerson* (HC, 1981)). Failure to disclose known risks associated with the treatment cannot therefore give rise to a battery but may be actionable in negligence (*Sidaway v Governors of the Bethlem Royal Hospital* (HL, 1985) and *Chester v Ashfar* (2004)).

Contributory negligence

In *Barnes v Nayer* (CA, 1986) it was considered that this could afford a defence in an appropriate case, but that it would not be available where the defendant's retaliatory act was wholly disproportionate to the claimant's misconduct.

Necessity

The basis of this defence is that the defendant was obliged to act as they did in order to prevent greater harm either to their person or a third party. The giving of emergency treatment to one who is unable to consent, for example, may be justified on this ground (*F v West Berkshire Health Authority* (HL, 1989)). The defence is not available where the occasion of necessity is brought about by the defendant's negligence, and once this matter is raised it is for the defendant to show that he or she was not negligent (*Rigby v Chief Constable of Northamptonshire* (HC, 1985)).

Self-defence

An individual may use such reasonable force as is necessary to protect their person or their property, and to prevent the entry of, or to eject, a trespasser upon their land. The use of reasonable force to prevent crime is statutorily sanctioned (Criminal Law Act 1967, s.3(1)), so a defence is available to one who goes to assist another under attack. Self-defence failed in the case of soldiers who were not being threatened with being shot when they fired their guns (*Bici v Ministry of Defence* (2004)).

Lawful arrest

This cannot be false imprisonment, nor will there be a battery by one who uses no more force than is reasonable to effect a lawful arrest. Detailed consideration of the law relating to powers of arrest, much of which is to be found in the Police and Criminal Evidence Act 1984, is not here possible; it is worth noting, however, that at common law any person may take reasonable steps to stop or prevent an actual or reasonably apprehended breach of the peace, and such steps may include the detention of a man against his will (*Albert v Lavin* (HL, 1982)).

LEGISLATION HIGHLIGHTER

Protection from Harassment Act 1997

Section 3(1) of the Act creates a statutory tort of harassment and provides remedies by way of damages and injunction. Damages may be awarded for consequential anxiety and financial loss (s.3(2)). There must be an actual or apprehended course of conduct by the defendant which amounts, or would if pursued amount, to harassment of the plaintiff and which the defendant knows or ought to know amounts to harassment (s.1(1)).

The legislation is very widely drawn and may potentially impact upon numerous spheres of everyday life, including the conduct of the press, conduct in employment (in *Majrowski v Guy's and St Thomas's NHS Trust* (HL 2006) it was held that an employer could be vicariously liable under the Act for harassment committed by one of its employees in the course of employment), disputes between neighbours and family members, and the activities of protesters (though in *Huntingdon Life Sciences Ltd v Curtin* (HC, 1997) it was said that Parliament had not intended to prevent individuals from exercising a legitimate right to protest about matters of public concern and that the Act should be interpreted accordingly).

Revision Checklist

You should now understand:

- trespass requires a *direct* and *intentional* interference, for example, unwanted touching or hitting or a person. The tort of negligence covers *un*intentional or negligent conduct and *in*direct interference;

- an assault is the reasonable apprehension of an *immediate* battery; a battery can take place without an assault and even the slightest force may amount to a battery, for example, an unwanted kiss;

- an imprisonment usually involves some positive act and if a reasonable means of escape is available to the claimant there may be no false imprisonment;

- the principle of *Wilkinson v Downton* applies to cases of the deliberate infliction of emotional harm;

- the Protection from Harassment Act 1997 protects against repeated harassment and situations involving a "course of conduct" causing emotional harm.

QUESTION AND ANSWER

Question

(a) Dan threw a stone at Ana which hit her in the eye. He also carelessly left his garden hose on the pavement outside his house causing Sylvia to fall over it. Which forms of action in tort are open to Ana and Sylvia?

(b) Niamh quietly crept up behind Patrick and hit him on the back of the head with a stone. Has she committed an assault? Has she committed a battery?

(c) A large crowd was jostling at the bus stop and as Josh went to board the bus he bumped into Zak, causing him to fall to the ground. Can Zak sue Josh in battery?

Approach to the answer

(a) Trespass requires a *direct* and *intentional* interference (*Reynolds v Clarke* (1725)) so the question is whether Dan's conduct in throwing the stone amounted to a direct and intentional interference? The tort of negligence covers *un*intentional or negligent conduct and *in*direct interference (*Letang v Cooper* (1965))—did Dan's conduct in leaving his garden hose on the pavement outside his house amount to unintentional or negligent conduct and an indirect interference?

(b) When Niamh crept up behind Patrick did he apprehend an immediate battery? Did the stone hitting Patrick on the back of the head amount to a battery? (*Thomas v National Union of Mineworkers* (1985))

(c) Would jostling at a bus stop amount to conduct generally accepted in the ordinary conduct of everyday life (*Collins v Wilcock* (1984))? If yes, then Josh's conduct would not constitute a battery.

Negligence: Duty of Care

. . . .

2

INTRODUCTION

Negligence as a tort may be defined as the breach of a duty of care, owed by the defendant to the claimant, which results in damage to the claimant. The tort of negligence requires that each of the elements duty, breach and damage must be established. The concept of duty of care serves to define the interests protected by the tort of negligence by determining whether the type of loss suffered by the claimant in the particular way in which it occurred is actionable. The loss in question may arise through misfeasance or non-feasance, and may consist of personal injury, damage to property, or what is categorised as pure economic loss. It may, in addition, consist of psychiatric damage (which was, until recently, more commonly termed "nervous shock") which has traditionally been treated as essentially different in kind to other forms of personal injury. In this chapter the development of the *duty of care* and the tests for establishing if a duty exists will be discussed, Ch.3 will examine what amounts to *breach of tha*t duty, and *damage* (causation and remoteness) will be the subject of Ch.4. However, it might be useful at this point to note that the elements of negligence frequently overlap and some-times fail to provide a clear answer as to whether a claim should be allowed.

Figure 3: Elements of Negligence

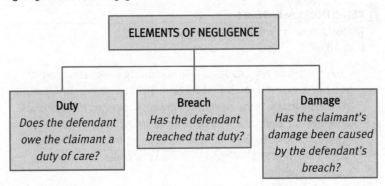

Note: the elements of negligence frequently overlap.

In *Lamb v Camden LBC* [1981] Q.B. 625, Lord Denning said: "it is not every consequence of a wrongful act which is the subject of compensation". Lines have to be drawn somewhere:

> "Sometimes it is done by limiting the range of persons to whom a duty is owed. Sometimes it is done by saying that there is a break in the chain of causation. At other times it is done by saying that the consequence is too remote to be a head of damage. All these devices are useful in their way. Ultimately, it is a question of policy for judges to decide".

ESTABLISHING A DUTY

As the law developed it came to be recognised that certain relationships gave rise to a legal duty, such that carelessness by one of the parties in that relationship which caused damage to the other would entitle that other to bring an action for damages. In this way a number of specific "duty situations" were created, and the claimant had either to prove that their case fell within one of these existing categories of relationship or to persuade the court to recognise a new duty situation.

Foreseeability, proximity and the "just and reasonable" requirement
In *Donoghue v Stevenson* (HL, 1932), Lord Atkin, in attempting to trace a common thread through existing authority, formulated a general principle (the "neighbour principle") for determining whether, in any given case, a duty of care should exist.

DEFINITION CHECKPOINT

The neighbour principle
Lord Atkin:

> "You must take reasonable care to avoid acts or omissions which you can reasonably foresee would be likely to injure your neighbour. Who then, in law, is my neighbour? The answer seems to be persons who are so closely and directly affected by my act that I ought reasonably to have them in contemplation as being so affected when I am directing my mind to the acts or omissions which are called in question."

The significance of the *Donoghue v Stevenson* principle was that it firmly established negligence as an independent tort and provided a basis for its expansion to cover situations not already governed by precedent where a relationship between the parties existed such as doctor-patient or innkeeper-guest. This is not to say, however, that cases in which no duty had been held to exist prior to 1932 would thereafter be decided differently simply on the basis that the damage in question was reasonably foreseeable, since it is clear from the neighbour principle itself, as emphasised in a number of subsequent decisions, that there must also be a sufficient *relationship of proximity* between the parties.

The term "proximity" means legal, rather than geographical, proximity and, according to Lord Keith in *Yuen Kun Yeu v Att Gen of Hong Kong* (PC, 1987), is referable to

> " ... such close and direct relations that the act complained of directly affects a person whom the person alleged to be bound to take care would know would be directly affected by his careless act." In addition to the two requirements of reasonable foresight and proximity, it must be just and reasonable to impose a duty upon the defendant (see, e.g. Lord Bridge in *Caparo Industries Plc v Dickman* (below)."

The unforeseeable plaintiff

Even where the courts are prepared to find that the circumstances are such as to be capable of giving rise to a duty, the claimant will still fail if he or she was an unforeseeable victim of the defendant's negligence. In imposing a duty it is not sufficient to establish that the circumstances give rise to a duty—the court must also be satisfied that the particular defendant owed a duty to the particular claimant. Thus, simply to say that a motorist owes a duty of care to other road users does not answer the question whether, in any given case, harm of the type suffered by the particular claimant was in the circumstances foreseeable.

KEY CASE

THE UNFORESEEABLE PLAINTIFF
In *Bourhill v Young* (HL, 1943), the plaintiff heard, but did not see, a crash caused by the defendant motorcyclist's negligence. The plaintiff later saw part of the aftermath of the accident and suffered nervous shock. She failed to establish the existence of a duty of care to prevent nervous shock—she was an "unforeseeable" plaintiff and harm to her of that type was not foreseeable.

The development of the *duty of care*

In *Hedley Byrne v Heller* (1964) (below), the House of Lords extended the neighbour principle to cover cases of pure economic loss not resulting from physical damage in circumstances where a "special relationship" arises between the parties. Later, in *Home Office v Dorset Yacht Co Ltd* (1970) some borstal trainees escaped from custody during the night when, it was alleged, the three officers in charge of them were asleep and caused damage to the plaintiff's yacht. It was argued by the Home Office that it would be contrary to public policy to hold it (or its officers) liable to a member of the public for the acts of others (the borstal trainees) by failing to restrain them. The majority of the House of Lords concluded that a duty of care was owed on the grounds that a "special relationship" existed. In extending Lord Atkin's neighbour principle, Lord Reid suggested that a duty of care based on reasonable foreseeability ought to apply in all cases unless there was some justification or valid explanation for its exclusion. This approach, seen as a liberating principle, was affirmed by the House of Lords in *Anns v Merton LBC* (1978) which held that the test for the existence of a duty of care is to be approached in two stages.

Anns—two stage test for establishing a duty

Lord Wilberforce extended the neighbour principle based on reasonable foresight and introduced a two-stage test which is approached by asking:

First, was the harm foreseeable, thereby bringing the plaintiff within the neighbour principle? If so, was there any valid policy reason to deny the existence of a duty of care in this case?

Under the first stage of Lord Wilberforce's test, the plaintiff, having established foreseeability of harm, raised the presumption of the existence of a duty of care. This meant that, at the second stage of the test (the policy stage) the courts were left to restrict the scope of negligence liability by reference to policy considerations. *Anns* was seen as a liberating principle; for example in *McLoughlin v O'Brian* (1983) (below) the policy arguments, which were said to justify the restrictions on liability, were criticised. Lord Bridge, dismissing the floodgates argument, said:

> "I believe that the floodgates argument … is, as it always has been, greatly exaggerated".

This period of expansion of negligence liability reached its high-water mark in *Junior Books v Veitchi Co Ltd* (1983) where the House of Lords went one step further than *Anns* and allowed a claim in negligence where there was no allegation that the factory floor in question was dangerously defective; the defect in question was one of quality. *Anns* was overruled by the House of Lords in *Murphy v Brentwood District Council* (1990) but judicial concerns about the expansion of the duty of care and a rejection of Lord Wilberforce's test had already marked a retreat from the broad approach. In *Governors of the Peabody Donation Fund v Sir Lindsay Parkinson & Co Ltd* (1985) the House of Lords warned against the more liberal approach of the Wilberforce test, and in subsequent decisions the courts have sought to reassert limits on the scope of liability that had traditionally been recognised in the case law.

DEFINITION CHECKPOINT

Judicial criticism of Anns
Yuen Kun Yeu v Att Gen of Hong Kong (1988)
Lord Keith:

"In view of the direction in which the law has since been developing, their Lordships consider that for the future it should be recognised that the two-stage test in Anns is not to be regarded as in all circumstances a suitable guide to the existence of a duty of care."

In *Caparo v Dickman* (1990), the House of Lords rejected the broad approach taken by Lord Wilberforce in *Anns* and approved *Sutherland Shire Council v Heyman* (1985) in which Brennan J. and said that the law should develop "incrementally by analogy with established categories." In *Caparo,* the plaintiffs brought an action for substantial losses they suffered on shares purchased in reliance on an audit which was negligently prepared by the auditors. The auditors were held to owe no duty of care in respect of the accuracy of the accounts to either members of the public or existing shareholders when they rely on such an audit to invest in the company; there was not sufficient proximity between the plaintiffs and the defendants. Also, the audit was prepared for the purpose of enabling the shareholders as a body to exercise control over the company; it was not prepared for the purpose of providing information for investors. Their Lordships ruled that the relationship of proximity is not always enough to determine whether a defendant is under a duty of care; it is still necessary to consider the scope of that duty and the controlling principle that the imposition of a duty of care should be "fair, just and reasonable" in all the circumstances.

KEY CASE

THE *CAPARO* CRITERIA
Their Lordships ruled that that the relationship of proximity is not always enough to determine whether a defendant is under a duty of

care; it is still necessary to consider the scope of that duty and the controlling principle that the imposition of a duty of care should be "fair, just and reasonable" in all the circumstances.

Under this test, for a duty of care to arise:

(i) the loss must be reasonably foreseeable;

(ii) there must be a relationship of proximity between the parties; and

(iii) it must be fair, just and reasonable that the law should impose a duty—this enables the court to take account of any underlying policy concerns.

In *Sutradhar v NERC* (2006), the question was whether the defendant was under a positive duty to test for arsenic when testing water in Bangladesh for minerals which might be harmful to fish. The boundaries between the concepts in *Caparo* were referred to by Lord Hoffman who expressed the view that they are somewhat porous. He said:

"In particular, the requirement that the imposition of a duty should be fair, just and reasonable may sometimes inform the decision as to whether the parties should be considered to be in a relationship of proximity and may sometimes provide a special reason as to why no duty should exist, notwithstanding that the relationship would ordinarily qualify as proximate.

In this case the House of Lords held that there was a failure by the defendant to assume responsibility because the relationship between the defendant and the harm suffered by the claimant (drinking contaminated water in Bangladesh) did not come even remotely within the proximity required to establish a duty. The defendant had no control whatever, whether in law or in practice, over the supply of drinking water in Bangladesh.

However, if there is a sufficiently close proximity between defendant and the claimant's harm the defendant may be held to assume a duty of care. In *Barrett v Ministry of Defence* (1995), there had been a pattern of excessive drinking amongst soldiers at a remote Navy base. A soldier collapsed after a bout of heavy drinking and the duty officer arranged for him to be taken to his room where he was left unchecked. The soldier later died due to choking on vomit. The Navy was not liable for preventing the deceased from excessive drinking or for anything that happened prior to his collapse but when the soldier collapsed the Navy assumed responsibility and was liable in negligence. Its supervision of the deceased following his collapse was inadequate and the measures taken fell short of the standard reasonably to be expected.

The present position

Whether a duty is capable of existing in any particular case does not often cause a problem since the issue will be governed by precedent, but in a novel case the three formal requirements (foreseeability, proximity, and the just and reasonable criterion) must all be satisfied, regardless of the nature of the damage (*Marc Rich & Co v Bishop Rock Marine Co Ltd* (HL, 1996)). In *Marc Rich*, no duty of care was owed by a marine classification society (a non-profit making organisation) when one of its employees approved the seaworthiness of a ship which sank a few days later with the loss of the claimants' cargo. It was assumed that the defendants had acted negligently and that the necessary proximity between the parties existed but the House of Lords stated that on grounds of policy it would not be fair, just and reasonable to impose a duty in this type of case. The law of international trade, under-pinned by a network of contracts and supported by insurance cover, already covered the events which occurred. To allow this to be evaded to the claimant's advantage by imposing liability on the marine classification society could undermine the whole system of international trade in the future. In *Perrett v Collins* (HC, 1998) a passenger injured in an aircraft accident, allegedly caused by the unairworthy condition of the aircraft, claimed in negligence against the inspector who had certified that the aircraft was fit to fly. The defendant sought to rely on the reasoning in *Marc Rich* but the Court of Appeal held that *Marc Rich* was based upon broad policy considerations relating to the organisation of maritime trade which were peculiar to that situation. In the present case the inspector had an independent and critical role because the aircraft could not lawfully fly unless such a certificate had been issued. He therefore owed a duty to potential passengers to use reasonable care in inspecting the aircraft and issuing the certificate.

However, inextricably interconnected as these requirements are, the relationship of one with the other is far from clear. In *Davis v Radcliffe* (PC, 1990), for example, Lord Goff said that proximity referred to such a relation between the parties as rendered it just and reasonable that a duty should be imposed, and Lord Oliver in *Caparo Industries Plc v Dickman* (HL, 1990) suggested that lack of proximity could in some cases be attributed to a failure of the just and reasonable requirement. Further, the relative significance to be attached to each requirement will depend upon a variety of factors including, inter alia, the status of the parties and their relationship with one another, the nature of the harm suffered, and the particular way in which that harm arises.

Figure 4: Questions relevant to establishing the elements of a duty of care

What is the relationship between the parties and the nature of the harm suffered?
The relative significance to be attached to each requirement will depend upon a variety of factors including, *inter alia*, the status of the parties and their relationship with one another, the nature of the harm suffered, and the particular way in which that harm arises

Was the claimant's physical harm the result of a positive act on the part of the defendant?
Where positive conduct by the defendant causes direct physical injury to the claimant or the claimant's property, reasonable foresight of such harm will generally be sufficient to satisfy the other criteria for the existence of a duty (see, e.g. Lord Oliver in *Murphy v Brentwood District Council* (HL, 1990)).

Does the claim involve pure economic loss or an omission to act?
Where the claimant's claim is in respect of *pure economic loss*, or where the defendant has failed to prevent damage by *omitting* to act, mere foreseeability of the harm is never sufficient to establish a duty; in cases of this type, questions of proximity and whether it would be just and reasonable to impose a duty assume much greater significance and must be weighed more carefully in the balance.

The language used by judges in dealing with the duty issue tends to mask the fact that the decision whether or not a duty exists as a matter of law is ultimately based upon policy, a fact which has now come to be more openly acknowledged. As Lord Pearce observed in *Hedley Byrne & Co v Heller & Partners Ltd* (HL, 1964):

> "How wide the sphere of the duty of care in negligence is to be laid depends ultimately on the courts' assessment of the demands of society for protection from the carelessness of others."

In other words, the concepts of proximity and what is just and reasonable, flexible and elusive as they are (and quite incapable of definition), merely serve as convenient tools which the courts can manipulate in order to achieve the result which they perceive the merits of the case to justify.

The rest of this chapter deals with some of the more well-defined circumstances in which no duty, or a duty of limited scope only, has been held to exist.

PURE ECONOMIC LOSS

Financial loss consequent upon negligently inflicted injury to the person or to property is ordinarily recoverable, but problems arise with "pure" economic loss, i.e. financial loss unaccompanied by other damage.

DEFINITION CHECKPOINT

Restriction of liability for negligent words
The courts are wary in cases of financial loss resulting from negligent statements of burdening the defendant with liability "in an indeterminate amount for an indeterminate time to an indeterminate class" (per Cardozo C.J. in *Ultramares Corp v Touche* (1931). Liability for harm caused by negligent *behaviour* is normally recoverable but where harm is caused by negligent *words* the courts are now inclined to approach the issue on a case by case basis, identifying discrete categories of liability. Cases of financial loss may arise as a result either of negligent information or advice, or of negligent conduct, although the distinction between word and deed is not always clear.

Thus, attempts have been made to establish general principles in order to limit both the potential range of claimants and the circumstances in which claims will be entertained, though with limited success.

A. Negligent Statements
Prior to 1964 liability for misstatements existed in contract, in the tort of deceit (*Derry v Peek* (HL, 1889)), or for breach of a fiduciary duty (*Nocton v Lord Ashburton* (HL, 1914)). In *Hedley Byrne & Co Ltd v Heller & Partners Ltd* (HL, 1964) the plaintiffs wanted to know if they could safely advance credit to their client, X. The plaintiffs' bankers sought references from the defendants, X's bankers, who gave favourable reports "without responsibility". The plaintiffs relied on the information and suffered financial loss when X went into liquidation. It was held that no duty arose because of the disclaimer, but that, in appropriate circumstances, a duty could arise.

KEY CASES

TESTS IMPOSED AS THE BASIS OF LIABILITY FOR NEGLIGENT STATEMENTS

(1) In *Hedley Byrne* their Lordships accepted that reasonable foresight of the harm was not in itself sufficient because of the potentially far-reaching effect of the spoken (or written) word, and spoke of the need for a "special relationship". It appeared that such a relationship would exist where, to the defendant's knowledge (actual or constructive), the plaintiff relied upon the defendant's skill and judgement or his ability to make careful enquiry, and it was reasonable in the circumstances for the plaintiff to do so. The essence of *Hedley Byrne* could thus be equated with the concept of "reasonable reliance".

(2) In *Caparo Industries Plc v Dickman* (HL, 1990) Lord Bridge said that, in order for a duty to arise, it was necessary to show that the defendant knew that his statement would be communicated to the plaintiff, either as an individual or as a member of an identifiable class, specifically in connection with a particular transaction or transactions of a particular kind, and that the plaintiff would be very likely to rely on it in deciding whether or not to enter into the transaction.

Subsequent developments

There has also been a tendency to explain the existence of a duty as resting upon a voluntary assumption of responsibility by the defendant. Thus, in *Henderson v Merrett Syndicates Ltd* (HL, 1994), it was held that where a person assumed responsibility to perform professional or quasi-professional services for another who relied on those services, the relationship between the parties was in itself sufficient to give rise to a duty on the part of the person providing those services. This broad statement of principle cuts across the traditional distinction between negligent statements and negligent acts in the context of liability for professional negligence. Although in many instances the relationship between the parties will be contractual, it was held in *Henderson* that this did not preclude the existence of a tortious duty.

Most of the cases have involved professional advisers, and the view of the majority in *Mutual Life and Citizens' Assurance Co Ltd v Evatt* (PC, 1971) was that the duty was limited to such persons, or to those holding themselves out as possessing a comparable skill and competence. The minority view, on the other hand, was that the duty would arise whenever a businessman in the course of his business gave information to a person who let it be known that he was seeking considered advice upon which he intended to act. This more liberal approach found favour in *Esso Petroleum Co Ltd v Mardon*

Figure 5: Negligent Statements

Negligent statements: relevance of the defendant's knowledge (actual or constructive) of the purpose for which the information is required	
Auditors	**Surveyors**
The scope of the duty in the context of auditors is restricted to situations which fall within the purpose for which the information is provided, so that where the defendant is specifically requested to prepare a report for the purpose of showing it to an actual or prospective bidder in a proposed take-over, there is no reason in principle why the defendant ought not to be liable.	In contrast to the position of auditors, surveyors appointed to value a house for mortgage purposes may owe a duty to the purchaser even though the primary purpose of the valuation is to enable the lender to decide whether to advance a loan (*Yianni v Edwin Evans & Sons* (HC, 1982), approved in *Smith v Eric S. Bush* (HL, 1989) and *Harris v Wyre Forest DC* (HL, 1989)).

Reason for this Distinction

This distinction has been justified on the basis that valuers are paid for their services at the mortgagor's expense and must know that, in the case of a typical house purchase, the majority of buyers in fact rely upon their report and cannot afford an independent valuation. The duty appears to be confined, however, to the person in respect of whose application the report is prepared and does not extend to subsequent owners of the property (*Smith v Bush*). A warning note was also sounded in *Smith v Bush* that the duty would not necessarily apply to commercial property or to houses at the more expensive end of the market, where the purchaser might be expected to obtain their own independent survey.

DEFINITION CHECKPOINT

Hedley Byrne does not apply to information or advice tendered "off the cuff" or on a purely social occasion, nor is there any general duty to volunteer information. However, the duty has been held to apply to pre-contractual negotiations (*Esso Petroleum Co Ltd v Mardon* (CA, 1976)), though where the claimant is induced to contract as a result of a negligent misstatement he may, apart from a possible action in tort, sue under s.2(1) of the Misrepresentation Act 1967. The advantage of the statutory action is that the defendant has the burden of proving that he or she had reasonable grounds to believe, and did believe up to the time the contract was entered into, that the facts represented were true (see *Howard Marine & Dredging Co Ltd v A. Ogden & Sons Ltd* (CA, 1978)

(CA, 1976), although the fact that the adviser is not in the business of giving advice of the type sought may be relevant in determining whether the plaintiff was reasonably entitled to rely on it for the particular purpose in question or whether, for example, he might reasonably have been expected to undertake further enquiries or obtain independent advice. For a more detailed break-down of the factors which may be relevant to the existence of a duty, see Neill L.J. in *James McNaughton Papers Group Ltd v Hicks Anderson & Co* (CA, 1991).

The application of Hedley Byrne

Provided that the defendant is aware of the existence of the claimant either as an individual or as a member of an ascertainable class, there is clearly no need for the defendant to know the identity of the claimant. A crucial ingredient of the duty is the defendant's knowledge (actual or constructive) of the purpose for which the information is required. In *Caparo Industries Plc v Dickman* (HL, 1990), it was held that, in preparing the statutory audit of the accounts of a public company, the defendants owed no duty to the plaintiffs either as potential investors or as existing shareholders. The purpose of the audit was to report to the shareholders to enable them to exercise their rights in the management of the company, not to provide information which might assist them in making investment decisions. It follows from this that auditors owe no duty to existing or potential creditors of the company (*Al Saudi Banque v Clark Pixley* (HC, 1989), approved in Caparo). Similarly, it was held in *Al-Nakib Investments (Jersey) Ltd v Longcroft* (HC, 1990) that information in a prospectus inviting shareholders to subscribe for additional shares by way of a rights issue can be used only for that specific purpose, and not for the purpose of deciding to buy additional shares in the stock market (see also *James McNaughton Papers Group Ltd v Hicks Anderson & Co* (CA, 1991)).

Reliance by a third party

There are situations in which a duty of care will be imposed upon A who makes a statement to B, as a result of which B acts upon it to C's financial detriment. Although it is well established that, in performing a service for their client, a solicitor generally owes no duty of care to third parties (see, e.g. *Clarke v Bruce Lance & Co* (CA, 1988)), it was held in Ross v Caunters (HC, 1980) that a solicitor who failed to inform his client, the testator, that the spouse of a beneficiary should not witness the will was liable to an intended beneficiary for the loss of her bequest. In *White v Jones* (HL, 1995) a majority of the House of Lords held the defendant solicitors liable for failing to carry out their client's instructions regarding his will, with the result that the plaintiffs (the intended beneficiaries) lost their legacy. One of the principal arguments in support of the imposition of a duty in these cases was that to hold otherwise would lead to the unjust result that the solicitor would escape liability for the consequences of his or her negligence, because the deceased testator and their estate had suffered no loss and would therefore have no claims (other than for nominal damages for breach of contract). A solicitor also owes a duty to an intended beneficiary under a will notwithstanding the fact that the estate may also have a claim against the negligent solicitor. In *Carr-Glynn v Frearsons* (CA, 1998) a first instance decision which held that no duty was owed where the effect of the solicitor's negligence is to cause a loss to the estate, since it is unacceptable that the defendant should be at risk of two separate claims for identical loss, was overruled by the Court of Appeal. In the opinion of the majority in *Spring* economic loss in the form of failure to obtain employment was clearly foreseeable if a careless reference was given and there was clear proximity of relationship as between employer and employee, so that it was fair, just and reasonable that the law should impose a duty on the employer. By analogy with *Spring* it has been held that, in carrying out a pre-employment medical assessment on behalf of a company, a doctor could owe a duty to the would-be employee (*Baker v Kaye* (HC, 1997)).

Figure 6: White v Jones

The duty under *White v Jones* is not confined to cases relating to wills

Pensions and Life Insurance	Employment References
In *Gorham v British Telecommunications Plc* (CA, 2000), Mrs Gorham sued Standard Life for breach of a duty of care owed to her and her children. Her deceased husband had been incorrectly advised that the BT pension scheme was preferable to a personal pension. However, on his death she and the children received considerably less because of the negligent advice given to her husband. The Court of Appeal held that if an insurance company owed a duty of care to the customer, this duty was also owed to the customer's dependant wife and family where he had intended to create a benefit for them on his death.	In *Spring v Guardian Assurance Plc* (HL, 1994) an employer supplying a reference about an employee to a prospective employer was held to owe a duty to the employee to avoid making untrue statements negligently or expressing unfounded opinions, even if honestly held or believed to be true. In the opinion of the majority in *Spring*, economic loss in the form of failure to obtain employment was clearly foreseeable if a careless reference was given and there was clear proximity of relationship as between employer and employee, so that it was fair, just and reasonable that the law should impose a duty on the employer.

In *Patchett v Swimming Pool & Allied Trades Association Ltd* (SPATA) (2009), the Court of Appeal considered liability for statements on a website which the claimant alleged were inaccurate and misleading. Here, financial loss was suffered when the installer of a swimming pool became insolvent before the pool was completed and the question was whether the defendant, SPATA, owed a duty of care to internet users for statements on its website. The Court of Appeal found there was no assumption of responsibility, because the degree of reliance by its customers which SPATA intended, or should reasonably have expected, was limited by its advice in a statement to customers to obtain an information pack for further details. It was held that the statements on the website had to be taken as a whole and it was reasonable to expect potential customers to have regard to all the information available on the website. In these circumstances, it would not be fair, just and reasonable to hold that SPATA owed the claimants a duty of care and that to find such a duty would be an unwarranted extension of existing case law.

B. Negligent Acts

There was originally no liability for pure economic loss caused by negligent acts (*Cattle v Stockton Waterworks Co* (HL, 1875)), although economic loss consequent upon damage to the plaintiff's property has always been recoverable.

KEY CASE

No RECOVERY FOR "PURE" ECONOMIC LOSS

In *Spartan Steel & Alloys Ltd v Martin & Co (Contractors) Ltd* (CA, 1973), the defendants negligently damaged a power cable cutting off the electricity supply to the plaintiffs' factory, as a result of which the plaintiffs suffered: (1) damage to their property reflected in loss of profit thereon and, (2) pure loss of profit during the interruption to the supply. The plaintiffs succeeded in the first part of their claim (resulting from damage to their property) but failed to recover the profit which they would have made but for the power cut (pure economic loss).

Although *Hedley Byrne*, which made a major inroad upon the principle that economic loss was generally not recoverable in tort, was originally confined to mis-statements, there followed a trend towards the formulation of a broader principle, applying to both statements and acts, which would permit recovery where there was no prospect of indeterminate liability (see, e.g. *Ross v Caunters* (HC, 1980)). This development blurred the distinction between statements and acts, and reached its highwater mark in *Junior Books Ltd v Veitchi Co Ltd* (HL, 1983). While it is the case that the *Hedley*

Byrne duty can arise in the context of the provision of professional services (*Henderson v Merrett Syndicates Ltd* (HL, 1994)), the search for a generalised principle covering all cases of economic loss has largely been abandoned.

> **DEFINITION CHECKPOINT**
>
> *Incremental approach for existence of a duty*
> In the development of the duty of care, the above cases show current judicial thinking is that the law should develop incrementally by analogy with established categories of duty, with the result that economic loss caused by negligent acts is normally irrecoverable unless the case can, exceptionally, be brought within the parameters of *Hedley Byrne*.

Damage to third party property
In some cases physical damage to property belonging to a third party may prevent the claimant from carrying on their business (e.g. *Spartan Steel*, above). In other cases it will adversely affect their contract with the third party, rendering that contract less valuable or more expensive than expected (*Leigh & Sillavan Ltd v Aliakmon Shipping Co Ltd* (HL, 1986); *Candlewood Navigation Corp Ltd v Mitsui OSK Lines Ltd* (PC, 1986)). In neither case can the claimant recover because of the long-established rule that no claim will lie in respect of foreseeable economic loss, unaccompanied by physical damage to property in which the plaintiff has a proprietary or possessory interest.

Acquiring defective property
In this situation the claimant acquires ownership of property and subsequently discovers that it is defective, with the result that he or she must expend money in repairing or replacing it.

> **DEFINITION CHECKPOINT**
>
> Economic loss, caused as it is by a defect in quality, may be recovered against a party who owes the loser a relevant contractual obligation, but has traditionally been regarded as irrecoverable in tort. The claimant cannot bring such a claim within ordinary *Donoghue v Stevenson* principles because that case is concerned with dangerously defective chattels which cause personal injury or damage to property other than the defective product in question (see Ch.6).

This fundamental principle was seriously eroded by *Dutton v Bognor Regis U.D.C.* (CA, 1972) and *Anns v Merton London BC* (HL, 1978), in both of which damages were held to be recoverable by a building owner against a local authority which had negligently inspected and approved defective foundations. Even if the damage (i.e. cracks in the fabric of the building caused by settlement) could be characterised as physical, that would still not come within the orthodoxy of *Donoghue v Stevenson*, which had hitherto been confined to chattels causing damage to other property. Lord Wilberforce in *Anns* justified the decision on the basis that the cause of action arose when the building became an imminent danger to the health and safety of the occupier, who could then recover the cost of averting that danger.

During the 1980s the duty imposed by *Anns* on local authorities was gradually restricted, so that it did not apply for the benefit of property developers or non-resident owners (*Governors of the Peabody Donation Fund v Sir Lindsay Parkinson & Co Ltd* (HL, 1985); *Investors in Industry Commercial Properties Ltd v South Bedfordshire DC* (CA, 1986)). In *D. & F. Estates Ltd v Church Commissioners for England* (HL, 1988), the House of Lords clearly had difficulty in reconciling *Anns* with established tort principles. Lord Oliver thought that the decision was peculiar to the construction of a building, and agreed with Lord Bridge that it was logically explicable only on the ground that, in the case of a complex structure such as a building, the constituent parts could be treated as separate items of property distinct from that part of the whole which gave rise to the damage, thus bringing the issue within ordinary *Donoghue v Stevenson* principles. For example, where defective foundations caused cracking in walls and ceilings, the latter could be regarded as "other property" for the purposes of an action.

KEY CASE

OVERRULING OF *ANNS*

This whole issue of duty of care was considered by seven Lords of Appeal in *Murphy v Brentwood DC* (HL, 1990). On similar material facts their Lordships unanimously overruled *Anns* in so far as it imposed a duty on local authorities, on the ground that where a defect in a building was discovered before any personal injury or damage to property other than the defective house itself had been done, the expense incurred by the building owner in rectifying the defect (or in vacating the premises) was pure economic loss and therefore irrecoverable in tort. In other words, once a dangerous defect is discovered it merely constitutes a defect in quality, and to permit recovery in tort would be to introduce a transmissible warranty of quality in the absence of any contract.

PSYCHIATRIC ILLNESS

According to Lord Ackner in *Alcock v Chief Constable of South Yorkshire* (HL, 1991), shock "involves the sudden appreciation by sight or sound of a horrifying event, which violently agitates the mind". It must manifest itself in some recognisable psychiatric or physical illness; mere grief or emotional upset is not actionable, save that mental distress suffered as a result of negligently inflicted injuries may be taken into account in the assessment of damages for pain and suffering. Lord Ackner also made it clear that, as the law presently stands, there can be no recovery for psychiatric illness "caused by the accumulation over a period of time of more gradual assaults on the nervous system".

Figure 7: Shock victims

Adopting Lord Oliver's classification in Alcock, shock victims may fall into one of two broad groups:	
1 those who are unwilling participants in the events causing shock (primary victims)	2 those who are merely passive and unwilling witnesses (secondary victims)

With regard to the first group his Lordship said that if the defendant's negligent conduct foreseeably puts the plaintiff into that position it follows that there will be a sufficiently proximate relationship between them, though if personal injury of some kind to the plaintiff is reasonably foreseeable as the result of an accident, the defendant is liable for psychiatric injury (even though no physical injury occurs), and the plaintiff need not prove that injury by shock was foreseeable because the defendant must take his victim as he finds him (*Page v Smith* (HL, 1995)).

However, following *White* (below) it may now be the case that the category of primary victims is limited to those who were exposed to the risk of physical injury and those who were not actually in physical danger but who believed themselves to be so. It remains unclear whether cases like *Dooley v Cammell Laird & Co* where the plaintiff crane driver not himself in physical danger suffered shock when, because of the defendant's negligence, the load he was lifting fell into the hold of a ship where his fellow employees were working. In *White v Chief Constable of South Yorkshire Police* (HL, 1998),

Figure 8: Injury by shock—three types of primary victim

> 1. Those who are put in reasonable fear for their own safety (as in *Dulieu v White & Sons* (HC, 1901))

> 2. Rescuers (see, e.g. *Chadwick v British Transport Commission* (CA, 1967))

> 3. Those who reasonably believe that they are about to be, or have been, the involuntary cause of another's death or injury (see, e.g. *Dooley v Cammell Laird & Co Ltd* (HC, 1951))

> Persons in these categories will recover if shock to them was reasonably foreseeable or if personal injury of some kind was foreseeable (in which case it need not be proved that psychiatric injury was foreseeable (*Page v Smith, above*)).

it was held that in claims for psychiatric injury employees are in no special position just because the incident was due to the negligence of the employer. Unless the employees are exposed to the risk of physical harm they remain "secondary victims" (see below). Nor are there special rules for rescuers engaged in rescuing others endangered by the defendant's negligence: unless they had been exposed to personal danger they are subject to the control mechanisms in *Alcock*. Although the majority held that in order to claim for psychiatric injury rescuers must have been exposed to physical danger or would need to satisfy the *Alcock* criteria, *Chadwick* (above) was distinguished on its facts. By entering the wrecked train carriages Mr Chadwick had been objectively exposed to physical danger and had therefore been within the range of foreseeable personal injury. However, where the claimant falls within the second of Lord Oliver's groups a more complex analysis is required.

KEY CASE

WHERE THE CLAIMANT FALLS WITHIN THE SECOND OF LORD OLIVER'S GROUPS A MORE COMPLEX ANALYSIS IS REQUIRED.
In *Alcock v Chief Constable of South Yorkshire* it was held that in order to recover for psychiatric injury the plaintiff must prove the following:

(a) that his relationship to the primary victim was sufficiently close that it was reasonably foreseeable that he might suffer shock if he apprehended that the victim had been, or might be, injured;

(b) that he was temporally and spatially close to the scene of the accident or its immediate aftermath;

(c) that he suffered shock through sight or hearing of the accident or its immediate aftermath.

In following the path taken by Lord Wilberforce in *McLoughlin v O'Brian* (HL, 1982) the House of Lords has made it clear that shock cases fall within a distinct category subject to special rules and that reasonable foresight of shock alone is not sufficient to give rise to a duty.

Figure 9: Alcock criteria applied

Application of the above *Alcock* criteria	
Requirement (a)	**Requirements (b) and (c)**
With regard to requirement (a) the plaintiff must generally show that he had a relationship of "love and affection" with the primary victim, though this might be presumed in the case of parents and spouses (and, per Lord Keith, fiancés) unless there is evidence to the contrary. Less close relations such as brothers and brothers-in-law do not have the benefit of the presumption and must therefore adduce evidence of the closeness of the emotional tie. Despite this general requirement three of their Lordships expressed the view that a bystander might succeed if he or she witnessed at close hand a particularly horrific catastrophe, provided that a person of reasonable fortitude would be likely to suffer shock but such a possibility was rejected by the Court of Appeal in *McFarlane v E.E. Caledonia Ltd* (CA, 1994).	Requirements (b) and (c) rule out the possibility of a claim by one who is informed of the event by a third party and who does not come upon the scene of the accident or its immediate aftermath. A point directly in issue in Alcock was whether a person who witnessed the events of a disaster on television (or radio) could be regarded as sufficiently proximate in time and space. Their Lordships held that, on the facts, such a person could not, because broadcasting guidelines forbade the suffering of identifiable individuals to be televised, and any perception of the actual consequences of the disaster to his relatives came later. In principle, however, Lords Ackner and Oliver thought that there could be circumstances where the simultaneous broadcast of a disaster would be equivalent to direct sight or hearing.

In a unanimous decision in *Palmer v Tees Health Authority* (1999), the Court of Appeal held that no duty of care was owed to the mother in respect of psychiatric injury following the abduction, sexual assault and murder of her four-year-old daughter by a psychiatric out patient. Although she was involved in the search for her daughter and in the vicinity at the time the body was discovered, she had not witnessed the events herself and did not therefore satisfy the immediate aftermath test. (The other reason for denying liability in this case was "lack of proximity" based on the decision in *Hill v Chief Constable of West Yorkshire* (1988) (below) where it was held that the police do not owe a duty of care in negligence to the victims of crime.) In *AB v Thameside & Glossop Health Authority* (1997) the defendant health authority wrote to inform a number of patients of the slight risk that they might have been exposed to the HIV infection. Some recipients of the letters alleged that they suffered psychiatric illness as a result of the communication of bad news by letter rather than face-to-face. Although a duty of care was conceded, the Court of Appeal held that the defendant had not been negligent in deciding to break the news in the way that it did. The categorisation of those claiming to be primary or secondary victims of psychiatric injury is a concept still to be developed in different factual situations.

KEY CASE

RELUCTANCE TO GRANT "BLANKET IMMUNITY"

In *W. v Essex County Council* (HL, 2000), their Lordships held that the Court of Appeal had been wrong to strike out the parents' claim on the grounds that they were secondary victims in respect of the psychiatric harm they had suffered upon discovering that their children had been sexually abused and thought it possible that the parents could establish a duty on the basis that they were primary victims. It should also be noted that since the enactment of the Human Rights Act 1998 the courts have shown a reluctance to grant "blanket immunity" and exclude a duty of care on grounds of policy. In *W. v Essex County Council*, the House of Lords ruled that it was not clear and obvious that the claim for psychiatric injury would fail and the parents had, at least, an arguable case (see below).

OMISSIONS

As a general rule the defendant does not owe a duty to take positive action to prevent harm to others. Thus, the rescuer who goes to the assistance of others in peril is certainly under no legal obligation to do so. So, too, the failure of a public authority to exercise a statutory power (or even a statutory duty) will not normally give rise to a common law duty (*Stovin v Wise* (HL, 1996)). The House of Lords further held that the mere existence of statutory powers and duties did not create a parallel common law duty and a highway authority's failure to paint a marking or to erect a road sign warning of a dangerous stretch of road did not give rise to a duty of care to the claimant (*Gorringe v Calderdale* (2004)).

DEFINITION CHECKPOINT

The term "omission" in this context is taken to mean passive inaction, since tortious negligence can invariably be characterised as a failure to take reasonable precautions.

EXCEPTIONS TO THE RULE

Most of the cases involving liability for nonfeasance are concerned, directly or indirectly, with the extent to which a defendant is under a duty to prevent harm to the claimant caused by the independent act of a third party. It may be the nature of the relationship between the parties which gives rise to the duty, such as employer and employee (*Hudson v Ridge Manufacturing Co Ltd* (HC, 1957), though the duty does not extend to protecting the employee from economic loss; *Reid v Rush & Tomkins Group Plc* (CA, 1989)), or occupier and visitor (see Ch.8). Alternatively, there may be a special relationship between the defendant and third party such that there is a positive obligation to control the third party. Examples of such a relationship include gaoler and prisoner (*Home Office v Dorset Yacht Co Ltd* (HL, 1970)), parent and child (*Carmarthenshire CC v Lewis* (HL, 1955)) and employer and employee (*Hudson v Ridge Manufacturing Co Ltd* (HC, 1957)). Liability might also arise where the defendant negligently causes or permits to be created a source of danger, and it is reasonably foreseeable that third parties may interfere with it and thereby cause damage (as in *Haynes v Harwood* (CA, 1935)); or where the defendant fails to abate a known risk created by third parties upon his or her property (*Sedleigh-Denfield v O'Callaghan* (HL, 1940); see Ch.11).

Where the wilful wrongdoing of a third party causes damage then, in the absence of any of the exceptional cases referred to above, it is very unlikely that the defendant will be liable. Thus, in *P. Perl (Exporters) Ltd v Camden London BC* (CA, 1983) the defendants were held not to owe a duty to make their premises secure in order to prevent thieves from breaking in thereby gaining access to, and stealing from, neighbouring occupiers.

KEY CASE

NO LIABILITY FOR PURE OMISSIONS

Liability for acts of third parties was further considered by the House of Lords in *Smith v Littlewoods Organisation Ltd* (HL, 1987) where the defendants bought a disused cinema with the intention of demolishing it to make way for a supermarket. While the premises were empty, vandals gained access and attempts were made to start a fire, though neither the defendants nor the police knew of this. A fire was eventually started which spread and caused damage to adjacent property belonging to the plaintiffs, whose claim was unanimously rejected.

- Lord Goff said that there was no general duty of care to prevent a third party from causing damage to the plaintiff by deliberate wrongdoing, however foreseeable such harm might be, because the common law does not normally impose liability for pure omissions. His Lordship concluded that none of the exceptional circumstances which might give rise to a duty applied and, since the defendants were unaware of the presence of the vandals, the risk was therefore not foreseeable.

- Lords Brandon and Griffiths said that the duty owed by the defendants was to take reasonable care to ensure that the cinema was not, and did not become, a source of danger to neighbouring occupiers, but since there was nothing inherently dangerous on the premises, and because the defendants did not know of the vandals' activities, the risk was unforeseeable. Lord Mackay, too, adopted the test of reasonable foresight, but indicated that there might be circumstances where the risk would have to be "highly likely" before it could be regarded as reasonably foreseeable; in this case, he said, whilst it was probable that persons might attempt to enter the vacant premises, it was by no means a probable consequence of the vacation of those premises that they would be set on fire.

In *Mitchell v Glasgow City Council* (2009), the House of Lords applied *Smith* and held that liability for the criminal act of a third party would arise only where the person who was said to be under that duty had by his words or conduct assumed responsibility for the safety of the person who was at risk. Here the question was whether the local authority had assumed a responsibility to protect one of its social housing tenants who, following a long campaign of abuse and threats, was murdered by a fellow tenant. Although the local authority had been aware that the victim's neighbour might resort to violence after being informed that he risked being evicted, the required element of a relationship of responsibility was absent, as it would not be "fair, just and reasonable" to impose this duty on a public authority coping with an onerous burden of anti-social behaviour amongst tenants.

SPECIFIC IMMUNITIES

Advocates
In *Hall (Arthur JS) & Co v Simons* (HL, 2000), the public policy decision in *Rondel v Worsley* (HL, 1969) that advocates enjoyed immunity from liability for the negligent conduct of a case in court was held to be no longer justified. Justification for the immunity had been based upon the policy ground that, in order to fulfil his duty to the court and to the administration of justice, the advocate had to be free from the threat of negligence actions by dissatisfied clients. The case concerned proceedings alleging negligence by solicitors and, at first instance, the judge struck out the claims on the policy ground that the defendants were entitled to rely on the advocates' immunity, recognised by the House of Lords in *Rondel v Worsley*. The Court of Appeal held that the claims should not have been struck out and the solicitors appealed against this decision. The seven-member House of Lords dismissed the appeals and held that because of the changes in society and in the law which have taken place since the decision in *Rondel v Worsley*, the propriety of maintaining such immunity could no longer be justified. The advantages which accrued to the public interest from advocates' immunity in negligence must be balanced with the normal right of an individual to be compensated for a legal wrong and there is no longer sufficient public interest to justify the maintenance of this immunity. Their Lordships were unanimous in their decision to abolish the immunity in civil proceedings and (by a majority) to abolish it in criminal proceedings.

The police
In performing the function of investigating and preventing crime the police owe no duty of care to an individual member of the public. In such circumstances even where harm was reasonably foreseeable, there is insufficient proximity between the police and the victim (*Hill v Chief Constable of West Yorkshire* (HL, 1988).

KEY CASE ON PUBLIC POLICY

A GENERAL DUTY OF CARE ON POLICE DEEPLY DAMAGING TO POLICE OPERATIONS

In *Hill v Chief Constable of West Yorkshire* (1988), the mother of the last victim of a mass murderer claimed damages on the basis that the police had negligently failed to apprehend the murderer before her daughter was killed. The House of Lords found that although harm was reasonably foreseeable, there was insufficient proximity between the police and the victim for a duty of care to arise. It was also held that a general duty of care to protect all members of the public from the consequences of crime would be impracticable and, on grounds of public policy, deeply damaging to police operations.

Hill was applied in *Brooks v Commissioner of Police for the Metropolis* (2005), where the House of Lords rejected a claim in negligence against the police by a friend of Stephen Lawrence who witnessed Stephen's racist murder. He was unable to recover for the post-traumatic stress he suffered as the result of the way he was treated by the police following the murder, first as a suspect and later as a witness but not as the victim of crime. The public policy immunity granted in Hill was extended beyond the failure of police to apprehend criminals to include police failure to act on warnings in *Osman v Ferguson* (1993). The police failed to act on warnings that a teacher was a known threat to his victims. The plaintiff and his father were subsequently shot by the teacher and although the Court of Appeal was prepared to accept that in the circumstances of this case a sufficient relationship of proximity existed between the plaintiff's family and the police, the *Hill* immunity was applied and the case failed on grounds of public policy.

KEY CASE

BLANKET IMMUNITY AND HUMAN RIGHTS

In *Osman* following the rejection of their claim, the applicants brought a case against the United Kingdom alleging a violation of their rights under the European Convention of Human Rights. Subsequently, in *Osman v UK* (1998) the European Court of Human Rights held that a rule forbidding action against the police regardless of the circumstances and effectively granting a "blanket immunity" in negligence was in breach of Art.6 of the European Convention (the right to a fair trial). The Convention does not prevent courts taking into account public policy issues and although a public interest in protecting police from civil claims could be asserted, this must be balanced with other competing public interests. Under the Human Rights Act 1998 (incorporating the European Convention on Human Rights into UK law) courts are required to balance whether granting such immunity to a defendant is proportionate to the interference with the claimant's human rights.

The police do not, however, have total immunity; in *Swinney v Chief Constable of Northumbria Police* (CA, 1996) it was held that the immunity could be displaced by other, more compelling, policy considerations. In that case the plaintiff supplied confidential information to the police about a serious crime, naming a person who, to the knowledge of the police, was of a violent disposition. As a result of police negligence, that information came into the hands of the person named, and the plaintiff suffered psychiatric injury in consequence of the threats made against him. It was held that the police could owe a duty in these circumstances, since it was in the public interest that informants should be encouraged in their activities without fear that their identity might become known to the suspect. Although the court refused to strike out the claim, the plaintiff failed when the case proceeded to trial on the ground that there had been no breach of duty. The police, in leaving the information in a locked briefcase in a locked care, had not been negligent: *Swinney v Chief Constable of Northumbria Police* (No 2) (1999). However, it should be noted that in *Smith* (below), the Court of appeal remarked that in cases involving the police the very proximity of the parties can not only create a duty of care, but can overcome the public policy considerations which would otherwise bar the claim (as in *Swinney*) and said that whether under Art.2 or at common law, it cannot be a valid ground of distinction that an informer is entitled to protection while a witness is not.

Where the police owe no duty under the common law, a positive obligation to protect life under the Human Rights Act 1998 (Convention Art.2 right to life and the Art.8 right to private and family life) may be relied.

Rescue services

The Court of Appeal has ruled that there is no proximity of relationship between the fire brigade and a building owner: fire brigades are not under a common law duty of care to answer an emergency call nor under a duty to take reasonable care to do so. Unless the fire service negligently increased the damage or caused additional damage, liability in negligence in tackling a fire will not arise (*Capital and Counties Plc v Hampshire CC* (CA, 1997)). Similar reasoning was applied in *Harris v Evans* (CA, 1998) where the plaintiff sued for the economic losses he had suffered when the advice of the specialist inspector from the Health and Safety Executive had been inconsistent with the Executive's policy. The Court of Appeal held that it was not fair, just and reasonable to impose a duty on the Health and Safety Executive: the

Figure 10: Justification for the Hill immunity

The justification for the *Hill* immunity against police liability was considered by the House of Lords in *Van Colle v Chief Constable of Hertfordshire and Smith v Chief Constable of Sussex* (2008) where the question was whether the Court of Appeal had been correct to find that the police were not immune from negligence liability in the two cases.

In *Van Colle*, a prosecution witness was shot dead shortly before he was due to give evidence at trial. The Court of Appeal found that the police were, or should have been, aware of the real and immediate threat to the witness and that they had failed to take preventive measures to protect his life. This case was not brought under common law negligence; it was based upon human rights and litigated under Art.2 of the ECHR and compensation was therefore payable for breach of Art.2. The chief constable appealed against this finding.	In *Smith*, the claimant, who had repeatedly informed the police that his former partner had threatened to kill him, brought an action under the common law. He claimed that the police had ample evidence of these threats and had no excuse for not preventing his partner from carrying out the threatened hammer attack which caused him serious injuries. This was a claim in common law negligence.

Both appeals were allowed:
- in *Van Colle*, the *Osman* test, that the police knew or ought to have known "at the time" of the shooting of "a real and immediate risk to the life" of an identified individual from the criminal acts of a third party was not met;
- in *Smith*, the balance of advantage in this difficult area lay in preserving the principle set out in *Hill* that imposition of liability would result in defensive policing and, in the absence of special circumstances, the police owed no common law duty of care to protect individuals against harm caused by criminals;
- in the context of the future of the *Hill* immunity, it is important that the dissenting views in these cases are borne in mind.

imposition of a duty of care would probably have a detrimental effect by producing an unduly cautious and defensive approach by inspectors. This analysis has been adopted at first instance in respect of an alleged bungled rescue attempt by the coastguard (*OLL Ltd v Secretary of State for Transport* (HC, 1997)).

In *Kent v Griffiths* (CA, 2000) the Court of Appeal held that in certain circumstances an ambulance service could be liable in negligence. Although no duty is owed to the public at large to respond to a call for help, once a 999 call in a serious emergency has been accepted, the ambulance service assumes responsibility and has an obligation to provide the service for a named individual at a specified address.

Public bodies

In *X (Minors) v Bedfordshire CC* (HL, 1995), the House of Lords ruled that there is no duty of care on local authorities in carrying out their discretionary statutory functions. Nevertheless, where the conduct results from an improper exercise of that discretion, liability may arise. The question then arises as to whether it is fair, just and reasonable to impose a duty of care in negligence upon a body exercising a public function. The impact of litigation on a local authority exercising its public function could lead to that function being performed in a detrimentally defensive manner and contrary to the public interest. In *Barrett v Enfield London BC* (HL, 1999), concerning a claim for the various psychiatric problems the plaintiff suffered as a result of the authority's negligence during his time in their care, the House of Lords reversed the Court of Appeal's decision to strike out the claim. In the light of *Osman* (above) the claimant is entitled to have his or her case tried and the facts found before excluding a duty simply because the actions of the local authority involved the exercise of discretion. The decision in *X (Minors) v Bedfordshire CC* involved the exercise of statutory discretion as to whether or not to take the plaintiff into local authority care.

The distinction between *Barrett* and *X* is that in *Barrett* the alleged negligence took place after the child had been taken into the local authority's care. Having taken the child into care it was at least arguable that the local authority could be liable for negligence in its decisions concerning his foster placements and supervision.

In Z v UNITED KINGDOM (2001), the European Court of Human Rights held that failure by a United Kingdom local authority to provide children with appropriate protection against serious long-term neglect and abuse amounted to inhuman and degrading treatment in breach of Art.3 of the European Convention of Human Rights. The Court further held that the applicants had not been afforded an effective remedy in

TORT

breach of Art.13 of the Convention concerning the right to an effective remedy before a national authority.

Figure 11: Public bodies

Public bodies—the same action may give rise to a duty to one of the parties involved in a case but not to another.

In *JD v East Berkshire Community Health Trust* (HL, 2005), a boy's allergic reaction was interpreted wrongly by the social service department as indicating mistreatment by his mother and the child was put on the at-risk register for some months until the mistake was discovered. The mother contended that the health care professionals' duty to exercise due skill and care in the investigation of suspected abuse extended to the child's parents as primary carers as well as to the child. The mothers claim was dismissed on grounds of public policy. Health professionals, acting in good faith in what they believed were the best interests of the child, should not be subject to potentially conflicting duties when deciding whether a child might have been abused. It was not fair, just and reasonable to impose such a duty, *Caparo Industries Plc v Dickman* (1990) applied.

JD was distinguished in *Merthyr Tydfil CBC v C* (2010), where the children in question had been sexually abused by a neighbour's child. The mother of the children claimed that she had suffered psychiatric harm caused by the local authority's negligence in failing to properly deal with her reports of abuse. The local authority claimed that owing a duty of care to a parent would potentially conflict with the duty of care that it owed to the children and sought to rely on the decision in JD. The Court said that the decision in JD did not lay down any general principle that, where an authority owed a duty of care to a child, it could not as a matter of law at the same time owe a duty of care to parents of that child; a duty of care may be owed to parents as well as children, provided the parents are not suspected of abuse.

In *Phelps v Hillingdon London BC* (HL, 2000) it was held that an educational psychologist, employed by the local authority, could be under a duty of care to the plaintiff for failing to diagnose her dyslexia. In reversing the Court of Appeal decision, the House of Lords further held that Hillingdon could be vicariously liable for the educational psychologist's breaches of duty. *Phelps* was applied in the case of *A v Essex CC* (2003) where, although it was not fair, just and reasonable on professionals involved in compiling reports for adoption agencies to impose a duty of care to the adopting parents, the adoption agency was found vicariously liable for the failure of its social workers to communicate information to the adopting parents which the agency decided they should have.

Unborn children

Burton v Islington Health Authority (1993) held that a duty of care is owed to an unborn person, which becomes actionable on the live birth of the child. The **Congenital Disabilities (Civil Liability) Act 1976** provides that a child who is born alive but disabled as a result of an occurrence before its birth may have a cause of action in negligence. The Act has replaced the common law for births that occurred after July 22, 1976, the date of its enactment (and was inapplicable in *Burton* because the plaintiff was born before the Act came into force). It was held in *McKay v Essex Area Health Authority* (CA, 1982) that the common law recognises no claim for "wrongful life" whereby a child claims that s/he would not have been born at all, but for the defendant's negligence. To allow a child to recover damages for the pain and suffering of being alive at all was against public policy. In *Thake v Maurice* (1986), the Court of Appeal rejected the contention that public policy would bar the award of damages to parents following the birth of a healthy child after the father had undergone a vasectomy. It ruled that claims by parents for "wrongful birth" after the failure of negligently conducted sterilisations or abortions are recognised by the courts. Initially, in *Udale v Bloomsbury Area Health Authority* (HC, 1983) Jupp J. refused a mother compensation towards the upkeep of the child and said the birth of a child was a blessing and the financial cost of such a blessing was irrecoverable. It offended society's notions of what is right and the value afforded to human life. Jupp J. was overruled on the policy issue by the Court of Appeal in *Emeh v Kensington Area Health Authority* (1985) where their Lordships expressed a disinclination to place limits on the scope of the duty owed to the mother by reference to what was "socially unacceptable". In *Goodwill v British Pregnancy Advisory Service* (1996), no duty of care was owed to the plaintiff in respect of her partner's vasectomy operation because the defendants had not voluntarily assumed responsibility to her nor could they have known that their advice to the patient would be communicated to his future sexual partners.

KEY CASE

MCFARLANE V TAYSIDE HEALTH BOARD (HL, 1999) held that claims in respect of the financial costs of bringing up a healthy child following advice about, or performance of, negligent sterilisation are not recoverable. According to Lord Slynn, claims in respect of the costs of bringing up a healthy child born as a consequence of a failed sterilisation fall into the category of economic loss. Although some potential costs (for example, relating to the mother's pain and suffering during pregnancy) are recoverable, the economic cost of bringing up a healthy child is not recoverable: it would not be fair, just and reasonable to impose this duty on the doctor or the hospital.

In *Parkinson v St James and Seacroft University NHS Trust* (CA, 2001), McFarlane was distinguished and the parents of a disabled child born as the result of a negligent sterilisation were allowed to claim the extra costs of bringing up the child. In *Rees v Darlington Memorial Hospital NHS Trust* (HL, 2003), a seriously disabled mother of a healthy child claimed the additional costs of bringing up the child. At first instance the trial judge held that the House of Lords decision in *McFarlane* precluded a disabled parent from recovering the economic costs of bringing up a healthy child born as the result of a negligently performed sterilisation. The Court of Appeal, however, said there was a crucial difference in the case of a seriously disabled parent who, unlike an able-bodied one, would be in need of assistance to discharge their basic parental responsibility of looking after a child properly and safely and held that it was fair, just and reasonable that the mother should recover the additional costs. Nevertheless, the House of Lords allowed an appeal by a 4:3 majority on the ground that no exception to the principle in *McFarlane* was justified, even when the parent of the child was seriously disabled. In stating that the law must take the birth of a normal healthy baby to be a blessing and not a detriment, the House reaffirmed its unanimous decision in *McFarlane*. In addition to the award of damages for the pregnancy and birth, however, the House of Lords made a conventional award of £15,000 to recognise that a legal wrong had been done and to mark the loss of the right to limit one's family.

Affirmative Duty to Prevent Harm

In *Watson v British Boxing Board of Control* (CA, 2001), a non-profit making organisation controlling the rules of boxing and the licensing of boxers was held to owe a duty of care to inform itself adequately about the risks inherent in a blow to the head and to ensure the provision of adequate resuscitation facilities at the ringside. In *Vowles v Evans* (CA, 2003), a referee of a rugby match, acting in an amateur capacity, owed a duty of care to players when carrying out his refereeing duties. In applying the rules of the game, it was fair, just and reasonable that the players should be entitled to rely on the referee for their safety. It was further noted that it was possible for the referee or Welsh Rugby Union, the body who appointed him, to take out insurance cover against third party liability.

Revision Checklist

You should now understand:

- the function of duty of care as the first of the three main elements of a claim in negligence;

- how the duty concept is determined by proximity and foreseeability;

- the just and reasonable requirement;

- the role of policy, special duty situations and specific immunities.

QUESTION AND ANSWER

Question

Sami, a youth worker, took a party of teenagers to Roundwood Hill during the October half-term holiday for a day's nature ramble. Even though Sami assured the teenagers' parents they would return home immediately after lunch, he decided to take the party to visit an ancient Roman Tower. Although the visit to the Tower only took 15 minutes, when the party went to come downhill a thick mist suddenly enveloped the Hill. Sami had not reminded the teenagers to take warm clothes and he had also forgotten to bring with him his map and compass.

The temperature dropped rapidly and visibility was very poor but it was not until dusk began to fall that the teenagers became scared. Some of the teenagers had mobile phones but it was impossible to obtain a signal on the Hill so they could not raise the alarm. After rambling aimlessly for some considerable time they took shelter in a clearing on the Hill to wait for the rescue services. Orla, one of the older teenagers, disobeyed Sami's instructions to remain with the group and decided to find her own way home. Ten minutes after she left they heard a loud scream. Orla had missed her footing and fallen over the edge of a cliff. She suffered a broken leg.

Meanwhile, when Sami failed to return home at the expected time, his wife contacted the police and a local search party set off to find the group. As they were searching, Jordan, a member of the rescue party, heard Orla crying. He decided not to wait for the other members of the rescue team to join him and he tried to lift Orla single-handedly. They both slipped and Orla suffered facial injuries a result of the second fall.

On arrival at the local hospital Orla was informed that her face would be severely scarred as a result of the injuries. Max, the consultant plastic surgeon, advised her of a silicone treatment that would help to eliminate some of the scarring. When Orla asked if the treatment had any associated risks Max said: "well, nothing is ever 100 per cent safe but you need have no worries about this treatment. I have used the silicone treatment on many of my patients and it has always been completely successful." Although Max was not negligent in carrying out the treatment, Orla has suffered an allergic reaction to the silicone which has left her face permanently scarred.

Discuss the possible rights and liabilities of the parties (if any) in each of the above situations.

Approach to the answer

Planning your answer is particularly important in a negligence question because problem questions frequently contain a number of different issues which sometimes involve a number of potential claimants and defendants. As you read through the question, each of the separate issues/items of damage should first be identified together with potential claimants and defendants.

Each issue should then be isolated and dealt with separately as you work through the elements of the tort. Remember that an answer to a problem question should not only outline the relevant legal principles—the discussion must actually apply these principles to the facts in the question and focus on answering the question/advising the parties.

A problem question in negligence normally requires a consideration of each of the different elements of the tort and the approach taken in this outline answer is to consider these separate elements at the end of the relevant chapters on negligence.

In this question Orla suffered: (1) broken leg for which Sami will be the potential defendant; (2) facial injuries for which Sami and/or

Jordan may be potentially liable and; (3) facial scarring for which Max may be liable.

(1) Orla—broken leg

The first issue to be addressed is whether Sami is under a duty of care to Orla. Orla will argue that she is owed a duty of care by Sami on the ground that he ought reasonably to have foreseen that she would be likely to suffer personal injury as a result of his acts or omissions (Lord Atkin in *Donoghue v Stevenson*—the neighbour principle). Even if there is clearly foreseeable harm and proximity, the question of whether it would be fair, just and reasonable for a duty to be imposed on Sami will need to be considered (*Caparo Industries plc v Dickman* (1990)). We are told that Sami is acting in a voluntary capacity so this is relevant to the question of whether it would be fair, just and reasonable for a duty to be imposed on him. In a case involving physical loss which was clearly foreseeable (*Marc Rich & Co v Bishop Rock Marine* (1996)) the House of Lords found that no duty was owed to the owner of the cargo which was lost. The defendant was a non-profit making entity created and operating for the purpose of promoting the safety of lives at sea and it was not fair, just and reasonable in these circumstances to impose a duty. However, in *Watson v British Boxing Board of Control* (2001), which involved a claim for personal injury, the fact that the Board was a non-profit making organisation (like the defendant in the *Marc Rich*) was not enough to deny the justice of finding liability. The Court of Appeal held the fact that *British Boxing Board of Control* was a non-profit making organisation without insurance was irrelevant to its liability because of the reliance placed upon the Board by boxers and concluded that it was fair, just and reasonable to impose a duty of care. The teenagers (depending on their precise age) would have relied on Sami for their safety and on this basis it is likely that Sami will be under a duty of care to Orla.

Note: In a negligence problem once a *duty of care* has been established the next issue to be considered is whether Sami has *breached* this duty. This element will be addressed at the end of Ch.3.

Negligence: Breach of Duty

3

INTRODUCTION

The reasonable man

Once it is established that the defendant owed to the particular plaintiff a duty of care, it must then be proved that the defendant was in breach of duty. Negligence was defined in *Blyth v Birmingham Waterworks Co* (Ex., 1856) as:

> "the omission to do something which a reasonable man, guided upon those considerations which ordinarily regulate the conduct of human affairs, would do, or doing something which a prudent and reasonable man would not do".

As a matter of law, therefore, the standard of care required of the defendant is that of the hypothetical, reasonable man and, whilst no man is expected to attain perfection, that standard is objective in the sense that it generally takes no account of the idiosyncrasies of the person whose conduct is in question (*Glasgow Corp v Muir* (HL, 1943)). However, whether the defendant has reached the required standard in any given case is a question of fact, so that previous decisions should not be relied upon as precedents for what constitutes negligence.

The standard of reasonable care is therefore invariable in the sense that the law does not recognise differing degrees of negligence, but it is an infinitely flexible concept enabling the court in any given situation to impose standards ranging from very low to very high.

DEFINITION CHECKPOINT

What is reasonable care?

- The standard required of a participant in a competitive sport vis-a-vis spectators and fellow players may be described as low (see, e.g. *Wooldridge v Sumner* (CA, 1963)).
- High standards are imposed on motorists and the Court of Appeal in *Nettleship v Weston* (CA, 1971) held that the learner driver must exercise the skill of a reasonably competent, experienced driver.
- A driver who loses control of the vehicle being driven on account of some disabling condition of which he or she knew or ought to have

known, will be liable, but not if the driver is wholly unaware of it (*Mansfield v Weetabix Ltd* (CA, 1997)). The imposition of such high standards may be justified where the defendant is engaged in a high-risk activity, and there can be little doubt that, in some instances, compulsory liability insurance has influenced the court in fixing the level of care.

THE CONCEPT OF RISK

What is reasonable conduct varies with the particular circumstances, and liability depends ultimately on what the reasonable man would have fore-seen, which in turn may depend upon what particular knowledge and experience, if any, is to be attributed to him (*Roe v Minister of Health* (CA, 1954)). However, although a defendant is not negligent if the consequences of his or her conduct were unforeseeable, it does not necessarily follow that such a defendant will be liable for all foreseeable consequences. In practice, the courts evaluate the defendant's behaviour in terms of risk, so that he or she will be adjudged negligent if the claimant is exposed to an unreasonable risk of harm.

Figure 12: Risk-balancing factors

> ### RISK—BALANCING FACTORS
>
> The defendant's behaviour is evaluated in terms of risk and the following factors must be weighed in the balance to deter-mine if the claimant was exposed to an unreasonable risk of harm
>
> - the magnitude of the risk;
> - the social utility or desirability (if any) of the activity in question; and
> - the cost and practicability of precautionary measures to minimise or eliminate the risk.
>
> In performing this balancing act the court will decide what weight is to be given to each of these factors and will make a value judgment as to what the reasonable man would have done in the circumstances.

Compensation Act 2006
A perception that society is becoming "risk averse" and concerns about the emergence of a "compensation culture" led to a fear that many worthwhile activities would be curtailed because of the deterrent effect of potential

liability. One of the aims of the Compensation Act 2006 is to address this concern and to serve as a reminder to judges to consider carefully the impact which decisions about potential negligence liability might have in deterring the organisation and pursuit of worthwhile activities.

LEGISLATION HIGHLIGHTER

Section 1 of the Act deals with the deterrent effect of potential liability and provides:

"A court considering a claim in negligence or breach of statutory duty may, in determining whether the defendant should have taken particular steps to meet a standard of care (whether by taking precautions against a risk or otherwise), have regard to whether a requirement to take those steps might—

(a) prevent a desirable activity from being undertaken at all, to a particular extent or in a particular way, or

(b) discourage persons from undertaking functions in connection with a desirable activity."

In *Cole v Davis-Gilbert* (2007), the Court of Appeal said that there was a danger in setting too high a standard of care as it could lead to inhibiting consequences, namely the reduction in or prohibition of traditional activities on village greens. *Harris v Perry* (2008) also illustrates the reluctance of courts to perpetuate a culture which is excessively risk-averse. Here the Court of Appeal held that the trial judge had imposed too high a standard of care on parents in finding that a bouncy castle required uninterrupted supervision to prevent injury occurring.

Magnitude of the risk

The degree of care which the law exacts must be commensurate with the risk created. Two factors are involved here, namely the likelihood that harm will be caused and the potential gravity of that harm should the risk materialise. In *Bolton v Stone* (HL, 1951) the plaintiff was standing in the road when she was struck by a cricket ball which had been hit out of the defendants' ground. There was evidence that this had happened six times in the preceding 30 years, so the risk was one of which the defendants were aware and which was therefore foreseeable. Nevertheless the defendants were held not liable because the risk was so small that they were justified in not taking further measures to eliminate it.

Gravity of that harm to a particular *claimant*

The relevance of the potential gravity of the consequences to a particular claimant is illustrated in *Paris v Stepney BC* (HL, 1951), where a one-eyed garage worker became totally blind after being struck in the eye by a metal chip which flew from a bolt which he was trying to hammer loose. The defendant employers were held liable for failing to provide him with safety goggles, even though they were justified in not providing such equipment to a person with normal sight. Although the risk was small, the injury to this particular plaintiff was very serious.

Where the claimant consents to injury, for example, by an opponent in a boxing ring, he does not consent to injury resulting from inadequate safety arrangements by the sport's governing body after being hit. In *Watson v British Boxing Board of Control* (2001), the Board breached its duty in failing to inform itself adequately about the risks inherent in a blow to the head and by failing to require resuscitation equipment to be provided at the ringside with persons capable of operating it. In *Smoldon v Whitworth* (CA, 1997), applying the test for the level of care adopted in *Condon v Basi* (Ch.5), the referee of a colts rugby match was held liable to the plaintiff, who was injured as the result of a collapsed scrum. In *Vowles v Evans* (CA, 2003) the court held the threshold of referee liability to be a high one and the standard of care required depended on all the circumstances of the case.

The degree of risk to which the plaintiff is exposed will also depend, as is evident from *Paris*, upon any physical abnormality from which he may suffer so that, if such abnormality is or ought to be known to the defendant, that is a factor which must be taken into account. Thus, if a hole is dug in the pavement, adequate steps must be taken to prevent blind people from falling into it (*Haley v London Electricity Board* (HL, 1965)).

Social utility

The purpose to be served, if sufficiently important or desirable, may justify the assumption of what might otherwise be regarded as an abnormal risk.

UTILITY OF THE CONDUCT

A LOWER STANDARD OF CARE MAY SOMETIMES BE JUSTIFIED

In *Watt v Hertfordshire CC* (CA, 1954), for example, a fireman was injured by the movement of a heavy jack whilst travelling in a lorry which was not properly equipped to carry it. The jack was urgently needed to save the life of a woman who had become trapped under a bus, and in weighing the risk against the benefit to be achieved the defendants were held to be justified in exposing the plaintiff to that risk.

On the other hand, the laudable object of saving human life or limb has its limits and is plainly self-defeating if the danger risked is too great, so that a fire authority has been held negligent where a fire engine passed through a red traffic signal on its way to a fire and caused a collision (*Ward v L.C.C.* (HC, 1938)).

Cost of precautions

The risk has to be weighed against the cost and practicability of minimising or overcoming it. In *Latimer v A.E.C. Ltd* (HL, 1953) a factory floor became slippery with oil and water after a heavy rainfall caused flooding. Despite taking such steps as they were able, the defendants could not entirely eradicate the danger and the plaintiff slipped and was injured. The defendants were held not liable because the risk was not so great as to require the drastic step of closing the factory until the floor dried out.

CHARACTERISTICS OF THE DEFENDANT

It has already been noted that the legal standard generally takes no account of the personal characteristics of the particular defendant, and a defendant cannot therefore claim to have done his or her incompetent best. Inexperience or lack of intelligence or slow reactions provide no excuse to a charge of negligence. Nor, for that matter, will a defendant be able to avail of some lower standard of care on account of a physical disability. A partially sighted driver owes the same duty as one with normal sight, and the fact that he or she has a reduced field of vision merely imposes an obligation to proceed with greater caution.

> **DEFINITION CHECKPOINT**
>
> *What is reasonable varies according to the circumstances*
> The "reasonable man" is expected to know those things that common experience teaches and, in appropriate cases, can be expected to anticipate that others may be careless. Two types of defendant, children and those professing a particular skill (below) require special mention.

Children

As far as children are concerned, there is no defence of minority as such and a child is as responsible for its torts (through its guardian ad litem) as a person of full age. Thus, a boy of 16 has been held negligent in the use of an air rifle (*Gorely v Codd* (HC, 1967)). However, as in cases of contributory negligence, it was held in *Mullin v Richards* (CA, 1998) that the standard of care is that which can reasonably be expected of an ordinary child of the defendant's age.

KEY CASE

PARENTS AND TEACHERS HAVE A RESPONSIBILITY FOR CHILDREN
In *Carmarthenshire CC v Lewis* (HL, 1955), a lorry driver was killed when he swerved to avoid a young child who wandered from his nursery school on to the road. The defendants were liable for the teacher's negligence on the ground that where a young child does cause injury by conduct which in an adult would be classed as negligent then, more often than not, a parent or other responsible person, such as a teacher, will be liable. This is not vicarious liability but a primary liability arising from a failure to exercise proper supervision and control.

Professionals

Persons holding themselves out as having a particular skill or profession must attain the standard of the reasonably competent person exercising that skill or profession. The level of skill demanded, however, will vary according to the extent of the risk. For example, the do-it-yourself enthusiast fixing a door handle in his home must reach the standard of a reasonably competent carpenter doing that type of work, but not of a professional working for reward (*Wells v Cooper* (CA, 1958)). If, however, the work is of a technical or complex nature, and there is a risk of serious injury should it not be properly done, the defendant may be expected either to employ an expert or to display the same degree of skill.

A member of a profession discharges their duty by conforming to the standards of a reasonably competent member of that profession and inexperience is no excuse. Thus, a doctor must act in accordance with a practice accepted as proper by a body of responsible and skilled medical opinion, and is not negligent merely because there is a body of opinion which would take a contrary view.

KEY CASE

IN THE CASE OF PROFESSIONALS THE STANDARD SET BY THE PROFESSION
ITSELF

Bolam v Friern Barnet Hospital Management Committee (HC, 1957), held
the appropriate test for judging the standard of professional behaviour
is not that of the ordinary man; the defendant is judged by the standard of the ordinary skilled person exercising and professing to have
that special skill. A defendant is not negligent if he acts in accordance
with a practice accepted as proper by a responsible body of professional opinion skilled in the particular form of treatment. It has since
been held that:

* where there is more than one accepted method of doing things,
  both or all of which are regarded as proper by a skilled body of
  opinion, the judge is not entitled to make a finding of negligence
  on the basis of his preference for one method rather than another
  (*Maynard v West Midlands Regional Health Authority* (HL, 1984).
* the duty of the doctor is the same whether the matter be one of
  treatment, diagnosis or advice (*Sidaway v Governors of the Bethlem
  Royal Hospital* (HL, 1985); *Chester v Ashfar* (HL 2004)).

Although the Bolam test applies to professions generally, it has on occasions
been suggested, in relation only to the medical profession, that practitioners
themselves are the final arbiters in determining standards of professional
competence. In *Bolitho v City and Hackney Health Authority* (HL, 1997) the
House of Lords made it clear, however, that this is not so, holding that a
doctor could be liable for negligent treatment or diagnosis despite a body of
professional opinion supporting his conduct. The court had to be satisfied
that that body of opinion was reasonable or responsible in that it could
withstand logical analysis, although their Lordships accepted that, in the vast
majority of cases, the fact that experts in the field were of a particular opinion
would demonstrate its reasonableness. It remains the case that the effect of
the Bolam test is to make proof of professional negligence extremely difficult
where the defendant has followed an accepted practice.

An error of judgment by a professional may or may not be negligent,
depending upon whether it was such as a reasonably competent practitioner
might make (*Whitehouse v Jordan* (HL, 1981)).

WHAT IS REASONABLE IS JUDGED BY THE STANDARDS AT THE RELEVANT TIME, NOT LATER KNOWLEDGE

It is part of the professional's duty to keep abreast of new developments and techniques, as what is reasonably foreseeable may depend upon the state of existing knowledge within that profession at the time. Thus, in *Roe v Minister of Health* (CA, 1954) an anaesthetist was not negligent in failing to appreciate the risk of percolation of a preservative through invisible cracks in glass ampoules in which the anaesthetic was stored, because such a danger was not known to exist at the time.

EVIDENCE OF NEGLIGENCE

It is for the claimant to prove, on a balance of probabilities, that the defendant was negligent, subject to the proviso that proof that a person stands convicted of an offence is conclusive evidence in civil proceedings that he or she did commit it unless the contrary is proved (Civil Evidence Act 1968, s.11). The effect of this provision is to shift the burden of proof where the claimant proves that the defendant has been convicted of an offence involving conduct complained of as negligent, such as careless driving.

In order to discharge the burden of proof, the claimant must usually prove particular conduct on the part of the defendant which can be regarded as negligent. The claimant will not be able to do so, however, if he or she does not know how the accident was caused and, in such a case, the *maxim res ipsa loquitur* (the thing speaks for itself) may be relied on. This is simply a rule of evidence by which the claimant, who is unable to explain how the accident happened, asks the court to make a prima facie finding of negligence which it is then for the defendant to rebut if he or she can. After a long history of uncertainty on the issue, the Privy Council has now held that there is no shift in the legal burden of proof (*Ng Chun Pui v Lee Chuen Tat* (PC, 1988)).

With regard to the first requirement, if the cause of the accident is known then the doctrine does not apply because all that need then be done is to decide whether, on the facts, negligence is proved (*Barkway v South Wales Transport Co Ltd* (HL, 1950)). The operation of the second requirement is illustrated in *Easson v L.N.E.R.* (CA, 1944) where it was held that the doors of a long distance express train could not be said to be under the continuous control of the defendants, so that a child who fell out of the train could not rely on the maxim. Control by the defendant depends on the probability of

Figure 13: res ipsa loquitur (the thing speaks for itself)

> *res ipsa loquitur* (the thing speaks for itself)
>
> Three conditions are necessary for the application of the doctrine, according to *Scott v London and St. Katherine Docks Co* (EC, 1865):

> 1   there must be an absence of explanation as to how the accident happened

> 2   the "thing" which causes the damage must be under the control of the defendant (or someone for whose negligence he is responsible)

> 3   the accident must be such as would not ordinarily occur without negligence.

outside interference. If the facts establish that such interference was improbable, the defendant will be regarded as being in control.

DEFINITION CHECKPOINT

Res ipsa loquitur

Whether the accident is such as would not ordinarily have happened without negligence is to be judged in the light of common experience. Thus *res ipsa loquitur* has been applied:

- where a plaintiff went into hospital with two stiff fingers and came out with four stiff fingers (*Cassidy v Ministry of Health* (CA, 1951).
- where there was no evidence of negligence for a plane crash in which the appellant's husband was killed, the Privy Council said that the aircraft was airworthy when it took off and held that the doctrine of *res ipsa loquitur* applied to her claim. The maxim of *res ipsa loquitur* was said to be potentially of great importance in plane crashes because of the difficulty of proving of negligence in these cases (*George v Eagle Air Services Ltd* (2009).

If the maxim applies (and it need not be specifically pleaded) the defendant may be able to rebut the inference of negligence if it can be shown how the accident actually occurred, and that explanation is consistent with no negligence on the defendant's part, or a defendant may be able to provide a reasonable explanation of how the accident could have happened without negligence, in which case one of the essential conditions for the application of the maxim is not satisfied.

You should now understand:

- The second step in a claim in negligence is for the claimant to show (on the balance of probabilities) that the defendant has breached his duty of care and fallen below the standard of care required in the circumstances;

- The standard of care in negligence is objectively assessed—the standard is measured against that *the reasonable man*;

- The *reasonable man* test is modified in the case of professionals; the standard applied to doctors is set down in the *Bolam* test; and

- The balancing factors which judges use to determine whether or not the defendant has fallen below the standard of care in the circumstances.

QUESTION AND ANSWER

Question—see page 45

Orla—broken leg
Having concluded that Sami is under a duty of care to the teenagers, the next question is whether he is in breach of duty. In addressing this question the legal standard of care and the application of that standard to the particular facts should be explained. The degree of risk and the ease with which Sami could have taken precautions to guard against it will be relevant. The standard of care required by the common law is that of the reasonable man. This was defined in *Blyth v Birmingham Waterworks Co.* (1856) as the omission to do something that a reasonable man would do or doing something which a reasonable and prudent man would not do. The question for the court is not "did the defendant act reasonably?", but "in all the circumstances, would a reasonable person behave as the defendant did?". In terms of the weather, the time of year might be relevant and the extent to which a violent rainstorm might be foreseeable. In *Glasgow Corp. v Muir* (1943), the accident, while it could have been foreseen as

a possibility, was not a reasonable probability to the extent that the manageress should have been expected to clear the hall of children in anticipation. However, in this case the rainstorm might be foreseeable and practicability of taking precautions (taking a map, compass and mobile phone, warn about suitable clothing) was not unreasonable to expect. In *Bolton v Stone* (1951) it was held that where some precautions are required the standard of care that can reasonably be expected will vary according to the magnitude of the risk, the purpose of the defendant's activity and the practicability of precautions. In the context of the potential severity of the injury in the present circumstances, it would seem that Sami is in breach of duty. Also see *Latimer v AEG* and *Paris v Stepney BC*.

Orla—facial injuries

In addition to a claim against Sami, Orla may also have a claim in negligence against Jordan, the rescuer. There are many situations in which the defendant may have held himself out as having a particular skill; the law in these situations imposes the standard of care of the reasonable practitioner of the skill which the defendant purports to have, so Jordan will be expected to have the skill of a competent rescuer. However, here where Sami, by his negligence, risked the safety of the teenagers so that it is reasonably foreseeable that a person such as Jordan would attempt a rescue (*Haynes v Harwood* and *Baker v Hopkins*) he could remain liable for Orla's injuries. The risk which Jordan took in not waiting for the other members of the rescue team to join him also has to be balanced against the end he set out achieve and, if sufficiently important, he may be able to claim this justified the risk. In the present circumstances, an emergency concerning a matter of life or limb (*Watt v Hertfordshire County Council*) may justify a lower standard of care.

Finally, the implications for future cases of these particular circumstances, where Sami and Jordan are acting in a voluntary capacity, will need to be considered in the context of the Compensation Act 2006. Under the Act, the court may take into account factors such as who can best bear the loss and the implications of a particular decision for society as a whole. This can include considerations of whether Sami and Jordan are insured and what is fair and just on the particular facts. A court considering a claim in negligence or breach of statutory duty may, in determining whether the defendant should have taken particular steps to meet a standard of care (whether by taking precautions against risk or otherwise), have regard to whether a requirement to take those steps might prevent a desirable activity from being undertaken at all, to a particular extent or in a particular way, or discourage persons from undertaking functions in connection with a desirable activity. In *Cole v Davis-Gilbert* (2007), the Court of Appeal said that there was a danger in setting too high a standard of care as it could lead to inhibiting consequences, namely the reduction in or prohibition of traditional activities on village greens. Scott Baker L.J. pointed out: "Accidents happen, and sometimes they are what can be described as pure accidents in the sense that the victim cannot recover damages for the resulting injury because fault cannot be established." It is unlikely that Jordan will be found to have breached his duty.

Note: In a negligence problem once *a duty of care* has been established and that duty is found to have been *breached*, the next issue to be considered *causation of damage*. This issue will be addressed at the end of Ch.4.

Negligence: Causation and Remoteness of Damage

INTRODUCTION

The issues of causation and remoteness are relevant to the law of tort generally but are dealt with in the context of negligence because that is where most of the problems have arisen. Unless the claimant can prove that the defendant's tort caused the loss suffered, the action will fail or, in the case of torts actionable per se, only nominal damages will be recovered. Even if the claimant can prove a sufficient causal connection the claim will still fail if the defendant's breach is not a cause in law of the damage or, to put the matter another way, if the damage is too remote.

FACTUAL CAUSATION

It must first be established that the breach was a cause of the damage, not necessarily the sole or principal cause provided it "materially contributed" to the damage (*Bonnington Castings Ltd v Wardlaw* (HL, 1956)). In determining this issue it is usual to employ the "but for" test, the function of which is not to allocate legal responsibility, but merely to eliminate those factors which could not have had any causal effect.

> "If the damage would not have happened but for a particular fault then that fault is the cause of the damage; if it would have happened just the same, fault or no fault, the fault is not the cause of the damage" (per Denning L.J. in *Cork v Kirby Maclean Ltd* (CA, 1952)).

KEY CASE

THE "BUT FOR" TEST

In *Barnett v Chelsea & Kensington Hospital Management Committee* (HC, 1969), the failure of a casualty officer to examine a patient, who later died of arsenic poisoning, was held not to have been a cause of death because evidence showed that the patient would probably have died in any event. The "but-for" test will not, however, always solve the problem as is apparent where two simultaneous wrongs are done to the claimant, each of which would in itself be sufficient to cause the damage. In this case the test leads to the absurd result that neither breach is a cause of the damage, whereas in practice both will be held to have caused it.

Difficulties may also arise where the precise cause of the damage is unknown. In *McGhee v National Coal Board* (HL, 1972), the claimant contracted dermatitis as a result of exposure to abrasive dust at work. His employers were not at fault for the exposure during the normal course of his work, but were negligent in failing to provide washing facilities with the result that he was caked in dust for longer than necessary as he cycled home. The plaintiff succeeded on the ground that it was sufficient to show that the defendants' breach materially increased the risk of injury, even though medical knowledge at the time was unable to establish the breach as the probable cause. This decision had potentially far-reaching effects, particularly for cases of medical negligence, and an attempt was made at first instance in *Hotson v East Berkshire Area Health Authority* (HL, 1987) to extend the principle so as to impose liability in respect of the loss of a chance of recovery.

> ### DEFINITION CHECKPOINT
> *Damage must be proved on a balance of probabilities—no recovery for "loss of chance"*
> *Hotson* establishes that there is no recovery for "loss of chance" in tort. The plaintiff injured his hip in a fall and, as a result of negligent medical diagnosis, suffered a permanent deformity the risk of which would, had proper treatment been given, have been reduced by 25 per cent. The trial judge's decision to award that percentage of the loss was upheld in the Court of Appeal but reversed by the House of Lords on the ground that the plaintiff had not proved his case on a balance of probabilities. Had he been able to do so, their Lordships made it clear that there was no principle of law which would have justified a discount from the full measure of damages, incidentally demonstrating that, ignoring any possibility of contributory negligence, the plaintiff's claim is determined on an "all or nothing" basis.

Any suggestion that McGhee's case establishes a new principle was decisively rejected by the House of Lords in *Wilsher v Essex Area Health Authority* (HL, 1988), where their Lordships simply said that the court in *McGhee* had properly concluded that the breach of duty had materially contributed to the injury. *McGhee* was applied in *Fairchild v Glenhaven Funeral Services Ltd* (HL,

2002), where the evidence showed more than one employer to have contributed to the claimant's inhalation of asbestos dust causing mesothelioma (a form of cancer)—they did not need to satisfy the "but for" test.

The issue of causation arose in *Bailey v Ministry of Defence* 2008 where the question was whether the damage suffered was the result of the claimant's state of weakness because of the negligence in her post-operative care at the MoD's hospital or a non-negligent cause, each of which had made a material contribution to her overall weakness. The Court of Appeal held that it was enough for a patient to establish that, on the balance of probabilities, a lack of post-operative care and what flowed from that made a material contribution, namely something greater than negligible, to the overall weakness of her condition and the resulting brain damage. The Court referred to *Hotson* and said that if the evidence demonstrated on a balance of probabilities that the injury would have occurred as a result of a non-negligent cause, the claimant would have failed to establish causation.

KEY CASE

DAMAGE RESULTING FROM MULTIPLE CAUSES

The claimants in *Fairchild* had developed the mesothelioma after being exposed to asbestos dust during the course of employment with more than one employer but because of the current limits of human science, it could not be proved which employer's breach of duty was the cause of the disease. The Court of Appeal found that the employees had failed to prove on the balance of probabilities which period of employment had caused or materially contributed to the cause of the disease. However, the House of Lords allowed the appeal and held that if a claimant is unable to prove, on the balance of probabilities, that the defendant's breach of duty was the cause of the disease, it was sufficient to prove that the defendant materially increased the risk of harm. Although the appeal raised conflicting policy considerations, their Lordships considered that the injustice of denying a remedy to employees who had suffered grave harm outweighed the potential unfairness of imposing liability on successive employers who could not be proved to have caused the harm.

Barker v Corus UK (2006) also concerned exposure to asbestos on three separate occasions. Here the circumstances differed from *Fairchild* in that the negligence for one of these exposures was that of the claimant himself during short periods when he worked as a self-employed plasterer. The question arose as to whether the *Fairchild* principle could apply in this situation and whether the defendant was liable for all the damage suffered by the claimant or only for its contribution to the risk that materialised. The House of Lords partially reversed the ruling in Fairchild and held that although a defendant could still be liable without proof of causation, his liability only extended to the relative proportion to which he could have contributed to the chance of the outcome. This decision was seen as a victory for employers' insurers but it met with strong resistance from trade unions and victim groups. The Government responded by introducing the Compensation Act 2006 to restore the *Fairchild* approach to liability in cases of mesothelioma. Section 3 sets out the provisions for dealing with cases where the victim has contracted mesothelioma as a result of exposure to asbestos.

LEGISLATION HIGHLIGHTER

Section 3(1) of the Compensation Act 2006 was interpreted in *Sienkiewicz v Grief (UK) Ltd.* (2009) where an office employee, who had been exposed to asbestos dust in the factory where she worked for 18 years, died of mesothelioma. Although there was only one employer, the woman had also been exposed to asbestos dust in the environment of the town where she lived. The trial judge said that since there was another potential cause which did not arise from the tort of the employer, the claimant should have to prove causation on the normal balance of probabilities test and he found that she failed to discharge this test. The Court of Appeal allowed the claimant's appeal and said that in mesothelioma cases a claimant could establish causation by showing that the workplace exposure to asbestos had materially increased the *risk* of the employee developing the disease. The Court further said the intention of Parliament was to reflect the common law requirements of causation in mesothelioma cases, which required proof of causation by reference to a material increase in risk.

In terms of proving causation, it has been held by the House of Lords that a doctor who failed to warn a patient of a small risk inherent in surgery, was liable to the claimant when that risk eventuated. The decision in favour of the claimant could not be based on conventional causation principles because the risk of which she should have been warned was not created or increased by the failure to warn and the operation had not been performed negligently. However, the claimant satisfied the test for causation in negligence as she could prove that, had she been properly informed, she would not have consented to the operation but would have obtained further advice before making her decision (*Chester v Afshar* (2005)).

DEFINITION CHECKPOINT

The but for test does not provide a simple solution where there are a number of possible causes of the damage

Causation becomes more complex where successive acts cause damage:

> In *Baker v Willoughby* (HL, 1970) the plaintiff's leg was injured through the defendant's negligence, and some time later, before the trial of the action, he was shot during a robbery in the same leg which then had to be amputated. It was held that the plaintiff's right of recovery was not limited to the loss suffered only before the date of the robbery, but that he was entitled to the damages that he would have received had there been no subsequent injury.

By contrast:

> In *Jobling v Associated Dairies Ltd* (HL, 1980) the defendants' negligence caused a reduction in the plaintiff's earning capacity. Three years later, but before trial, the plaintiff was found to be suffering from a complaint, wholly unrelated to the original accident, which totally incapacitated him. The defendants were held liable only for the loss up to the time of the plaintiff's disablement.

In *Baker*, the later act was tortious whereas in *Jobling* it was a natural event, but the distinction is not very compelling. The decision in the former case is perhaps justifiable on the ground that to have applied the "but for" test in its full rigour would have left the plaintiff undercompensated. For even had the robbers been sued they would have been liable only for depriving the plaintiff of an already damaged leg.

REMOTENESS OF DAMAGE

It is not for every consequence of the defendant's wrong that the plaintiff is entitled to compensation. In order to contain the defendant's liability within reasonable bounds a line must be drawn, and those consequences which fall on the far side of that line are said to be too remote or, to put the matter another way, are regarded as not having been caused in law by the defendant's breach of duty.

Competing tests for remoteness of damage

- In *Re Polemis* (CA, 1921), a ship's cargo of benzine had leaked filling the hold with inflammable vapour. Stevedores unloading the vessel negligently dropped a plank into the hold, and the defendant employers were held liable for the destruction of the ship in the ensuing blaze because that loss was a *direct* (albeit unforeseeable) consequence of the negligence. Whilst not denying the relevance of foreseeability to the existence of a duty, the case did decide that it was not relevant in determining for what consequences the defendant should pay.

- The above approach was, however, disapproved by the Privy Council in *The Wagon Mound* (PC, 1961), which substituted a test of *reasonable foresight* of consequence for that of directness. The defendants negligently discharged into Sydney Harbour a large quantity of fuel oil which drifted to the plaintiffs' wharf where welding was in progress. The plaintiffs discontinued their operations, but later resumed following an assurance that the oil was in no danger of igniting. A fire did eventually break out, however, causing damage to the plaintiffs' wharf and to two ships upon which work was being done. It was found as a fact that some damage to the wharf was reasonably foreseeable by way of fouling of the slipway but that, in view of expert evidence, it was unforeseeable that the oil would ignite. The defendants were accordingly held not liable.

A number of points may be noted here. First, the courts have come to accept *The Wagon Mound* as representing the law. Secondly, the foreseeability of an event and the likelihood or otherwise of its occurring are quite different matters, and whilst the latter may be relevant to the issue of breach of duty (see Ch.3), the degree of foresight is generally irrelevant to the question of remoteness (see, however, the section in this Chapter on intervening acts). Thus, in *The Wagon Mound (No.2)* (PC, 1967) an action brought by the owners of the vessels damaged in the fire succeeded because it was found as a fact, on different evidence, that although the risk of fire was very slight, it was nonetheless foreseeable. Thirdly, although *The Wagon Mound (No.2)* held that foreseeability was the test for remoteness in cases of nuisance also it is unclear how far, if at all, the principle applies to other torts. It would appear not to apply where the defendant intends to cause injury because that "disposes of any question of remoteness" (*Quinn v Leathem* (HL, 1901)), but whether torts of strict liability are governed by foreseeability is a matter of controversy. Finally, the general tendency is to adopt a liberal approach to foreseeability, so that neither the extent of the harm nor the precise manner of its infliction need be foreseeable, provided it falls broadly within a fore-seeable class of damage. Taken in conjunction with the "egg-shell skull" principle, this means that, in practice, the same result would often be achieved whichever of the competing tests is applied.

Manner of occurrence

> ### DEFINITION CHECKPOINT
> *Reasonable foreseeability of damage of the relevant "kind" is not too remote*
> - In *Hughes v Lord Advocate* (HL, 1963), post office employees neg-ligently left a manhole uncovered with a canvas shelter over it, surrounded by paraffin lamps. The plaintiff, aged eight, took one of the lamps into the shelter and knocked it into the manhole. By an unusual combination of circumstances there was a violent explo-sion in which the boy was badly burned. Although the explosion was unforeseeable, the defendants were held liable because burns from the lamp were foreseeable, and it was immaterial that the precise chain of events leading to the injury was not.
> By contrast:
> - In *Doughty v Turner Manufacturing Co Ltd* (CA, 1964), the defen-dants' employee dropped an asbestos cover into a vat of molten liquid which, due to an unforeseeable chemical reaction, erupted and burned a fellow worker standing nearby. It was held that, even if injury by splashing were foreseeable (which was doubted), the eruption was not, and the plaintiff failed. This case is clearly at odds with *Hughes*, because if it is accepted that some injury by burning was foreseeable, then it ought not to matter that the way in which it occurred was not. On the balance of authority, *Hughes* is to be preferred.

Type of damage

The precise nature of the damage need not be foreseeable, provided it is of a type which could have been foreseen. The difficulty in defining damage "of a type" is illustrated by two contrasting cases. In *Bradford v Robinson Rentals Ltd* (HC, 1967), a van driver sent on a long journey in an unheated vehicle in severe weather was able to recover for frostbite because, although not in itself foreseeable, it was within the broad class of foreseeable risk arising from exposure to extreme cold. In *Tremain v Pike* (HC, 1969), the defendant's alleged negligence caused his farm to become rat-infested with the result that the plaintiff contracted a rare disease by contact with rat's urine. It was held that, even if negligence had been proved, the plaintiff could not succeed because although injury from rat bites or food contamination was foreseeable, this particularly rare disease was entirely different in kind. The decision in *Bradford* is a more accurate reflection of the current tendency to adopt a liberal approach to this issue.

Extent of damage; the "egg-shell skull" rule

Subject to what has been said above, it matters not that the actual damage is far greater in extent than could have been foreseen. Thus, in *Vacwell Engineering Co Ltd v B.D.H. Chemicals Ltd* (CA, 1971) the plaintiffs purchased a chemical manufactured and supplied by the defendants, who failed to give warning that it was liable to cause a minor explosion upon contact with water. The plaintiffs' employee placed a large quantity of the chemical in a sink whereupon an explosion of unforeseeable violence extensively damaged the premises. Since the explosion and consequent damage were foreseeable, even though the magnitude and extent thereof were not, the defendants were held liable.

A similar rule operates where the claimant suffers foreseeable personal injury which is exacerbated by some pre-existing physical or psychic abnormality.

DEFINITION CHECKPOINT

The "egg-shell skull" principle

The so-called "egg-shell skull" principle which survives *The Wagon Mound* (PC, 1961) means that a defendant must take his victim as he finds him. Liability is imposed upon the defendant for harm which is not only greater in extent than, but which is of an entirely different kind to, that which is foreseeable. In *Smith v Leech Brain & Co Ltd* (HC, 1962) a workman who had a predisposition to cancer received a burn on the lip from molten metal due to a colleague's negligence. The defendants were held liable under the "egg-shell skull" principle for his eventual death from cancer triggered off by the burn.

The principle applies equally to:

- a claimant who suffers from nervous shock (*Brice v Brown* (HC, 1984)) and
- a claimant with an "egg-shell personality" (*Malcolm v Broadhurst* (HC, 1970)).

In *Robinson v Post Office* (CA, 1974), the principle was applied to a plaintiff who suffered serious damage due to an allergy to medical treatment, which was foreseeably required as a result of an injury caused by the defendants' negligence. According to *Liesbosch Dredger v S.S. Edison* (HL, 1933) the "egg-shell skull" rule does not apply where the plaintiff's loss is aggravated by his own lack of financial resources. However, this decision was the subject of strong criticism and it has now been disapproved by the House of Lords. In *Lagden v O'Connor* (2004), the defendant negligently drove into the 10-year-old car of the claimant, who did not have the financial resources to pay for a hire car while his car was off the road so he entered into a credit agreement which involved greater expense. The court found that this additional expense was at least broadly foreseeable and, in stating that the wrongdoer must take his victim as he finds him, Lord Hope said: "The rule applies to the economic state of the victim in the same way as it applies to his physical and mental vulnerability."

INTERVENING CAUSES

In some cases the claimant's damage is alleged to be attributable not to the defendant's breach of duty, but to some intervening event which breaks the chain of causation. Such an event is called a *novus actus interveniens* and is usually dealt with as part of the issue of remoteness because even though the damage would not have occurred "but for" the defendant's breach, it may still be regarded in law as falling outside the scope of the risk created by the original fault.

Claimant's intervention

KEY CASES

WHERE DAMAGE IS CAUSED BY A COMBINATION OF THE CLAIMANT'S OWN ACT AND THE DEFENDANT'S BREACH

- In *McKew v Holland & Hannen & Cubitts (Scotland) Ltd* (HL, 1969), as a result of an injury caused by the defendants' negligence, the plaintiff's leg would give way without warning. Whilst descending a steep flight of steps without assistance or support, his leg gave way and he fell and fractured his ankle. The defendants were held not liable for this further injury because, although foreseeable, the plaintiff's conduct was so unreasonable as to amount to a *novus actus*.
- In *Sayers v Harlow UDC* (CA, 1958), a faulty lock on the door of a public lavatory cubicle caused the plaintiff to become trapped inside. She fell and injured herself when the toilet-roll holder onto which she had climbed in order to get out gave way, and damages were reduced under the **Law Reform (Contributory Negligence) Act**

1945 (see Ch.5) for the unreasonable manner in which she had attempted her escape.

These two cases illustrate the different approach that may be taken where the damage is caused by a combination of the claimant's own act and the defendant's breach. Whether the issue is seen as one of novus actus or of contributory negligence (which is the more common approach) will depend upon the nature and quality of the claimant's conduct, and it may be that a positive act is more likely to break the causal chain than a mere omission (cf. *Knightley v Johns* (CA, 1982); see below).

On any view of the matter McKew seems to be a harsh decision. In *Spencer v Wincanton Holdings Ltd (Wincanton Logistics Ltd)* (2009), the employer admitted liability for the first injury but sought to rely on *McKew*, arguing there was no liability to pay damages for a second accident which resulted in the employee becoming wheelchair dependent, because it had been caused by his own unreasonable conduct when he pulled into a petrol station to fill his car with petrol without wearing his artificial leg or using his sticks. The Court of Appeal held that there was *no novus actus* that broke the chain of causation: the employee's contributory conduct towards the second accident had been below the standard of unreasonableness required to break the chain of causation and contributory negligence was available to deal with the sharing of responsibility.

DEFINITION CHECKPOINT

There may be instances where even a deliberate act by the claimant will not relieve the defendant of responsibility

- In *Pigney v Pointer's Transport Services Ltd* (HC, 1957), the defendants were held liable to a plaintiff whose husband committed suicide as a result of mental depression brought on by an injury caused by the defendants' negligence.
- In *Corr v IBC Vehicles* (2008), following a near-fatal accident at work as a result of the defendant's negligence, the claimant's husband suffered ongoing physical and psychological problems. In these circumstances the suicide is merely the culmination of the depression and the House of Lords upheld a Court of Appeal decision allowing an appeal against the judge's finding that the deceased's subsequent suicide was not reasonably foreseeable: depression as a result of the accident was within the compensable damage flowing from the injury and the chain of causation had not been broken by the intentional act of suicide.

In any event, the above decisions are presumably justifiable on the basis of the "egg-shell skull" principle (see also *Reeves v Commissioner of Police of the Metropolis* (HL, 1999), Ch.5).

As far as rescuers are concerned (see Ch.5), there is generally no question of categorising the plaintiff's conduct as a *novus actus* (*Haynes v Harwood* (CA, 1935)), unless the danger has passed, in which case it is arguable that a duty is no longer owed (see *Cutler v United Dairies (London) Ltd* (CA, 1933)). It makes no difference in principle whether the rescuer acts on impulse or after conscious reflection (*Haynes v Harwood*, per Greer L.J.).

Intervention of third party

According to Lord Reid in *Dorset Yacht Co Ltd v Home Office* (HL, 1970), the intervention of a third party must have been something very likely to happen if it is not to be regarded as breaking the chain of causation. However, this dictum should be interpreted in the light of its proper context, namely the potential liability of a defendant for the criminal act of another, because a less stringent test may be applied in the case of non-wilful intervention by the third party.

KEY CASE

NEGLIGENT CONDUCT IN THE INTERVENING ACT OF A THIRD PARTY IS MORE LIKELY TO BREAK THE CHAIN OF CAUSATION THAN NON-NEGLIGENT CONDUCT

In *Knightley v Johns* (CA, 1982), the defendant negligently caused a crash on a dangerous bend in a one-way tunnel. The police inspector at the scene of the accident forgot to close the tunnel to oncoming traffic as he ought to have done in accordance with standing orders, so he ordered the plaintiff officer to ride back on his motorcycle against the flow of traffic in order to do so, and the plaintiff was injured in a further collision. It was said that, in considering whether the intervening act of a third party breaks the chain of causation, the test is whether the damage is reasonably foreseeable in the sense of being a "natural and probable" result of the defendant's breach. A deliberate decision to do a positive act is more likely to break the chain than a mere omission; so too, tortious conduct is more likely to break it than conduct which is not. In this case the inspector's errors amounted to tortious negligence which could scarcely be described as the natural and probable consequence of the original collision, and the defendant was therefore not liable.

It must be decided in each case whether the nature of the intervening actor's conduct was such as to eclipse the causative effect of the original wrong. In *Rouse v Squires* (CA, 1973), the negligence of the first defendant in causing a motorway crash was held to be an operative cause of the death of the plaintiff who, whilst assisting at the scene of the accident, was run down by the negligent driving of the second defendant. By contrast, in *Wright v Lodge* (CA, 1993) the defendant's negligence caused a lorry driver to collide with his car, as a result of which the lorry was involved in a further collision. It was found that the lorry driver had driven recklessly (not merely carelessly), and his driving was therefore held to be the sole legal cause of the damage arising from the second accident.

A question which as yet remains unresolved is the extent to which negligent medical treatment or diagnosis may break the chain of causation, although the answer will no doubt depend upon the extent to which the practitioner has departed from the requisite standard of care. In *Prendergast v Sam & Dee Ltd* (HC, 1988), the negligent misreading by a pharmacist of a doctor's prescription did not relieve the doctor of his duty to write in a reasonably legible hand, and liability was apportioned between them.

DEFINITION CHECKPOINT

Intervening conduct in the context of the risk created by the defendant's negligence

In dealing generally with the question of what amounts to a *novus actus*, the answer is sometimes to be found by considering whether the intervening conduct was within the ambit of the risk created by the defendant's negligence. For example, an incursion of squatters is not one of the risks attendant upon undermining the foundations of a building (*Lamb's* case); but the act of a rescuer who goes to assist another put in peril by the defendant's negligence clearly is within the risk created by that negligence and is not therefore a *novus actus* (*Haynes v Harwood* (CA, 1935); see Ch.5).

Intervening natural force

The defendant will not normally be liable for damage suffered as the immediate consequence of a natural event which occurs independently of the breach. In *Carslogie Steamship Co Ltd v Royal Norwegian Government* (HL, 1952), the defendants were held not liable for storm damage suffered by a ship during a voyage to a place where repairs to collision damage caused by the defendants' negligence were to be done, even though that voyage would not have been undertaken had the collision not occurred.

It will be apparent from the foregoing discussion that, in the case of intervening acts, foreseeability may be a rough guide in assessing relative degrees of responsibility but it can never be the sole criterion of liability. A number of the cases evince a notable lack of consistency of approach and precision in the use of language, which serves only to mask the policy factors at play in the judicial process.

You should now understand:

- Causation of damage is the third element of a claim in negligence; if there is no causal connection between the claimant's damage and the defendant's conduct the claim will not succeed;

- The "but for" test of causation is the primary means of establishing factual causation but in some situations this test is insufficient;

- The chain of causation may be broken by unreasonable or unforeseeable acts or events (*novus actus interveniens*);

- Causation in fact and causation in law (or remoteness of damage) must be distinguished; foreseeability of damage of the relevant type is required—otherwise the claimant's damage is too remote.

QUESTION AND ANSWER

Approach to answer

Orla—broken leg

Having concluded that Sami is in breach of duty, the next issue is to determine, applying the "but for" test, whether Orla's broken leg is a direct consequence of Sami's breach. Applying the "but for" test (*Barnett v Kensington & Chelsea Hospital*) would indicate that Sami's breach caused Orla's damage (which is of a foreseeable kind and therefore not too remote (*The Wagon Mound*). We do not have Orla's precise age but Sami would be liable for her broken leg unless he could claim that her refusal to follow his instruction to remain with the group constituted a *novus actus interveniens*, thereby breaking the chain of causation between his negligence and Orla's damage. Sami would rely on *McKew v Holland* (1969) and say that Orla's own unreasonable conduct broke the chain of causation, but he may not succeed in this argument on the basis of the decision in *Weiland v Cyril Lord Carpets*, where the defendants were found liable because the plaintiff had not acted unreasonably.

Alternatively, Sami may seek to argue contributory negligence on Orla's part. The principle of contributory negligence is that a person has responsibility for his actions and it is just and equitable that the reduction in damages should take account of the relative blame-worthiness of the claimant's conduct. However, although in *Gough v Thorne* (1966) the fact that a 13-year-old girl had relied entirely on the driver's signal to cross the road did not constitute contributory negligence, Orla's conduct will be judged as that of an adult.

Orla—facial scarring

If a defendant has injured someone who consequently requires medical attention, he is likely to be liable for the consequences of that treatment, even if unforeseeable. In *Robinson v Post Office* (1974), the plaintiff suffered a severe allergic reaction to an anti-tetanus injection he needed and although the court found some carelessness on the doctor's part in administering the injection, liability remained with the plaintiff's employer. On this basis Sami would remain liable for Orla's injuries but if Max's conduct in treating Orla is sufficiently unreasonable it may amount to a *novus actus interveniens* which breaks the chain of causation between Sami's breach and Orla's injury (*Knightley v Johns* (1982)). If Max's conduct does amount to a *novus actus interveniens* even though has not acted negligently in performing the operation, the "but for" test of causation may be satisfied on grounds of policy. In *Chester v Afshar* (2005) it was held that even where the treatment has not been negligent but a risk that eventuates falls within the scope of a duty to warn, the doctor remains liable.

Should Max be found liable for Orla's permanent scarring, the question of remoteness of damage will arise. A defendant is not liable for all the direct losses which result from his breach of duty; the kind of harm sustained by the claimant must be reasonably foreseeable, the *Wagon Mound* (1961). However, in *Hughes v Lord Advocate* (1963) it was held that if the kind of damage suffered is reasonably foreseeable, the precise manner in which it occurred need not have been. If Orla can show that the kind of damage she suffered (scarring) was of a type which was foreseeable then Max will be liable.

Defences to Negligence: Contributory Negligence, Volenti Non Fit Injuria and Ex Turpi Causa

5

INTRODUCTION—CONTRIBUTORY NEGLIGENCE

At common law a claimant whose injuries were caused partly by their own negligence could recover nothing. To succeed in this defence it is not necessary for the defendant to prove that the claimant owed a duty of care but simply that the claimant "did not in his own interest take reasonable care of himself and contributed, by this want of care, to his own injury" (per Lord Simon in *Nance v British Columbia Electric Ry* (PC, 1951)). Since the Law Reform (Contributory Negligence) Act 1945, contributory negligence is no longer a complete bar to recovery but, in accordance with s.1(1) of the Act, will result in a reduction of damages "to such extent as the court thinks just and equitable having regard to the claimant's share in the responsibility for the damage".

> **LEGISLATION HIGHLIGHTER**
>
> Section 1(1) of the Law Reform (Contributory Negligence) Act 1945 provides:
> Where any person suffers damage as the result partly of his own fault and partly of the fault of any other person or persons, a claim in respect of that damage shall not be defeated by reason of the fault of the person suffering the damage, but the damages recoverable in respect thereof shall be reduced to such extent as the court thinks just and equitable having regard to the claimant's share in the responsibility for the damage.

The Act applies where the damage is attributable to the fault of both parties, and "fault" is defined in s.4 to mean "negligence, breach of statutory duty or other act or omission which gives rise to a liability in tort or would, apart from this Act, give rise to the defence of contributory negligence".

Causation

The damage suffered must be caused partly by the fault of the claimant and it is therefore irrelevant that the claimant's fault was nothing to do with the accident. Thus, reductions have been made for failing to wear a seat belt or a crash helmet, and for travelling in a vehicle with a drunk driver. To put the matter another way, a claimant's damage must be within the foreseeable risk to which he or she unreasonably exposed themselves. In *Jones v Livox Quarries Ltd* (CA, 1952) the plaintiff, contrary to instructions, stood on the rear towbar of a vehicle and was injured when another vehicle ran into the back of it. It was held that this was one of the risks to which he had exposed himself and his damages were reduced accordingly.

DEFINITION CHECKPOINT

Damage must be caused partly by the fault of the claimant
- In *Badger v Ministry of Defence* (2006), the deceased's lung cancer was caused by asbestos fibres to which he been exposed during his employment, however, his failure to stop smoking despite warnings about the risk of cancer constituted contributory negligence.

On the other hand:
- In *Westwood v Post Office* (1974), an employee fell through a rotten floor in a room housing dangerous machinery which bore a notice forbidding him to enter. No reduction was made because that was not a risk which the employee could have foreseen; the employer's argument that he should have anticipated the risk was rejected.

Standard of care

The claimant is expected to show an objective standard of reasonable care in much the same way as the defendant must to avoid tortious negligence. A claimant who ought reasonably to have foreseen that, if he or she did not act as a "reasonable man" they might be hurt themselves, is guilty of contributory negligence. Similar factors to those determining whether the defendant is in breach of duty (see Ch.3) are therefore relevant here.

Particular cases

1. Children

As a matter of law there is no age below which it can be said that a child is incapable of contributory negligence, but the degree of care to be expected must be proportioned to the age of the child.

DEGREE OF CARE TO BE EXPECTED MUST BE PROPORTIONED TO THE AGE OF THE CHILD

- In *Gough v Thorne* (CA, 1966), a 13-year-old girl who was knocked down by a negligent motorist when she stepped past a stationary lorry whose driver had beckoned her to cross, was held not guilty of contributory negligence.
- In *Morales v Eccleston* (CA, 1991), however, an 11-year-old who was struck by the defendant driver while kicking a ball in the middle of a road with traffic passing in either direction had his damages reduced by 75 per cent.
- In *Yachuk v Oliver Blais Co Ltd* (PC, 1949), a boy of nine was not contributorily negligent when he set fire to petrol supplied to him by the defendants, on the ground that it was foreseeable that he might meddle with it and he could not be expected to appreciate its dangerous properties.

2. Old or infirm persons
It seems that some latitude may be given to such persons in assessing whether they are guilty of contributory negligence. Thus, an elderly person who is unable to move quickly enough to get out of the path of a motorist who drives close by in the expectation that he is able to do so may not be penalised (*Daly v Liverpool Corp* (HC, 1939)).

3. Rescuers
It is not often that a rescuer will be found guilty of contributory negligence, bearing in mind that, in the face of imminent danger, his reaction is usually instinctive. Thus, in *Brandon v Osborne, Garrett & Co Ltd* (HC, 1924) the defendants negligently allowed a sheet of glass to fall from their shop roof and the plaintiff, believing her husband to be in danger, tried to pull him away and injured her leg. It was held that she was not contributorily negligent. A similar principle applies where the claimant is injured in trying to extricate him or herself from a perilous situation in which the defendant's negligence has placed them, even though with hindsight the claimant is shown to have chosen the wrong course of action (*Jones v Boyce* (1816), cf. *Sayers v Harlow UDC* (CA, 1958)). That a rescuer may be contributorily negligent, however, is illustrated by *Harrison v British Railways Board* (HC, 1981), although in this case the plaintiff was plainly at fault in not following an established work procedure designed to deal with the particular emergency in question.

4. Workers

In relation to actions for breach of statutory duty, this issue is dealt with in Ch.9. It seems clear from *Westwood v Post Office* (HL, 1974) that the more lenient approach towards employees is appropriate only where the action is founded upon the employer's breach of statutory duty and not upon ordinary negligence.

5. Car passengers

KEY CASE

FAILURE TO WEAR A SEAT BELT AND CONTRIBUTORY NEGLIGENCE

Froom v Butcher (CA, 1976) firmly established that failure to wear a seat belt is contributory negligence, provided of course that such failure causes or contributes to the injury. It was suggested that ordinarily there should be:

- a reduction of 25 per cent in respect of injuries which would have been avoided altogether; and
- a reduction of 15 per cent in respect of those injuries which would have been less severe.

Although these figures are guidelines only, they should, according to *Capps v Miller* (CA, 1989), generally be followed. So, too, a motorcyclist who fails to wear a crash helmet will have his damages similarly reduced (*O'Connell v Jackson* (CA, 1972)), although failure to fasten a helmet properly has been held to merit a slightly smaller reduction (*Capps v Miller*).

Even though there is no legal requirement to wear a cycling helmet, contributory negligence was argued in *Smith v Finch* (2009) where a cyclist sustained serious head injuries in a road accident caused by the defendant. The Court concluded that the judgment and observations of Lord Denning MR Court in *Froom v Butcher* should apply to the wearing of helmets by cyclists (however, contributory negligence failed here because the defendant was unable to show that a helmet would have prevented the claimant's serious head injuries or made them less severe).

It is also clear that to ride in a car in the knowledge that the driver has been drinking constitutes contributory negligence, even though the passenger himself is so intoxicated as not to appreciate that the driver is unfit to drive (*Owens v Brimmell* (HC, 1977)).

Apportionment

Apportionment is on a just and equitable basis according to the 1945 Act and, in assessing the claimant's reduction, the court may take into account both the causative potency of his act and the degree of blameworthiness (i.e. the extent to which the claimants conduct fell below the requisite standard of care) to be attached to it. There seem to be no hard and fast rules, however, and a good deal of judicial discretion is exercised in the matter. The Court of Appeal has held that no apportionment should be made unless one of the parties is at least 10 per cent to blame (*Johnson v Tennant Bros Ltd* (CA, 1954)), although the case seems to have been decided on the ground that the defendant's breach was not a cause of the damage (see *Capps v Miller* (CA, 1989)).

■ DEFINITION CHECKPOINT

Law Reform (Contributory Negligence) Act 1945 provides that there must be fault on the part of both parties
In *Jayes v IMI (Kynoch) Ltd* (CA, 1985), the plaintiff was adjudged 100 per cent contributorily negligent, but such a finding is illogical according to *Pitts v Hunt* (CA, 1990) because the 1945 Act does not apply unless both parties were at fault. The earlier case can presumably be explained on the basis that the plaintiff was solely to blame for the damage.

Where the same accident involves two or more defendants, any contributory negligence must be assessed by comparing the claimant's conduct with the totality of the defendants' negligence. The issue of the extent to which each defendant contributed to the damage should thereafter be dealt with in contribution proceedings (*Fitzgerald v Lane* (HL, 1988)).

One final point to note is that a defendant who seeks to rely on the defence must plead it (*Fookes v Slaytor* (CA, 1978)).

INTRODUCTION—VOLENTI NON FIT INJURIA

This maxim embodies the principle that a person who expressly or impliedly agrees with another to run the risk of harm created by that other cannot thereafter sue in respect of damage suffered as a result of the materialisation of that risk. The defence is commonly called consent or voluntary assumption of risk and, if successful, is a complete bar to recovery.

For the defence to apply, the defendant must have committed what would, in the absence of any consent, amount to a tort. The defendant must prove not only that the claimant consented to the risk of actual damage, but also that he or she agreed to waive their right of action in respect of that damage. The application of the defence is most straightforward in the case of intentional torts, as, for instance, where each party to a boxing match consents to being fairly struck by the other. Most of the problems in the past have arisen in negligence where the infliction of damage is a risk rather than a certainty, but in view of the power to apportion responsibility by a finding of contributory negligence, the defence is rarely successful today.

Knowledge of the risk

Mere knowledge of the risk does not amount to consent. It must be found as a fact that the plaintiff freely and voluntarily, with full knowledge of the nature and extent of the risk, impliedly agreed to incur it (*Osborne v L. & N. W. Ry.* (HC, 1888)). The claimant must therefore have genuine freedom of choice which predicates the absence of any feeling of constraint (*Bowater v Rowley Regis Corp* (CA, 1944)). One explanation for the lack of success of this defence to a negligence action is that, since the alleged consent usually precedes the defendant's breach of duty, the claimant cannot be said in these circumstances to have full knowledge and appreciation of the risk (*Wooldridge v Sumner* (CA, 1963), per Diplock L.J.).

Agreement

It has been suggested that an appreciation of, and willingness to take, the risk will not satisfy the requirements of the defence; there must, in addition, be evidence that the claimant has expressly or impliedly agreed to waive his or her right of action (see, e.g. *Nettleship v Weston* (CA, 1971) per Lord Denning). On the other hand the defence may apply where the claimant consciously assumes the risk of an existing danger created by the defendant, independently of any agreement (*Titchener v British Railways Board* (HL, 1983)).

> **LEGISLATION HIGHLIGHTER**
>
> An express antecedent agreement to relieve the defendant of liability for future negligence operates in effect as an exclusion notice and is therefore subject to the **Unfair Contract Terms Act 1977**.
>
> Section 2(1) renders void any purported exclusion of liability for death or personal injury caused by negligence and, in the case of other loss or damage, s.2(2) subjects such an exclusion to a test of reasonableness.

Section 2(3) further provides that a person's agreement to, or awareness of, such a notice is not of itself to be taken as indicating his voluntary acceptance of any risk.

It should be noted, however, that the above provisions only apply to business liability (see further Ch.8). In *Johnstone v Blooms-bury Health Authority* (CA, 1991), it was considered that, on the assumption that an express contractual term amounted to a plea of volenti, it could fall within the ambit of s.2(1) of the Act.

In some circumstances the conduct of the parties may enable an inference to be drawn that the claimant has impliedly agreed to waive his legal rights in respect of future negligence. For example, in *Morris v Murray* (CA, 1990) the defence applied when, in poor weather conditions, the defendant, who to the plaintiff's knowledge was extremely drunk, took the plaintiff for a spin in his aircraft and crashed almost immediately after take-off.

1. Sporting events

A spectator injured by a participant in a sporting event does not consent to negligence either by the participant or by the organiser, though he may be defeated by a valid exclusion notice (*White v Blackmore* (CA, 1972)). A spectator may be taken to have accepted those risks ordinarily incidental to the game (e.g. being hit by a cricket ball struck into the crowd), but in this case there is no negligence and volenti is therefore irrelevant. The potential liability of the participant depends upon the standard of care owed and, in *Wooldridge v Sumner* (CA, 1963), this was expressed by Diplock L.J. as a duty not to act with reckless disregard for the spectator's safety. This was criti-cised, however, in *Wilks v Cheltenham Home Guard Motor Cycle & Light Car Club* (CA, 1971) where it was said that the proper standard was one of rea-sonable care in all the circumstances, which might include the fact that the defendant is involved in a fast-moving, competitive sport in an all-out effort to win.

DEFINITION CHECKPOINT

Approach adopted to incidents between one player and another at sporting events:

- In *Condon v Basi* (CA, 1985), a "reckless and dangerous" tackle in a local amateur football match was held to be negligence.
- In *Watson v British Boxing Board of Control* (2001), it was pointed out that where the plaintiff consents to injury by an opponent in a boxing ring he does not consent to injury resulting from inadequate safety arrangements by the sport's governing body after being hit.

2. Workmen

CONSENT WILL NOT APPLY WHERE THE CLAIMANT HAS NO CHOICE BUT TO ACCEPT THE RISK; KNOWLEDGE OF THE RISK DOES NOT NECESSARILY IMPLY CONSENT

Smith v Baker & Sons (HL, 1891) held that a plea of *volenti* by an employer in an action by his employee for common law negligence is almost bound to fail because the unequal nature of the relationship is such that the employee does not exercise complete freedom of will (*Bowater v Rowley Regis Corp* (CA,1944)).

It has further been held that the defence is not available in an action for breach of an employer's statutory duty, though it may succeed where the employer is sued vicariously, provided that the person in breach is not superior in rank to the claimant such that his instructions are bound to be obeyed (*ICI Ltd v Shatwell* (HL, 1965)). In *Johnstone v Bloomsbury Health Authority* (CA, 1991), an express term in a contract of employment required the plaintiff to work 40 hours per week and to "be available" for a further average 48 hours per week overtime at the employer's discretion. In an action for breach of the employer's common law duty to take reasonable care for the plaintiff's health and safety, Leggatt L.J. took the view that the express term could not be overridden by the implied duty, and Browne-Wilkinson V.C. would have agreed if the term had imposed an absolute obligation to work those further hours, as opposed to giving a discretion. If this view is correct it would appear to undermine the proposition that *volenti* ought not, in principle, to afford a defence to the employer.

3. Car passengers

A passenger who accepts a lift with a driver who, to his or her knowledge, is inexperienced or whose ability to drive safely is otherwise impaired (e.g. through drink) cannot be held *volenti* to the risk, because s.149 of the Road Traffic Act 1988 prohibits any restriction on the driver's liability to his passenger as is required to be covered by insurance (*Pitts v Hunt* (CA, 1990); cf. travelling in a plane with a drunken pilot as in *Morris v Murray* (CA, 1990)). Taking a lift with an inebriated car driver is, however, likely to amount to contributory negligence (*Owens v Brimmell* (HC, 1977)).

Section 149 of the Road Traffic Act (1988) prohibits any restriction on the driver's liability to his passenger as required by insurance. This means that the *volenti* defence is now excluded in claims arising from road traffic accidents.

4. Rescuers

If the defendant's negligence endangers the safety of others such that a rescue attempt is reasonably foreseeable, a duty is owed to the rescuer (*Haynes v Harwood* (CA, 1935)). It makes no difference that the person imperilled is actually the defendant rather than a third party (*Harrison v British Railways Board* (HC, 1981)), and the duty owed is wholly independent of any duty owed by the defendant to those who are rescued (*Videan v British Transport Commission* (CA, 1963)). Nor is there any rule of law to prevent a claim by a professional "rescuer", so that a fireman injured whilst fighting a negligently-started fire may recover (*Ogwo v Taylor* (HL, 1988)). In these situations volenti clearly does not apply. In the first place the rescuer acts under moral compulsion and does not therefore exercise freedom of choice, and secondly, since the defendant's negligence precedes the rescue the plaintiff cannot be said to consent to it and may not even be aware of it at the time (*Baker v T. E. Hopkins & Son Ltd* (CA, 1959)).

KEY CASE

DANGER INVITES RESCUE; RESCUERS ARE TREATED LENIENTLY WHERE THE RESCUE IS TO SAVE LIFE OR LIMB.
Chadwick v British Transport Commission (HC,1967) a rescuer who assisted at the scene of a train crash and who suffered nervous shock as a result of what he saw was held entitled to recover even though he was in no personal danger (for the position regarding psychiatric harm generally see Ch.2).

INTRODUCTION—EX TURPI CAUSA

Where the alleged wrong occurs while the claimant is engaged in criminal activity, the claim may be barred because *ex turpi causa non oritur actio* (no action can be founded on an illegal act).

In *Gray v Thames Trains Ltd* (2009), Lord Hoffman said the maxim expresses not so much a principle as a policy; that policy is not based upon a single justification but on a group of reasons, which vary in different situations: "The wider and simpler version was that you could not recover for damage which was the consequence of your own criminal act. In its narrower form, it was that you could not recover for damage which was the consequence of a sentence imposed upon you for a criminal act."

This principle may also apply where the claimant's conduct is immoral (*Kirkham v Chief Constable of Greater Manchester* (CA, 1990)). The difficulty is in determining which types of conduct are considered sufficiently heinous for the purposes of the defence. Some cases have said that it will apply where it would be impossible to determine an appropriate standard of care (e.g. *Pitts v Hunt* (CA, 1990)), while others have suggested that the plaintiff ought not to succeed if to permit him to do so would be an "affront to the public conscience" (*Kirkham v Chief Constable of Greater Manchester*).

In *Clunis v Camden and Islington Health Authority* (CA, 1998), the plaintiff, who had a long history of mental illness, was convicted of manslaughter and ordered to be detained in a secure hospital. He sued the defendant for negligence for failing to take reasonable care to provide him with after-care services following his discharge from hospital where he had been detained under the Mental Health Act 1983. It was held that, despite a successful plea of diminished responsibility at the criminal trial, his action was barred on grounds of public policy since he was directly implicated in the illegality and must be taken to have known that what he was doing was wrong (cf. *Meah v McCreamer* (HC, 1985)).

KEY CASES

- In *Vellino v Chief Constable of Greater Manchester Police* (CA, 2001), the claimant suffered brain damage when he attempted to escape from police custody by jumping from a window of his second floor. He claimed negligence on the part of the arresting officers, alleging that they had stood idly by and let him jump. The Court of Appeal held that the maxim *ex turpi causa* made the claim untenable because the defendant had to rely on his own criminal conduct in escaping lawful custody to found his claim.
- In *Gray v Thames Trains Ltd* (2009), as the result of a serious rail crash caused by the defendant's negligence, the claimant suffered severe psychological depression which led to his conviction of killing a man. His claim in damages for loss of earnings after he committed the manslaughter was allowed by the Court of Appeal on the ground that it was not defeated by *ex turpi causa* because the damages were not inextricably bound up with or linked to his criminal conduct. However, on appeal the House of Lords ruled that Gray's conviction for manslaughter precluded a claim for loss of

earnings during his detention by reason of the public policy expressed in the doctrine of *ex turpi causa*.

Both the degree of moral turpitude and the closeness of the causal connection between it and the claimant's damage are relevant factors. Thus, the principle was applied to a plaintiff car passenger injured by the defendant's negligent driving during the course of making their get-away from a burglary (*Ashton v Turner* (HC, 1981)); and to one who, having had a few drinks with the defendant, then rode as a pillion passenger on the defendant's motorcycle and encouraged him to drive in a reckless manner, in the knowledge also that the defendant did not hold a licence and was uninsured (*Pitts v Hunt* (CA, 1990)). In *Kirkham* (above) the defence was held not to apply to a claim based directly on the suicide of a man who was mentally disturbed, though it was considered that the position might be otherwise where the suicide was entirely sane; the same conclusions were reached in relation to the application of the *volenti* defence. However, it has now been held that neither defence can apply even where the suicide was of sound mind, provided that the defendant was under a duty of care to prevent a suicide attempt; nor can the plaintiff's conduct be regarded as a *novus actus interveniens* (see Ch.4) (*Reeves v Commissioner of Police of the Metropolis* (HL, 1999)).

According to Lord Denning a burglar bitten by a guard dog may be defeated by the maxim (*Cummings v Granger* (CA, 1977)), as may one who instigates an affray and gets "more than he bargained for" (*Murphy v Culhane* (CA, 1977)), though these decisions must now be read in the light of *Revill v Newbery* (CA, 1996); see Ch.8. In *Rance v Mid-Downs Health Authority* (HC, 1991), the plaintiff alleged that the defendants negligently failed to detect a foetal abnormality during pregnancy and to advise her of her right to terminate it, with the result that she gave birth to a seriously handicapped child. It was held that even if the defendants were negligent, they could not be liable because the pregnancy was so far advanced by the time of the alleged negligence that, as the law then stood, abortion would have been a criminal offence.

Revision Checklist

You should now understand:

- The conditions within which the three general defences apply in tort and the overlap between the defences;

- *Volenti* is a complete defence and contributory negligence is preferred because it is more flexible;

- *Volenti* is not easily established—the defendant must show that the claimant had full knowledge and consented to the nature and the extent of the risk; and

- *Ex turpi causa* prevents a claimant engaged in illegal activity from obtaining damages.

QUESTION AND ANSWER

Question

To what extent is a defendant in a tort action liable to a claimant who was engaged in an illegal activity at the time the injury was sustained?

Approach to the answer

Outline the effect of *ex turpi causa* (the claim is barred because no action can be founded on an illegal act) and the policy reasons underlying the defence—per Lord Hoffman *Gray v Thames Trains Ltd* (2009).

Discuss the factors taken into account in determining which types of conduct are considered sufficiently heinous for the defence to be established *Pitts v Hunt* (1990) and considerations such as:

(a) where it is impossible for the court to determine the appropriate standard of care in a particular case;

(b) the closeness of the connection required between the illegal activity of the claimant and the damage suffered—the damage must be a direct result of the illegal activity;

(c) where to permit the claimant to succeed would be an affront to the public conscience.

Liability for Dangerous Products

6

INTRODUCTION

Part I of the Consumer Protection Act 1987, which came into force on March 1, 1988 was enacted to give effect to an EC Directive of 1985, requiring the harmonisation of law on product liability throughout the Community. Subject to certain defences, the Act creates a regime of strict liability, although existing common law rights remain unaffected so that if, for some reason, the Act does not apply a claimant may still be able to sue in negligence.

STRICT LIABILITY UNDER THE 1987 ACT

Although a successful claim under the Act is not dependent upon proof of negligence, the claimant will have to prove that he or she suffered damage caused wholly or partly by a defect in a product.

Parties to the action and the meaning of "product"

No mention is made in the Act of who may be able to sue, so anyone who suffers damage would appear to be covered, whether a user of the product in question or not. As far as potential defendants are concerned, s.2(2) provides that the following are liable for the damage:

  (a) the producer of the product;

  (b) any person who holds himself out as producer by putting his name or trade mark or other distinguishing mark on the product;

  (c) an importer of the product into a Member State from a place outside the EC in order to supply it to another in the course of his business.

- "Producer" is defined in s.1(2) to mean either the manufacturer, or the person who won or abstracted the product (e.g. as in the case of mineral deposits) or, where the product has not been manufactured, won or abstracted but the essential characteristics of which are attributable to an industrial or other process having been carried out, the person who carried out that process. Furthermore, by s.2(3), the mere supplier (e.g. retailer) is liable if he fails within a reasonable time to comply with the plaintiff's request to identify one or more of the persons to whom s.2(2) (see above) applies, or to identify his own supplier.
- "Product" is defined in s.1(2) as any goods or electricity and, although the definition of "goods" in a later part of the Act is wide enough to cover fixtures in buildings and component parts of the building itself, there is no liability where goods are supplied by virtue of the creation or disposal of an interest in land. Component parts and raw materials also fall within the definition of "product" as distinct from the overall product in which they are comprised.

Thus, where X manufactures a product containing a defective component manufactured by Y which causes damage (e.g. a car with faulty brakes), both X and Y are jointly and severally liable. However, s.1(3) in effect provides that the mere supplier of a product containing component parts will not, by reason only of that supply, be treated as supplying those components. This means that liability under s.2(3) in respect of a product containing a defective component will only arise for failure to identify the producer or supplier of the finished product.

It has been noted that, where the essential characteristics of a product are attributable to an industrial or other process having been carried out, the processor may be liable as a producer within the meaning of s.1(2). The failure of the legislature to define "essential characteristics" or "industrial or other process" may present difficulties of interpretation, particularly with regard to foodstuffs.

Farmers and other suppliers of agricultural produce (defined in s.1(2) as "any produce of the soil, of stock-farming or of fisheries") had originally been exempt from liability unless, at the time of their supply of it to another, it could be said to have been through an industrial process. However, the exception for agricultural products and game was removed by EU Directive 1999/34 in respect of goods put into the market after December 2002.

LIABILITY FOR DANGEROUS PRODUCTS

The meaning of "defect"

According to s.3(1) a product is defective if its safety is not such as persons generally are entitled to expect. In *Tesco Stores v Connor Fredrick Pollock* (2006, CA), a small child suffered injury after swallowing detergent from a bottle which was supposed to have a child resistant cap. The cap was found to provide the level of protection that persons generally would be entitled to expect because the resistance required to open it was significantly more than a child could be expected to apply. The "safety" of a product expressly includes safety "with respect to products comprised in that product" (i.e. components and raw materials), and a product may be unsafe not only if there is a risk of personal injury but also if it poses a risk of damage to property.

LEGISLATION HIGHLIGHTER

In determining what persons generally are entitled to expect, s.3(2) provides that account shall be taken of all the circumstances including the following specific matters:

(a) the way in which and the purposes for which the product has been marketed, its get- up, and warnings and instructions for use accompanying it;

(b) what might reasonably be expected to be done with or in relation to the product;

the time when the product was supplied by its producer to another.

The reference in (a) to the purposes for which the product has been marketed may indicate that a balance has to be struck between known risks associated with a product and the benefits which it seeks to confer. Adopting this interpretation in the case of drugs, for example, a product which produces harmful side-effects is not necessarily defective if its disadvantages are outweighed by the long-term benefits. With regard to (b), a product which is clearly intended for a particular use may not be defective if it causes damage when put to an entirely different use. Similarly, where the defendant reasonably contemplates that something would be done to the product before use (e.g. testing), he may argue that there is no defect if that thing is not done (cf. *Kubach v Hollands* (HC, 1937); *Grant v Australian Knitting Mills Ltd* (PC, 1936)). The provision of appropriate warnings and instructions may clearly be relevant here, and there would therefore appear to be some overlap with (a) in this respect. As far as (c) is concerned, it should be noted that it is the time of supply by the producer to another which is relevant, not the time of supply to the consumer.

The concluding words of s.3(2) provide that the mere fact that a product supplied after that time is safer than the product in question does not require the inference that there is a defect. This clearly makes allowance for the fact that improved safety standards are constantly being developed, so that what is considered safe, say, in 1997, will not necessarily be so in 2003.

KEY CASE

FAULT BASED ARGUMENTS AGAINST LIABILITY ARE NOT RELEVANT IN A "NO-FAULT" REGIME

In *A v National Blood Authority* (2001), the claimants had been infected with Hepatitis C through blood transfusions which had used blood products obtained from infected donors. The defendants argued that the product was as safe as might be expected (and also there was no available test that could be used to detect defects in the particular transfusion; s.4(1)(e) below). Nevertheless, it was held that factors which would have been relevant in a negligence action were completely irrelevant when applying a strict liability principle and the defendants were found liable under the Consumer Protection Act. This interpretation of the Act, the decision would suggest that liability under the statute is considerably stricter than the common law.

In *Ide v ATB Sales Ltd* (2008) CA, the claimant had no recollection of his serious accident and there were no witnesses when the handlebar of his mountain bike snapped off. The bike had been imported into the UK by the defendants who argued that the claimant had failed to discharge the burden of proving that there was a defect in the bike that had caused his injury. It was held that since the claim was under the Consumer Protection Act it was not strictly necessary to make any finding as to the *specific* cause of the defect and the claimant was entitled to succeed.

Damage

Section 5(1) defines damage for the purposes of Pt I as death or personal injury, or loss of or damage to property (including land). Claims for property damage are, however, limited in several important respects. First, the defendant will not be liable for damage to the defective product itself, nor for damage to any product supplied with a defective component comprised in it (s.5(2)). A parallel may be drawn here with the common law, where such claims are regarded as being concerned essentially with the quality of the product so that, in the absence of a contract, there is generally no liability in tort on the ground that the loss is purely economic (*Muirhead v Industrial Tank Specialities Ltd* (CA, 1986); see Ch.2). Secondly, there is no liability unless, at the time of the damage, the property was "of a description of property ordinarily intended for private use, occupation or consumption" and was intended by the plaintiff mainly for such purposes (s.5(3)). A person who suffers damage to his business property must therefore sue in negligence. Finally, no claim will lie where its value does not exceed £275, excluding interest (s.5(4)).

Defences
The Act provides specific defences:

LEGISLATION HIGHLIGHTER

Section 4(1), paras (a)–(f), provides for the following defences:
(a) The defect is attributable to compliance either with a domestic enactment or with Community law.
(b) The defendant did not at any time supply the product to another. A broad definition is given to "supply" in a later Part of the Act to include not only the usual types of supply contract, but also gifts.
(c) The defendant supplied the product otherwise than in the course of his business and either he does not fall within s.2(2) (i.e. he is not a producer, "own-brander" or importer) or he does so only by virtue of things done otherwise than with a view to profit. Thus, for example, the producer of home-made wine who gives a bottle to a friend (or, indeed, who charges simply to cover the costs of his production) will be protected.
(d) The defect did not exist at the relevant time. By s.4(2) the "relevant time" means, in relation to electricity, the time at which it was generated; as far as all other products are concerned it means, in the case of the defendant to whom s.2(2) applies, the time when he supplied the product to another and, in the case of a supplier, the time of the last supply by a person who is within the ambit of that section.
(e) The state of scientific and technical knowledge at the relevant time was not such that a producer of products of the same description as the product in question might be expected to have discovered the defect if it had existed in his products while they were under his control. This is the so-called "development risks" or "state of the art" defence which has provoked considerable controversy, not least because it would appear to offer a wider protection than the corresponding provision of the Directive which it seeks to implement. Whereas Art.7(e) of the Directive would only allow the defence if the state of scientific and technical knowledge was not

such as to enable the existence of the defect to be discovered, s.4(1)(e) of the Act talks in terms of what might be expected to have been discovered by a producer of products of the same description as the product in question. The statutory language may thus lead to the inference that the defendant is to be judged by the standards of the hypothetical, reasonable producer of the same, or similar, products, which is tantamount to saying that the defendant will not be liable in the absence of negligence. The apparent discrepancy between the Directive and the Act was, however, referred to the European Commission, and the issue was taken to the European Court of Justice, who concluded that there was nothing to suggest that s.4(1)(e) could not be interpreted so as to achieve the purpose of Art.7(e) of the Directive. "Relevant time" bears the same meaning as in (d) above and will normally be the time of supply of the product by a person to whom s.2(2) applies.

(f) The defect constituted a defect in a product containing the defendant's component part (or raw material) and was wholly attributable to the design of the overall product or to compliance by the defendant with instructions given by the producer of the overall product. Apart from the above defences, the effect of s.6(4) is to preserve the plaintiff's contributory negligence as a partial defence to a claim against any person under the Act.

It has been noted that the claimant must prove that the damage was caused wholly or partly by the defect. It seems clear that there can be no question of categorising the damage as too remote but if, for example, the claimant seriously misuses the product, or an intermediary fails to follow clear instructions (e.g. to test before use), it is unlikely that the product would be found to be defective. Once it has been categorised as defective, however, failure by an intermediary to examine it will not defeat the action on grounds of causation.

Three final points are worthy of note:

(1) Although there is a limitation period of three years, this is subject to an overall long-stop period of 10 years from the relevant time (see above), after which no claim may be brought. Thus, for example, where a product manufactured and distributed in 2000 causes damage in 2011, a claim against the manufacturer will lie only in negligence.

(2) Section 7 of the Act prevents the defendant from limiting or excluding his liability, either contractually or otherwise.

(3) Section 1(1) states that the purpose of Pt I of the Act is to give effect to the Directive and that it should be construed accordingly. Any ambiguity in the Act should therefore be resolved, wherever possible, by

reference to the Directive and not merely in accordance with traditional canons of construction.

COMMON LAW NEGLIGENCE

Where the Consumer Protection Act does not apply, the claimant must rely upon existing common law remedies. If the claimant acquires defective goods under a sale or similar supply contract the first line of attack is to sue the supplier for breach of implied undertakings relating to quality. Although these contractual obligations are generally imposed only upon those who supply in the course of a business, they are strict and entitle the claimant to recover both in respect of goods which simply fail to work or which are less valuable than those contracted for, and where the defect causes personal injury or damage to property. If the claimant does not have a contract, however, or indeed where an action against the supplier is not viable (e.g. the supplier is in liquidation), an action in tort may be pursued.

The manufacturer's duty

KEY CASE

The source of the duty owed by a manufacturer to the ultimate consumer is to be found in the so-called narrow rule in **DONOGHUE V STEVENSON** (HL, 1932), expressed by Lord Atkin as follows:

"A manufacturer of products, which he sells in such a form as to show that he intends them to reach the ultimate consumer in the form in which they left him with no reasonable possibility of intermediate examination, and with the knowledge that the absence of reasonable care in the preparation or putting up of the products will result in an injury to the consumer's life or property, owes a duty to the consumer to take that reasonable care."

The term "products" includes not only comestibles, but such diverse items as lifts, hair-dye, motor vehicles, chemicals and underpants. The manufacturer's duty extends to the packaging of the product and to any labels, warnings or instructions for use which accompany it (*Vacwell Engineering Co Ltd v B.D.H. Chemicals Ltd* (HC, 1971)). If the manufacturer of a finished product incorporates a component made by another, he is under a duty to check on its suitability and may be liable for failure to do so should it turn out to be defective (*Winward v TVR Engineering* (CA, 1986)). Where products are already in circulation when the defect is discovered the manufacturer must take reasonable steps to warn of the danger or to recall the products (*Walton v British Leyland (UK) Ltd* (HC, 1978)).

Manufacturer and ultimate consumer

The term "manufacturer" has been judicially interpreted to include any person who actively does something to the goods to create the danger, such as assemblers, servicers, repairers, installers and erectors. In *Malfroot v Noxal Ltd* (HC, 1935), an assembler was held liable when the side-car which he had negligently fitted to a motor-cycle came adrift and injured the plaintiff. Mere suppliers may also come within the rule, even though they may be unaware of the danger and do nothing positive to create it. Thus, in *Andrews v Hopkinson* (HC, 1957) a second-hand car dealer was liable for failing to check that an 18-year-old car was roadworthy, with the result that the plaintiff was injured in a collision caused by a failure of the steering. Similarly, in *Fisher v Harrods* (HC, 1966) a retailer was held liable for supplying dangerous goods without first checking upon the reputability of his supplier.

DEFINITION CHECKPOINT

Apart from the end user of the product, an "ultimate consumer" is any person who may foreseeably be affected by it. In *Stennett v Hancock and Peters* (HC, 1939) the defendant was held liable for negligently fitting a metal flange to the wheel of a lorry, so that it came off while the vehicle was in motion and struck the plaintiff.

Intermediate examination and causation

The normal rules of causation and remoteness apply (see Ch.4) and, as elsewhere in negligence, difficulties may arise where the negligence of two or more defendants causes indivisible damage. According to Lord Atkin's formulation of the rule, the duty only arises where there is "no reasonable possibility of intermediate examination", which would suggest that there is no duty where such a possibility exists. From a conceptual point of view, however, it is perhaps preferable to deal with the issue of intermediate examination in terms of causation. Thus, failure by an intermediary to make an examination reasonably expected of him, may either break the chain of causation (assuming that the examination would, or should, have revealed the defect) or, given that the manufacturer originally created the danger, both manufacturer and intermediary will be liable, as in the Irish case of *Power v Bedford Motor Co* (1959). What is clear is that, if the intermediary's failure to examine is to be regarded as severing the causal chain, it must at least have been likely that an examination would be made, so that a mere foreseeable possibility of inspection will not suffice (*Griffiths v Arch Engineering Co Ltd* (HC, 1968)). If, of course, the intermediary acquires actual knowledge of the defect and fails to withdraw the product from circulation, the manufacturer will probably escape liability (*Taylor v Rover Co Ltd* (HC, 1966)), just as he will where the intermediary ignores a clear warning to test the product before use (*Kubach v Hollands* (HC, 1937)).

DEFINITION CHECKPOINT

Apart from anything that the intermediary may do in relation to the product, regard must equally be had to what the consumer himself does.

    Failure by the claimant to conduct an expected examination or a continued use of the product after discovery of the defect, may produce one of two consequences, depending upon the degree of fault:

- either the chain of causation will be broken (see, e.g. *Farr v Butters Bros* (CA, 1932)); or
- the loss may be apportioned under the Law Reform (Contributory Negligence) Act 1945.

The claimant will not be barred from recovery, however, where he has no effective choice in assuming a risk created by a defect of which he is aware (*Denny v Supplies and Transport Co Ltd* (CA, 1950)).

Proof of negligence and damage

The burden rests upon the claimant as in any other negligence action; however, despite judicial reluctance to allow the application of *res ipsa loquitur* (see Ch.3), damage caused by a defect in manufacture, as distinct from a defect in design, may easily give rise to an inference of negligence (*Grant v Australian Knitting Mills Ltd* (PC, 1936)). On the other hand, if it is equally probable that the defect arose after the manufacturing process and is wholly unconnected with anything that the manufacturer may have done, the plaintiff will fail (*Evans v Triplex Safety Glass Co* (HC, 1936)). The defendant will no longer escape liability, however, merely by showing that he had a foolproof system of manufacture and quality control, because the very fact of the defect may be evidence of negligence in the operation of the system by a servant for whom the defendant is vicariously liable (*Hill v J. Crowe (Cases) Ltd* (HC, 1978)).

What is the position where the defect is in the design of the product (as distinct from a manufacturing fault)?

Where the alleged defect is in relation to the design of the product, the claimant may face greater difficulty in that the issue of negligence is to be judged in the light of current knowledge which must be proved to have been such as to render the damage foreseeable (cf. the "state of the art" defence under s.4(1)(e) of the Consumer Protection Act 1987 where it is for the defendant to prove that such knowledge did not exist).

As far as damage is concerned, liability exists only in respect of personal injury or damage to other property, though consequential financial loss is also recoverable. Pure economic loss is, however, irrecoverable (*Muirhead v Industrial Tank Specialities Ltd* (CA, 1985)), and it is clear from *Murphy v Brentwood DC* (HL, 1990) that both damage to the product itself and "preventive damage" represented by the cost of avoiding apprehended physical damage to persons or property (e.g. by repairing or discarding the product) is regarded as pure economic loss (see further Ch.2). The difficulty remains of determining the circumstances in which a defective product can be said to have caused damage to "other" property.

KEY CASE

WHEN CAN A DEFECTIVE PRODUCT BE SAID TO HAVE CAUSED DAMAGE TO "OTHER" PROPERTY?

In *Aswan Engineering Establishment Co v Lupdine Ltd* (CA, 1987) the plaintiffs lost a quantity of waterproofing material when the plastic buckets in which it was contained collapsed as a result of exposure to high temperatures. In an action against the manufacturers of the buckets Lloyd L.J. thought that the contents could be regarded as property distinct from their container, thus bringing the case within *Donoghue v Stevenson* principles (though the claim failed on other grounds). If this analysis is correct, the plaintiff would seem to be in a better position at common law than under the 1987 Act (see s.5(2)).

Revision Checklist

You should now understand:

- English law on product liability has been developed both through the common law and the wider European Community context;

- The justifications for the imposition of strict liability on manu-facturers and producers for defective products which cause harm;

- The Consumer Protection Act 1987 sets down a strict liability regime for defective products on a wide range of potential defendants;

- The limits on the scope of the Act such as cases where the loss concerns damage to property not intended for private use and where the 10-year "cut-off" limitation period applies; these restrictions do not apply in common law negligence.

QUESTION AND ANSWER

Question

The most notable feature of the Consumer Protection Act 1987 is that it removes the need for a claimant who has been harmed by a defective product to establish fault on the part of the defendant but there are limitations on its scope. To what extent does the Act improve on the law of common law negligence in respect of product liability?

Approach to the answer

This question requires an analysis of the provisions the Consumer Protection Act 1987 with discussion of its limitations.

Outline the regime of strict liability under the Act which is not dependent upon proof of negligence.

Explain the meaning of "product" and the range of potential defendants who can be liable under the Act.

Discuss the meaning of "defect" and the factors taken into account in determining what persons generally are "entitled to expect".

Evaluate the defences available under the Act.

Consider the interpretation of the Act in cases such as *A v National Blood Authority* (2001) and *Ide v ATB Sales Ltd* (2008) which suggest that liability under the statute is considerably stricter than the common law. It should be noted that claims for damage are limited in several important respects under the Act and there is no liability for damage to business or where its value does not exceed £275 so that a claimant must rely on common law negligence for recovery of such losses.

Employers' Liability at Common Law

7

INTRODUCTION

This Chapter is concerned with an employer's personal liability for common law negligence *to* its employees in respect of harm suffered at work. The incidence of an employer's vicarious liability for the torts committed *by* its employees is dealt with in Ch.14. Since 1948 this country has had a national insurance system providing benefits to the victims of industrial accidents and to those who contract certain prescribed industrial diseases. Although the statutory scheme is not dependent upon proof of fault, it has not led to any diminution in the number of actions brought by employees against their employers. In addition to its common law duty there is a large body of statutory obligations cast upon the employer for the protection of its work-men, and it is not uncommon for an employee to sue both in negligence and for breach of statutory duty (see Ch.9). No civil action will lie, however, for breach by an employer of his statutory duty to insure against his liability to its workforce as required by s.1 of the Employers' Liability (Compulsory Insurance) Act 1969 (*Richardson v Pitt-Stanley* (CA, 1995)).

THE NATURE OF THE DUTY

At one time, by the doctrine of common employment, there was an implied term in a contract of service that employees accepted risks incidental to their employment. One of those risks was that they might be injured by the neg-ligence of a fellow employee for whom the employer was not, therefore, vicariously liable. As means were sought to mitigate the harshness of the doctrine, the concept developed of the personal nature of the duty owed by an employer to its workforce—a duty, in other words, which could not be discharged merely by entrusting its performance to another, no matter how apparently competent that other might be. Although the doctrine was abol-ished in 1948, the employer's personal duty survives and co-exists with his vicarious liability.

Traditionally, the duty is said to be threefold, as explained in the leading case of *Wilsons and Clyde Coal Co Ltd v English* (HL, 1938):

- "the provision of a competent staff of men
- adequate material
- a proper system and effective supervision".

The duty is not absolute but is discharged by the exercise of reasonable care and is thus similar to the duty of care in the tort of negligence generally.

Although most of the cases concern work accidents, the duty clearly extends to guarding against disease and gradual deterioration in health as a result of adverse working conditions (*Thompson v Smith's Shiprepairers (North Shields) Ltd* (HC, 1984)). An employer's liability to safeguard employees against these particular types of harm has expanded as the results of advances in medical and scientific knowledge about the effects of asbestos and repetitive strain injury.

DEFINITION CHECKPOINT

An employer's liability for psychiatric harm as the result of occupational stress is a developing area of liability.

An employer who becomes aware that stress at work is having an adverse effect on the mental health of an employee is under a duty to take positive steps to prevent the harm. See *Hatton v Sutherland* (CA, 2002) below.

However, an employer's liability does not extend to protecting the employee's economic welfare.

An employer's liability does not extend to the prevention of economic loss by, for example, advising the employee to take out insurance (*Reid v Rush & Tomkins Group Plc* (CA, 1989)), nor to the prevention of injury to health caused by self-induced intoxication (*Barrett v Ministry of Defence* (CA, 1995)). The various aspects of the duty will now be considered.

. . . .

COMPETENT STAFF

The abolition of the doctrine of common employment has drastically reduced the significance of this particular aspect of the duty, since employees will usually be able to sue their employer vicariously for the wrongdoings of a colleague. It remains important, however, where the wrongful act, such as an assault or violent horseplay, takes place outside the course of employment. In this case the employer may be liable for breach of its personal duty if he or she knew or ought to have known of his employee's vicious or playful tendencies (*Hudson v Ridge Manufacturing Co Ltd* (HC, 1957)). So, too, if an employee is instructed to perform a task for which he or she has not been properly trained and thereby injures a workmate, the employer may be liable, even though there might be difficulty in establishing negligence by the employee for the purposes of vicarious liability.

SAFE PLANT AND EQUIPMENT

The duty here is to take reasonable care to provide proper plant and equipment and to maintain them as such. This includes the provision of protective devices and clothing, and, in appropriate cases, a warning or exhortation from the employer to make use of such equipment (*Pape v Cumbria CC* (HC, 1992)).

KEY CASE

ALTHOUGH COMPLIANCE WITH A STATUTORY OBLIGATION IS EVIDENCE OF A DISCHARGE OF THE COMMON LAW DUTY, IT IS NOT CONCLUSIVE
In *Bux v Slough Metals Ltd* (CA, 1973), the plaintiff foundry worker lost the sight of one eye when splashed with molten metal. Although the employer had, in compliance with statutory regulations binding upon him, provided protective goggles, he was held liable for breach of his common law duty, which extended to persuading and even insisting upon the use of protective equipment. This case also demonstrates that compliance with a statutory obligation, whilst evidence of a discharge of the common law duty, is not conclusive of the matter. Most employees will now be protected by the Personal Protective Equipment at Work Regulations 1992, which impose a statutory duty to take all reasonable steps to see that protective equipment is properly used, though it is the employee's duty to use it.

With regard to injury caused by defective equipment, it was held in *Davie v New Merton Board Mills Ltd* (HL, 1959) that the duty to provide proper tools was satisfied by purchase from a reputable supplier. The decision has now been reversed, however, by the Employers' Liability (Defective Equipment) Act 1969, which renders an employer personally liable in negligence if two conditions are met: first, that the employee is injured in the course of his employment by a defect in equipment issued by the employer for the purposes of the employer's business; and, secondly, that the defect is attributable wholly or partly to the fault of a third party (whether identifiable or not). Strict liability is thus imposed upon the employer if his employee can prove that some third party, such as the manufacturer, was at fault, though contributory negligence is a defence. The manufacturer may now, of course, be strictly liable under the Consumer Protection Act 1987 (see Ch.6), but this does not in any way affect the employer's position under the 1969 Act.

KEY CASES

EQUIPMENT DEFINED AS "ANY PLANT AND MACHINERY, VEHICLE, AIRCRAFT OR CLOTHING"
- In *Coltman v Bibby Tankers Ltd* (HL, 1988) "equipment" for the purposes of the Act was widely defined to include a ship.
- It was further held in *Knowles v Liverpool City Council* (HL, 1993) that the word embraced any material furnished by the employer for the purposes of his business and was not confined to such things as tools and machinery, and their Lordships also considered that the Act would apply even though the employee was neither required to use, nor had in fact used, the equipment in question.

Apart from the 1969 Act the employee may be able to rely on the Provision and Use of Work Equipment Regulations 1992 which provide, inter alia, that employers must ensure that work equipment is so constructed or adapted as to be suitable for the purpose for which it is used or provided, and that such equipment is maintained in an efficient state, in efficient working order and in good repair. The definition of "work equipment", however, is not as wide as under the 1969 Act.

SAFE SYSTEM OF WORK

This is the expression used to describe such matters as the organisation of the work, the manner in which it is to be carried out, the number of men required for a particular task and the part that each is to play, the taking of safety precautions, and the giving of special instructions, particularly to inexperienced workers (see *Speed v Thomas Swift & Co Ltd* (CA, 1943)). In *Johnstone v Bloomsbury Health Authority* (CA, 1991) it was held that requiring the plaintiff to work such long hours as might foreseeably injure his health could constitute a breach of duty, although a majority expressed the view that the implied contractual duty to take reasonable care for an employee's safety is subject to any express term imposing an absolute duty to work certain specified hours.

KEY CASES

PSYCHIATRIC INJURY CAUSED BY "STRESS AT WORK"

- *Walker v Northumberland CC* (HC, 1995) held that a safe system of work extends to a duty to take extra steps to protect an employee against the risk of foreseeable psychiatric harm. There are no intrinsically stressful occupations and the special control mechanisms (as per *Alcock*) do not apply to claims for psychiatric injury arising from occupational stress. The question is simply whether the employer has breached his duty not to injure the health of his employees.

- In *Hatton v Sutherland* (CA, 2002), Hale Lady J. set down 16 guiding propositions relating to breach of duty and said that in all cases of occupational stress it is necessary to ask not only what the employer *could* but what the employer *should* have done. Also, whether the claim involves a public or a private sector employer, the resources and the size and scope of the operation will be relevant to this question.

Unless an employer knows of some particular problem or vulnerability of an employee he is usually entitled to assume that employees can withstand the normal pressures of a job. An employer's duty of care in respect of psychiatric harm is owed to workers as individuals and, since capacity to stress varies between employees, an employer must heed warnings from those who are less able. The test for liability takes account of the conduct of the reasonable and prudent employer, taking positive thought for the safety of his employees in the light of what he knew or ought to have known (*Barber v Somerset* (HL, 2004)). An employer was not fixed with knowledge of the vulnerability to stress where it was provided in a confidential medical questionnaire submitted to the occupational health department (*Hartman v South Essex Mental Health and Community Care NHS Trust* (CA, 2005).

Finally, it should be noted that the employer does not discharge his duty merely by providing a safe system unless reasonable steps are also taken to see that it is put into operation, and the employer must be mindful of the fact that workers are often careless of their own safety. On the other hand, it may not be necessary to warn or advise an experienced worker of the risks with which he should be familiar (*Baker v T. Clarke (Leeds) Ltd* (CA, 1992)).

WHERE AN EMPLOYEE IS WORKING OUTSIDE THEIR USUAL WORKPLACE THE EMPLOYER RETAINS PERSONAL RESPONSIBILITY FOR OPERATING A SAFE SYSTEM

- *McDermid v Nash Dredging and Reclamation Co Ltd* (HL, 1987)—even though the employer has devised a safe system, it will be liable upon proof of a negligent failure to put it into practice.
- *Jebson v Ministry of Defence* (2000)—the defendant employers were liable when the claimant, one of a group of soldiers returning in a drunken state from a night out, fell when he tried to climb onto the roof of the army truck. He claimed that in failing to have someone in the back of the truck to supervise him and his fellow soldiers the employers had breached their duty of care. It was held at first instance that although the defendant was in breach of a duty to supervise the soldiers, the damage was too remote because it was not reasonably foreseeable that the soldier would have tried to climb onto the roof. The Court of Appeal allowed the claimant's appeal and held that under the circumstances rowdy behaviour was foreseeable and the damage was not too remote.
- *Mulcahy v Ministry of Defence* (CA, 1996)—there may, however, in exceptional cases, be policy reasons for denying the existence of a duty, as in this case where it was held not to be fair, just and reasonable to impose upon the defendant a duty of care to a serviceman who, at the time of the accident, was engaging the enemy in hostilities.

SAFE PREMISES

It is clear that the employer's obligation includes making the premises as safe as the exercise of reasonable care and skill permits, but he is not required to eliminate every foreseeable risk if the burden in so doing is too onerous (*Latimer v A.E.C. Ltd* (HL, 1953)).

KEY CASE

THE DUTY TO PROVIDE A SAFE PLACE OF WORK APPLIES WHEN THE EMPLOYEE IS WORKING AWAY FROM THE EMPLOYER'S PREMISES
In *Wilson v Tyneside Window Cleaning Co* (CA, 1958), it was held that the duty exists equally in relation to premises in the occupation or control of a third party. In appropriate circumstances an employer may

therefore be expected to go and inspect the premises to see that they are reasonably safe for the work to be done upon them; but the fact that the employer does not have control of the premises is important in determining whether he has been negligent. As far as this aspect of the duty is concerned, most workplaces are now likely to be governed by the Workplace (Health, Safety and Welfare) Regulations 1992.

THE SCOPE OF THE DUTY

The duty arises only where the master-servant relationship exists so that it will not, for example, avail an independent contractor. It extends to those acts which are reasonably incidental to the employment and is owed to each employee individually, the consequence of which is that the personal circumstances of the employee must be taken into account, in so far as the employer knew or ought to have known of them.

KEY CASE

THE EMPLOYER'S NON-DELEGABLE DUTY IS OWED TO EACH EMPLOYEE
INDIVIDUALLY

In *Paris v Stepney BC* (HL, 1951), it was held that, where a garage worker known by his employer to be one-eyed was engaged on work involving a risk of injury to his remaining eye, the employer was under a duty to provide him with goggles. Finally, although the duty is frequently dealt with under its various sub-headings, it is to be remembered that there is in effect but a single duty to take reasonable care in the conduct of operations so as not to subject employees to unnecessary risks.

DELEGATION

Since the duty is personal it is said to be non-delegable, so that the employer does not discharge its obligation by entrusting its performance to another, whether that other be a servant or independent contractor (*Wilsons and Clyde Coal Co Ltd v English* (HL, 1938)). Although, as far as the employment of contractors is concerned, some doubt was cast upon this proposition by *Davie v New Merton Board Mills Ltd* (HL, 1959), the widely accepted view is that an employer who entrusts performance of his duty to a person other than a servant remains responsible for the defaults of that person (*McDermid v Nash Dredging & Reclamation Co Ltd* (HL, 1987); see, too, Employers' Liability (Defective Equipment) Act 1969).

You should now understand:

- The distinction between an employer's liability for harm caused *by* his employees (vicarious liability) and liability for harm caused *to* his employees (personal liability);

- The personal and non-delegable nature of the employer's responsibility for the safety of his employees;

- An employer's liability arises not only for failure to adopt a safe system of working but also when a safe system is operated negligently;

- Occupational stress is a developing area of liability; an employer who becomes aware that work-related stress is having an adverse effect on the mental health of an employee is under a duty to take positive steps to prevent the harm.

QUESTION AND ANSWER

Question

Consider the approach of the common law to the issues arising from work-related stress complaints by employees.

Approach to the answer

In *Walker v Northumberland CC* (1995), foreseeability of stress was identified as the key determinant in a claim for work related stress and the question is simply whether the employer has breached his duty not to injure the health of his employees. Claims for work-related stress arising from an employer's liability are not subject to the special control mechanisms as compared with the duty of care in respect of psychiatric injury (cf Alcock criteria etc).

The key authority is *Hatton v Sutherland* (CA, 2002) and the 16 guiding propositions relating to breach of duty set down by Hale Lady J. should be considered. Unless an employer knows of some particular problem or vulnerability of an employee he is usually entitled to assume that employees can withstand the normal pressures of a job.

In *Barber v Somerset* (2004), the House of Lords said the test for liability takes account of the conduct of the reasonable and prudent employer, taking positive thought for the safety of his employees in the light of what he knew or ought to have known.

In *Hartman v South Essex Mental Health and Community Care NHS Trust* (CA, 2005), an employer was not fixed with knowledge of the employee's vulnerability to stress where it was provided in a confidential medical questionnaire submitted to the occupational health department.

Occupiers' Liability

8

. . . .
THE OCCUPIERS' LIABILITY ACTS 1957 AND 1984

Introduction

The liability of occupiers towards persons injured on their premises is governed by two statutes. The Occupiers' Liability Act 1957 is concerned with liability to lawful visitors but the 1957 Act did not deal with trespassers so a subsequent statute, the Occupiers' Liability Act 1984 was enacted to govern the duty of an occupier to persons other than visitors (e.g. trespassers). The liability of an occupier in respect of loss or injury suffered by those who come lawfully upon his premises is primarily governed by the 1957 Act. Although it is clear that the duty imposed by the Act arises where damage results from the static condition of the premises, there is some doubt as to whether it applies where the plaintiff is injured in consequence of an activity conducted upon the premises (see *Revill v Newbery* (CA, 1996)). The balance of authority would suggest that it does, at least where the activity in question is an integral purpose of the occupation, rather than being merely ancillary to it.

KEY CASE

An illustration of how the general law of negligence applies to an activity on the premises is provided in *Slater v Clay Cross Co Ltd* (1956) by Lord Denning:

> "If a landowner is driving his car down his private drive and meets someone lawfully walking upon it, then he is under a duty to take reasonable care so as not to injure the walker and his duty is the same, no matter whether it is his gardener coming up with his plants, a tradesman delivering his goods, a friend coming to tea, or a flag seller seeking a charitable gift."

In any event, since the statutory duty is to take reasonable care, there is little or no difference between an action under the Act and one for breach of the common law duty of care. Section 2(1) of the Act provides:

> "An occupier owes the same duty, the 'common duty of care,' to all his visitors, except in so far as he is free to and does extend, restrict, modify or exclude his duty to any visitor or visitors by agreement or otherwise."

In any event, since the statutory duty is to take reasonable care, there is little or no difference between an action under the Act and one for breach of the common law duty of care.

LEGISLATION HIGHLIGHTER

Section 2(1) of the Act provides:

> "An occupier owes the same duty, the 'common duty of care,' to all his visitors, except in so far as he is free to and does extend, restrict, modify or exclude his duty to any visitor or visitors by agreement or otherwise."

The occupier

The Act contains no definition of "occupier" which is simply a term of convenience to denote a person who has a sufficient degree of control over premises to put him under a duty of care towards those who come lawfully on to the premises (*Wheat v Lacon & Co Ltd* (HL, 1966)). Control is thus the decisive factor, and it is immaterial that the occupier has no interest in the land. He may be an owner in occupation, a tenant, a licensee or any person having the right to possession and to permit others to enter the premises. For example, in *AMF International Ltd v Magnet Bowling Ltd* (HC, 1968), building contractors were held to be joint occupiers along with the building owners. But a landlord who lets premises by demise to a tenant is not the occupier thereof for the purposes of the Act, though he remains the occupier of those parts of the premises excluded from the demise, such as an entrance hall or common staircase in a block of flats (*Moloney v Lambeth London BC* (HC, 1966)).

KEY CASE

EXCLUSIVE OCCUPATION OF THE PREMISES IS NOT ESSENTIAL FOR LIABILITY; THERE MAY BE MORE THAN ONE OCCUPIER OF THE SAME PREMISES OR PART OF THE PREMISES.

The issue of multiple occupation was fully considered in the leading case of *Wheat v Lacon & Co Ltd* where the House of Lords held that the residential area of licensed premises was occupied both by the manager who lived there under licence from the brewers, and by the brewers, who could be regarded as occupying either vicariously through their servant (the manager) or because they retained control. It was also made clear that, although two or more people may owe the same common duty of care, the content of their duty might well differ according to the degree of control exercised.

The premises

By s.1(3)(a) of the Act, the statutory provisions extend to any fixed or movable structure, including any vessel, vehicle or aircraft. This is apt to include not only structures of a permanent nature but temporary erections such as ladders and scaffolding.

LEGISLATION HIGHLIGHTER

With regard to "vessels, vehicles and aircraft" the Act would appear to apply only to the structural state of the premises, so that where injury is caused to a passenger by, say, negligent driving, the appropriate cause of action is negligence at common law.

Visitors

The statutory duty is owed only to visitors who, by s.1(2), are those who would, at common law, have been either invitees or licensees. The common law distinction between these two categories of entrant is thereby abolished and the vital distinction (which remains unaffected by the Act) is as between the visitor and the trespasser. No difficulty arises where the occupier expressly invites or permits another to enter or use his premises, bearing in mind that such invitation or permission may legitimately be limited either to a particular part of the premises or for a specified purpose. It may be alleged, however, that the occupier has impliedly sanctioned the entry, and whether this is so is a question to be decided on the facts of each case. A tradesman, for example, has an implied licence to walk along a garden path to the front door for the purpose of promoting his business with the occupier, unless of course he has been clearly forbidden to do so. For a licence to be inferred there must be evidence that the occupier has permitted entry as opposed to merely tolerated it, for there is no positive obligation to keep the trespasser out. Moreover, repeated trespass of itself confers no licence (*Edwards v Railway Executive* (HL, 1952)). It must be said that in some cases the courts have been at pains to infer the existence of a licence.

| DEFINITION CHECKPOINT |

In some cases the courts have been at pains to infer the existence of an implied licence

In *Lowery v Walker* (HL, 1911), members of the public had for many years used the defendant's field as a short cut to the railway station. The defendant had not infrequently prevented them from so doing, but did nothing further until, without warning, he turned a savage horse loose in the field. The animal attacked and injured the plaintiff, who succeeded in his action on the basis that he was a licensee, not a trespasser. However, this and other cases were decided at a time when trespassers were afforded little or no protection and, in view of the more favourable treatment which they now receive (see later in this Chapter), the courts may be less favourably inclined to find an implied licence in a case such as Lowery.

Three further types of entrant must now be considered. First, those who enter premises for any purpose in the exercise of a right conferred by law are, by s.2(6) of the Act, treated as having the occupier's permission to be there for that purpose (whether they in fact have it or not) and are therefore owed the common duty of care. Secondly, s.5(1) provides that where a person enters under the terms of a contract with the occupier there is, in the absence of express provision in the contract, an implied term that the entrant is owed the common duty of care and, according to *Sole v W. J. Hallt Ltd* (HC, 1973), he may frame his claim either in contract or under the 1957 Act. It is further provided by s.3(1) that where a person contracts with the occupier on the basis that a third party is to have access to the premises, the duty owed by the occupier to such third party as his visitor cannot be reduced by the terms of the contract to a level lower than the common duty of care. Conversely, if the contract imposes upon the occupier any obligation which exceeds the requirements of the statutory duty, then the third party is entitled to the benefit of that additional obligation. Thirdly, those who use public (*Greenhalgh v British Railways Board* (CA, 1969)) or private (*Holden v White* (CA, 1982)) rights of way are not visitors for the purposes of the 1957 Act, though the user of a private right of way is now owed a duty under the Occupiers' Liability Act 1984 (see later in this Chapter). An owner of land over which a public right of way passes may be liable for misfeasance, but not negligent nonfeasance (*McGeown v Northern Ireland Housing Executive* (HL, 1994)).

Exclusion of the duty
It has already been seen that the duty owed to a contractual entrant is governed by the terms of the contract and that a person who enters under a contract to which he is not a party is owed, as a minimum, the common duty

of care. In the case of non-contractual entrants it is clear that, at common law, an occupier may be able to exclude or limit his liability by notice, provided that reasonable steps are taken to bring it to the visitor's attention and that, upon its proper construction, it is clear and unambiguous. Such was the decision in *Ashdown v Samuel Williams & Sons* (CA, 1956), where it was held that the plaintiff, who was injured by the negligent shunting of a railway wagon upon the defendant's premises, was defeated in her claim by exclusion notices erected by the defendant stating that persons entered at their own risk and that no liability would be accepted for injury or damage, whether caused by negligence or otherwise.

LEGISLATION HIGHLIGHTER

Despite the criticisms of the defeat of the claim by exclusion notices in Ashdown's case, s.2(1) of the 1957 Act clearly envisages the possibility of an exclusion of the duty and the decision was followed by a majority in *White v Blackmore* (CA, 1972). The principle is said to rest upon the basis that if an occupier can prevent people from entering his premises, then he can equally impose conditions, subject to which entry is permitted.

Exclusion will almost certainly not apply either where the visitor enters in the exercise of a right conferred by law, or where he has, in practical terms, no real freedom of choice (as, for example, where an employee enters the premises in the ordinary course of his employment: *Burnett v British Waterways Board* (CA, 1973)). Furthermore, some writers have argued that the Ashdown principle no longer applies in its full rigour on the ground that, if the duty owed to a trespasser (see later in this Chapter) represents a minimum standard below which the occupier cannot go, then that duty must also be owed to all entrants; for to suggest otherwise would be to accord to the trespasser a protection denied to the lawful visitor.

LEGISLATION HIGHLIGHTER

Whatever the present common law position may be, the power of the occupier to exclude or restrict his liability for negligence has been severely reduced by the Unfair Contract Terms Act 1977.

Section 2 of the Act provides that a person cannot, by reference to a contract term or to a notice, exclude or restrict his liability for death or personal injury caused by negligence; and, in the case of other loss or damage, he cannot exclude or restrict his liability for negligence unless the term or notice satisfies the requirement of reasonableness. By s.1(1) negligence includes a breach of the common duty of care imposed by the 1957 Act and it matters not whether liability arises directly or vicariously.

More importantly, the operation of s.2 of the 1977 Act is confined to those situations where there is "business liability" which is defined in s.1(3) as liability for breach of duty arising from things done in the course of a business or from the occupation of premises used for the business purposes of the occupier. There is no exhaustive definition of "business", though s.14 provides that it includes a profession and the activities of any government department or local or public authority. It should also be noted that s.1(3) has been modified by s.2 of the Occupiers' Liability Act 1984 which enables a business occupier to exclude liability to those whom he allows on to his land for recreational or educational purposes, provided that it is not part of his business to grant access for such purposes.

As a result of these provisions Ashdown's case would be decided differently today. But whether or not *White v Blackmore* (CA, 1972) is similarly affected is debatable, because in that case private land was used to stage a fund-raising event for charity, and it is not certain whether that would be classed as a business occupation.

The common duty of care

LEGISLATION HIGHLIGHTER

The common duty of care is defined in s.2(2) as:

"a duty to take such care as in all circumstances of the case is reasonable to see that the visitor will be reasonably safe in using the premises for the purposes for which he is invited or permitted to be there".

This is similar to the common law duty of care, and may extend to taking steps to see that a visitor does not deliberately harm other visitors by foreseeably likely misconduct (*Cunningham v Reading Football Club Ltd* (HC, 1991)). Whether the occupier has discharged it depends upon the facts, taking into account such matters as the nature of the danger, the purpose of the visit and the knowledge of the parties. In particular, there is express provision in the Act relating to children, those with special skills, warning notices and independent contractors, and these will now be considered in turn.

1. Children

The Act provides that the amount of care, or of lack of it, which the occupier may expect in the visitor is a relevant consideration, so that, by s.2(3)(a), the occupier must be prepared for children to be less careful than adults. At common law, where a child was injured by some especially attractive but potentially dangerous object which had allured him on to the land, the occupier could not be heard to say that the child was a trespasser in relation to the very thing which had attracted him in the first place.

LEGISLATION HIGHLIGHTER

Section 2(3)(a), provides that the occupier must be prepared for children to be less careful than adults.

KEY CASE

THE "ALLUREMENT" PRINCIPLE

In *Glasgow Corp v Taylor* (HL, 1922), a child of seven died after eating some poisonous berries which he had picked from a bush in a public park. The berries had a very tempting appearance to children, yet the defendant, though aware of their toxic nature, had neither erected a barrier around the bush nor given any warning. It was held that the defendants were liable because the berries constituted an "allurement" to children and the danger was not obvious to a child of that age.

If, on the other hand, there is no dangerous object or allurement upon the land the occupier will not normally be liable (*Latham v R. Johnson & Nephew Ltd* (CA, 1913)). In *Jolley v Sutton London BC* (2000), although the Court of Appeal found that a derelict boat had constituted an allurement and a trap, it held that even making full allowance for the unpredictability of children's behaviour it was not reasonably foreseeable that teenage boys would work under a propped up boat and the damage was held to be too remote because it occurred in an unforeseeable manner. However, in allowing an appeal against this decision, the House of Lords approached the question of what risk was foreseeable in much wider terms and said that the trial judge had been correct to consider the reasonable forseeability of the wider risk that children would meddle with a dilapidated boat and be at risk of physical injury.

Although an occupier must be prepared for children to be less careful than adults, the extent of the occupier's liability is a question of fact and degree and much depends on the particular circumstances of the case. In

Keown v Coventry Healthcare NHS Trust (2006), the trial judge found that a fire escape, which could be climbed from the outside, constituted an inducement to children habitually playing in the grounds of the hospital. However, allowing the defendant's appeal the Court of Appeal said that it would not be right to ignore a child's choice to indulge in a dangerous activity in every case merely because he was a child. In this case the claimant had not only appreciated that there was a risk of falling but also that what he was doing was dangerous and that he should not have been climbing the fire escape. In the case of very young children, to whom many ordinarily harmless things may pose a potential hazard, the courts at one time applied the doctrine of the conditional licence, a legal fiction whereby the child was regarded as a trespasser unless accompanied by a responsible guardian. A different approach was adopted, however, in *Phipps v Rochester Corp* (HC, 1955) (below).

KEY CASES

SUPERVISING VERY YOUNG CHILDREN; LIABILITY IS ALLOCATED BETWEEN PARENTS AND OCCUPIERS

- In *Phipps v Rochester Corp* (HC, 1955) the court considered that it was proper to have regard to the habits of prudent parents who will, where appropriate, either take steps to satisfy themselves that the place holds no danger for children, or not permit the child to wander without supervision.

- *Phipps* was followed in *Simkiss v Rhonnda BC* (CA, 1983) and is clearly consonant with the provisions of the 1957 Act which state that, in determining whether the occupier has discharged his duty, regard is to be had to all the circumstances. One of those circumstances must be what the occupier is reasonably entitled to expect of a young child's parents.

- In *Bourne Leisure Ltd T/A British Holidays v Marsden* [2009] EWCA Civ 671, the question was whether a holiday site owner was liable for the drowning of a child in a pond, by failing to warn of the dangers and bring the pond's location to the parent's attention. The Court of Appeal held that although an occupier ought reasonably to anticipate that small children might escape the attention of parents and wander into places of danger, it does not follow that the occupier is under a duty to take precautions against such dangers.

2. Special skills

Section 2(3)(b) provides that:

"an occupier may expect that a person, in the exercise of his calling, will appreciate and guard against any special risks ordinarily incident to it, so far as the occupier leaves him free to do so".

Thus, in *Roles v Nathan* (CA, 1963) the defendant was held not liable for the death of two chimney sweeps killed by carbon monoxide fumes while sealing up a flue in the defendant's boiler. Had they suffered injury by falling through a rotten floorboard the position would, of course, have been otherwise (*Woolins v British Celanese Ltd* (CA, 1966)). In *Salmon v Seafarer Restaurants Ltd* (HC, 1983), a fireman was entitled to recover damages when it was reasonably foreseeable that he would be injured while fighting a blaze caused by the occupier's negligence, despite the exercise of his special skills (approved in *Ogwo v Taylor* (HL, 1988)).

3. Warnings

Section 2(4)(a) of the Act, provides that an occupier may discharge his duty by warning his visitor of the particular danger, provided that the warning is sufficient to enable the visitor to be reasonably safe.

The occupier may, in accordance with s.2(4)(a) of the Act, discharge his duty by warning his visitor of the particular danger, provided that the warning is sufficient to enable the visitor to be reasonably safe. Warning notices should be distinguished from exclusion notices. By sufficient warning the occupier discharges his duty, whereas an exclusion purports to take away the right of recovery in respect of a breach. To be effective a warning must sufficiently identify the source of the danger and be brought adequately to the visitor's notice. Mere knowledge of the nature and extent of the risk is not necessarily a bar to recovery, though it may go towards establishing a defence of *volenti non fit injuria* or, more likely, contributory negligence (*Bunker v Charles Brand & Son Ltd* (HC, 1969); see Ch.5).

4. Independent contractors

Where a visitor suffers damage due to faulty construction, maintenance or repair work by an independent contractor employed by the occupier, s.2(4)(b) provides that the occupier will not be liable if it was reasonable to entrust the work to a contractor and he took such steps (if any) as he reasonably ought to see that the contractor was competent and had done the work properly. Assuming, therefore, that the occupier reasonably entrusted the work to a contractor whom he had checked to see was suitably qualified to do the job, he will not be liable for that contractor's defaults provided that he took reasonable steps, where necessary, to satisfy himself that the work was properly done.

DEFINITION CHECKPOINT

No liability if the occupier acted reasonably in entrusting the work to an independent contractor

- The occupier is not necessarily expected to check work of a technical nature (e.g. lift maintenance as in *Haseldine v Daw & Son Ltd* (CA, 1941)), but in the case of a complex project he may be under a duty to have the contractor's work supervised by a qualified specialist such as an architect or surveyor (*AMF International Ltd v Magnet Bowling Ltd* (HC, 1968)).
- Where the work is of a routine nature requiring no particular skill or expertise, the occupier may himself be expected to check it and will be liable for failing to do so (*Woodward v Mayor of Hastings* (CA, 1945)).

On a point of interpretation it was held in *Ferguson v Welsh* (HL, 1987) that the word "construction" in s.2(4)(b) was wide enough to embrace demolition and that the provision protected an occupier from liability for injuries to visitors not only after completion of the work, but also during its execution. The majority also held that where an occupier had notice of an unsafe system of work adopted by the contractor, he could be liable to an employee of the contractor injured thereby, although two of their Lordships thought that any such liability would be as joint tortfeasor rather than occupier.

KEY CASES

OCCUPIER'S DUTY TO CHECK ON THE COMPETENCY OF CONTRACTORS

- In *Bottomley v Tordmorden Cricket Club* (CA, 2003), the defendant club had allowed independent contractors to carry out a pyrotechnic display on its land. The claimant (an unpaid assistant of the independent contractors) suffered severe burns and other injuries during the display, and although the case was not about a risk caused by the state of the premises under the Occupiers Liability Act 1957, *Ferguson v Welsh* applied and the defendant occupier, along with the contractors (who had no public liability insurance) was liable in common law negligence.

- In *Naylor v Payling* (CA, 2004), the claimant suffered severe injuries whilst being forcibly ejected from a nightclub by a door attendant employed by the independent contractor responsible for security at the nightclub. The independent contractor had no public liability insurance and the claimant sued the defendant nightclub owner for failing to ensure that the independent contractor was insured. In this case, the defendant had not acted negligently in selecting the independent contractor and, it was held that, save in special circumstances, there was no free-standing duty to take reasonable steps to ensure that the independent contractor was insured.

Damage

LEGISLATION HIGHLIGHTER

Section 1(3)(b): the statutory provisions apply not only to personal injury but also to damage to property, including the property of those who are not visitors which is nevertheless lawfully on the premises.

In *AMF International Ltd v Magnet Bowling Ltd* (HC, 1968), it was held that financial loss consequential upon damage to property is also recoverable. The ordinary principles of causation and remoteness (see Ch.4) apply, so that a negligent occupier will not be liable if the accident was of an unforeseeable kind.

Defences
The provisions of the Law Reform (Contributory Negligence) Act 1945 apply and s.2(5) of the 1957 Act provides that an occupier is not liable in respect of risks which the visitor willingly accepts, thus allowing for the defence of *volenti non fit injuria* (see Ch.5). However, where there is business liability within the meaning of the Unfair Contract Terms Act 1977, s.2(3) of that Act provides that a person's agreement to or awareness of a notice purporting to exclude liability for negligence is not of itself to be taken as indicating his voluntary acceptance of any risk.

THE OCCUPIERS' LIABILITY ACT 1984

Persons to whom the 1984 Act applies

The 1984 Act governs the liability of an occupier to "persons other than his visitors" in respect of injury suffered by them on the premises due to the state of the premises or to things done or omitted to be done upon them. For the position with regard to activities on the premises see *Revill v Newbery* (CA, 1996).

The terms "occupier" and "premises" have the same meanings as for the purposes of the Occupiers' Liability Act 1957. The expression "persons other than his visitors" includes trespassers and persons exercising private rights of way, but those using public rights of way are specifically excluded.

The scope of the duty

Section 1(3) of the 1984 Act provides that the occupier owes a duty if:

(a) he is aware of the danger or has reasonable grounds to believe that it exists;

(b) he knows or has reasonable grounds to believe that the non-visitor is in the vicinity of the danger concerned or that he may come into the vicinity of the danger; and

(c) the risk is one against which, in all the circumstances of the case, he may reasonably be expected to offer the non-visitor some protection.

Whilst para.(c) clearly adopts an objective test, it would appear that paras (a) and (b) import a subjective element in that the existence of the duty depends upon the occupier's actual knowledge of facts which should lead him to conclude that a danger exists or that the non-visitor is in the vicinity. If the occupier is not aware of those facts he may not owe a duty, even though a reasonable occupier would have known of them.

DEFINITION CHECKPOINT

Interpretation of Section 1(3) of the 1984 Act is not far removed from the old common law duty of "common humanity" which took into account, along with the occupier's skill and resources, his actual knowledge of the trespasser's presence or of the likelihood of it (*British Railways Board v Herrington* (HL, 1972)).

Although it seems, from the objective wording of para.(c), that the individual occupier's skill and resources no longer come into the equation, the position is not entirely clear as regards what knowledge is required. For the purposes of s.1(3)(b) the fact that the occupier has erected a fence to keep people out does not mean that he had reasonable grounds to believe that they would enter the premises (*White v St Albans City Council* (CA, 1990)).

LEGISLATION HIGHLIGHTER

Where the duty arises s.1(4) states that the duty is to take such care as is reasonable in all the circumstances of the case to see that the non visitor does not suffer injury on the premises by reason of the danger concerned.

This is the usual standard in negligence generally, and whether the occupier has discharged his duty will depend upon the character of the entry, the age of the non-visitor, and the extent of the risk, including the burden that would be imposed upon the occupier in eliminating it.

KEY CASES

THE PRINCIPLE OF "INDIVIDUAL RESPONSIBILITY"
- In *Tomlinson v Congleton BC*, (HL 2004), an appeal was allowed against a Court of Appeal finding that, where the local authority was aware that its no-swimming policy was habitually being flaunted by members of the public, it was under a duty to provide effective protection against the grave risk of injury. The House of Lords, however, held that the risk of the claimant's injury had not arisen out of the state of the premises or things done or omitted to be done on them and found that the claimant's injuries had arisen from his decision to dive into a shallow lake when the risk was obvious. Lord Hoffman said the fact that such people take no notice of warnings cannot create a duty to take other steps to protect them.
- In *Keown v Coventry Healthcare NHS Trust* (CA, 2006), the defendants were not liable for an 11-year-old child's injury when he fell from the underside of the fire escape he had been climbing. In this case it was acknowledged that premises which were not dangerous to an adult could be dangerous for a child but the court said that it would not be right to ignore a child's choice to indulge in a dangerous activity in every case merely because he was a child. In this case the risk arose not out of the state of the premises but out of what the child chose to do.

- In *Rhind v Astbury* (2004), the claimant accepted that he was a trespasser when he dived into shallow water to retrieve a football, but he argued that his injury was caused by a fibreglass container on the bed of the lake which constituted a danger within the meaning of s.1(3) of the 1984 Act. The Court of Appeal held that the claimant had failed to establish a duty of care under s.1(3) since the defendant was unaware of the existence of the container and had no reasonable grounds for suspecting that the danger existed.

It is to be noted that the new statutory duty applies only to personal injury or death. Liability for loss of, or damage to, property is expressly excluded by s.1(8).

Defences

LEGISLATION HIGHLIGHTER

Section 1(5) of the Act provides that the occupier may, in appropriate cases, discharge his duty by taking reasonable steps to warn of the danger or to discourage persons from incurring the risk.

Whether a warning is effective will depend, among other things, upon the nature of the risk and the age of the entrant. What is adequate for an adult may not be so for a child, particularly if the danger is an allurement.

The defence of *volenti non fit injuria* is preserved by s.1(6) of the Act. It remains to be seen whether it will be more readily available as against trespassers, though there seems no reason why it should be. In any event the indication in *Titchener v British Railways Board* (HL, 1983) is that it will normally be limited to dangers arising from the state of the premises. The plaintiff was held to have willingly accepted the risk as his within the meaning of s.1(6) in *Ratcliffe v McDonnell* (CA, 1999) where, having drunk about four pints, he agreed to go swimming with two friends and climbed over the gate of a college open-air swimming pool. Although conscious of the word "Warning" he did not read the notice by the gate and took a running dive into the pool and suffered tetraplegic injuries when he struck his head. The Court of Appeal rejected the plaintiff's claim for damages on the ground that he was aware of the risk and had willingly accepted it.

Can ex turpi causa *act as a defence to an action by a trespasser?*
As far as the defence of *ex turpi causa* is concerned, it was held in *Revill v Newbery* (CA, 1996) that the fact that the plaintiff was a burglar did not take him outside the protection of the law, so that he was held entitled to succeed in negligence when the defendant unintentionally shot him (cf. Lord Denning in *Cummings v Granger* (CA, 1977); see Ch.5). There was, however, a substantial reduction of damages for contributory negligence. The court in Revill took the view that, since the discharge of the gun was an activity unconnected with the defendant's status as occupier, the 1984 Act was not strictly relevant, but nevertheless thought that the common law principles applicable were analogous to the relevant statutory provisions.

It is unclear whether the above case is authority for the proposition that *ex turpi* can never be a defence to an action by a trespasser, at least where the defendant is actively instrumental in causing the injury (cf. *Murphy v Culhane* (CA, 1977); see Ch.5). The actual decision may well have been quite different had the plaintiff been injured by some defect in the premises (e.g. by falling through a hole in the floor), or had the defendant not reacted so vehemently; in either case there may have been no duty, having regard to the requirement in s.1(3)(c) of the 1984 Act.

Exclusion notices

There is no mention in the Act of the possibility of excluding liability to the non-visitor, and the provisions of the Unfair Contract Terms Act 1977 do not apply to the 1984 duty. Trespassers pose particular problems because, depending upon the point at which they enter the premises, they may be less likely to see a notice than a lawful visitor. One suggested solution is that the duty under the 1984 Act is a minimum which cannot be excluded so that even the lawful visitor would be protected by it, even though he was aware of an exclusion notice (put up, for example, by a non-business occupier). The objection to this, it has been said, is that it would effectively deprive the occupier of his right to exclude liability entirely as against the lawful visitor, which right was given in the 1957 Act and was left intact, at least for the non-business occupier, by the 1977 Unfair Contract Terms Act.

Liability of independent contractor to trespasser

At common law, the liability of a contractor to the trespasser rests upon ordinary negligence principles. The fact that the claimant is a trespasser in relation to the occupier is not relevant except in so far as the trespasser's presence may be less foreseeable. Thus in *Buckland v Guildford Gas Light and Coke Co* (HC, 1949), the defendants, who had erected electricity cables on a farmer's land close to the top of a tree, were held liable for the death of a young girl who climbed the tree and was electrocuted. This decision is unaffected by the 1984 Act, but there are indications in Herrington's case that no distinction should be drawn in this respect between occupiers and non-occupiers, in which case the defendants in *Buckland* would now owe the duty of common humanity.

Revision Checklist

You should now understand:

- The scope of an occupier's liability and range of potential defendants including landlords, occupiers, and those involved in the construction process;

- The duty of care owed by occupiers to lawful visitors under the Occupiers' Liability Act 1957 (covers personal injury and damage to property);

- The duty of care owed by occupiers to trespassers under the Occupiers' Liability Act 1984 (imposes liability only for personal injury);

- The Occupiers' Liability Act 1957 is silent on the meaning of "occupier", "premises", and "lawful visitors" so these terms are interpreted by reference to the common law.

QUESTION AND ANSWER

Question

Sutton Builders took over an office block for redevelopment. They immediately erected a prominent notice outside the entrance to the premises stating: "Keep out—No admission to unauthorised persons".

Haris, a car salesman, misread his map and mistakenly drove his car onto the premises and parked close to the building. A piece of scaffold which had been negligently erected fell on his car and smashed the windscreen. When Clive, a surveyor from the Council, called at the premises to inspect the work in progress he realised that he had forgotten his safety helmet. Although aware of the risk of injury, Clive decided to proceed with the inspection anyway. He suffered severe head injuries when a piece of building equipment fell on him. Olga had taken her eight-year-old son, Danny, to play in the park which adjoined the premises. As Olga was checking her emails on her mobile phone Danny slipped away and wandered into the premises. He suffered a leg injury when he fell through a broken floor.

Advise the parties as to the principal issues of law which will arise under the Occupiers' Liability Acts of 1957 and 1984 if they attempt to recover their losses.

This question requires a discussion of the duty of care owed by occupiers to lawful visitors under the Occupiers' Liability Act 1957 (which covers personal injury and damage to property) and the duty of care owed by occupiers to trespassers under the Occupiers' Liability Act 1984 (which imposes liability for personal injury only). Each potential claimant should be considered separately:

Haris: As a person who is "other than a visitor" Sutton Builders would argue that Haris is a trespasser and therefore is governed by the Occupiers' Liability Act 1984. Section 1(3) of the 1984 Act provides that the occupier owes a duty to a trespasser if: (a) he is aware of the danger or has reasonable grounds to believe that it exists; (b) he knows or has reasonable grounds to believe that the non-visitor is in the vicinity of the danger concerned or that he may come into the vicinity of the danger; and (c) the risk is one against which, in all the circumstances of the case, he may reasonably be expected to offer the non-visitor some protection. Their duty was to take such care as is reasonable in all the circumstances to see that Haris did not suffer injury on the premises by reason of the danger concerned so whether Sutton Builders has discharged its duty will depend upon the extent of the risk of the scaffold falling and the burden that would be imposed in eliminating it. However, liability under the 1957 Act applies only to personal injury or death so liability for the broken windscreen (property damage) suffered by Haris is expressly excluded by Section 1(8).

Clive: as a lawful entrant the liability of Sutton Builders would be governed by the Occupiers' Liability Act 1984. Section 2(3)(b) provides that "an occupier may expect that a person, in the exercise of his calling, will appreciate and guard against any special risks ordinarily incident to it, so far as the occupier leaves him free to do so". Sutton

Builders may deny liability on this ground and seek to argue that as a surveyor from the Council, Clive should have appreciated and guarded against the risk of injury associated with his surveying work by wearing his safety helmet (*Roles v Nathan* (1963)).

Danny: in respect of the child's injury, s.2(3)(a) of the 1984 Act provides that the occupier must be prepared for children to be less careful than adults. However, the extent of the occupier's liability for children is a question of fact and degree and much depends on the particular circumstances of the case. Since Danny is a young child the court would consider whether Olga had taken proper steps in preventing him to wander without supervision. *Phipps v Rochester Corp* (1955); *Simkiss v Rhonnda BC* (1983); *Bourne Leisure Ltd T/A British Holidays v Marsden* (2009)

Breach of Statutory Duty

9

INTRODUCTION

Breach by the defendant of an obligation cast upon him by statute (other than one which expressly seeks to impose liability in tort) may, apart from giving rise to any criminal sanction laid down in the Act, also enable a person injured by the breach to bring a civil action for damages for "breach of statutory duty". This is a tort in its own right independent of any other form of tortious liability. Whether a claimant can sue depends on whether the statute, upon its proper construction, confers a right of civil action upon her and this is, in theory at least, a question of ascertaining the intention of Parliament.

WAS A RIGHT OF ACTION INTENDED?

As a preliminary step, then, the claimant must prove that the legislature intended to create a right to sue. In *Cullen v Chief Constable of the Royal Ulster Constabulary* (2003), the House of Lords upheld the previous decisions that the claimant could not rely on the tort of breach of statutory duty for the failure of the police to give him reasons for delaying his access to a solicitor, on the ground that the duty concerned could be enforced through judicial review. In a few instances Parliament has expressly made known its intention, but in the majority of cases the statute is silent on the issue. It is then for the courts to interpret the enactment in order to discover what that intention is and, to this end, certain guidelines have been established. It should be said at the outset, however, that there is considerable inconsistency in judicial approach to the problem, because, as Lord Browne-Wilkinson observed in *X v Bedfordshire CC* (HL, 1995), although the general principles applicable in determining whether an action lies are well established, the application of those principles in any particular case remains difficult.

DEFINITION CHECKPOINT

The following paragraph contains Lord Browne-Wilkinson's summary of the principles for breach of statutory:

The basic proposition is that a breach of statutory duty does not, by itself, give rise to a private law action. Such an action will arise, however, if it can be shown that, on the proper construction of the statute, the duty was imposed for the protection of a limited class of the public and that Parliament intended to confer upon members of that class a right to sue for breach. There is no general rule for determining whether the Act does create such a right, but if no other remedy is provided for its breach that is an indicator in the claimant's favour (though cf. *O'Rourke v Camden London BC* (HL, 1997)).

If the Act does contain other provision for enforcing the duty that is an indication of an intention that it was to be enforced by those means alone and not by private law action (*Cutler v Wandsworth Stadium Ltd* (HL, 1949); *Lonrho Ltd v Shell Petroleum Co Ltd (No.2)* (HL, 1982)).

However, the mere existence of some other statutory remedy is not decisive, since it is still possible to show that the protected class was intended to have a private remedy. A classic example is that a civil action will lie for breach of industrial safety regulations imposed upon employers, despite the imposition of criminal penalties (*Groves v Lord Wimborne* (CA, 1898)).

In *X v Bedfordshire CC*, two sets of appeals came before the House of Lords relating in the one set to an alleged breach of a local authority's statutory duties in respect of child welfare, and in the other of its duties with regard to the provision of education for children with special needs. It was held that, as in the case of legislation regulating the conduct of prisons (see *Hague v Deputy Governor of Parkhurst Prison* (HL, 1991)), no civil action lay on the grounds, inter alia, that although the legislation did in fact protect individuals adversely affected by the local authorities' activities, it was intended not for the benefit of those individuals but of society as a whole. Lord Browne-Wilkinson said that cases where a right of action has been held to arise are all cases in which the duty has been very limited and specific as opposed to general administrative functions imposed on public bodies, involving the exercise of administrative discretion.

In *Clunis v Camden & Islington Health Authority* (CA, 1998) the Court of Appeal held that breach of duty under the Act does not give rise to an action for damages. The plaintiff, who had a long history of mental illness, was convicted of manslaughter and claimed that he would have been prevented from committing the stabbing if the after-care services under the Mental Health Act 1983 had been provided by the defendant.

In conclusion, in determining whether, in any particular case, a civil action for breach of statutory duty will lie, the starting point is to look to precedent or for a clearly stated Parliamentary intention. In the absence of either, the above principles may assist, but it is in all cases a question of ascertaining the fundamental purpose the legislation intended to achieve, and that can only be done by a consideration of the enactment as a whole.

THE ELEMENTS OF THE TORT

Duty owed to the plaintiff

In establishing that breach of the particular duty will in principle ground a right of action the claimant will in most, if not all, cases have established that the obligation was imposed for the benefit of a limited class. He must then prove that, on the proper construction of the statutory provision, he is a member of that class.

LEGISLATION HIGHLIGHTER

In *Hartley v Mayoh & Co* (CA, 1954), the widow of a fireman electro-cuted while fighting a fire at the defendants' factory had no cause of action because the regulations existed for the benefit of "persons employed", and her husband was not such a person.

Similarly the expression "person employed or working on the premises" was held in *Napieralski v Curtis (Contractors) Ltd* (HC, 1959) not to include a person working for his own private purposes and after normal working hours. In contrast, the same expression has been held to cover a worker who was not acting within the course of his employment but was on a frolic of his own (*Uddin v Associated Portland Cement Manufacturers Ltd* (CA, 1965), approved in *Westwood v Post Office* (HL, 1974), where the plaintiff was a trespasser on that part of the premises to which the action related).

Defendant in breach of duty

The claimant must prove that the defendant was in breach, and this can only be ascertained by having regard to the precise wording of the Act to determine the nature of the obligation. Some obligations are absolute, such as that formerly contained in s.14(1) of the Factories Act 1961 requiring that "every dangerous part of any machinery shall be securely fenced", so that whether reasonable care was taken is irrelevant (see *John Summers & Sons Ltd v Frost* (HL, 1955), where compliance with the regulation would have rendered the machine unusable). Other safety provisions require measures to be taken "so far as is reasonably practicable", which is similar to the ordinary common law negligence formula with the important proviso that the burden is upon the defendant to prove that compliance was not reasonably practicable (*Nimmo v Alexander Cowan & Sons Ltd* (HL, 1967); *Larner v British Steel Plc* (CA, 1993)).

LEGISLATION HIGHLIGHTER

The provisions of the Factories Act and of other work safety legislation have been replaced by a unified series of regulations pertaining to particular aspects of work. As with the old legislation some of the duties contained in the regulations impose an absolute obligation, while others are qualified in some way, so similar problems of interpretation are likely to arise.

Damage of the contemplated type

For the claimant to succeed, the harm suffered must be of a type which the Act was designed to prevent. In *Gorris v Scott* (Ex., 1874), the plaintiff's sheep were swept overboard the defendant's vessel during a storm. The sheep were not penned, contrary to statutory regulations, but the plaintiff nevertheless failed in his action because the object of the regulations was to prevent the spread of disease, not to afford protection from the perils of the sea. So, too, it has been held that the aim of the fencing provisions of the Factories Acts is to prevent the operator from coming into contact with the machine and not to stop parts of the machine, or the materials on which it is working, from flying out and striking the operator (*Close v Steel Co of Wales* (HL, 1962); *Nicholls v F. Austin (Leyton) Ltd* (HL, 1946)). There has been a tendency in more recent times, however, to adopt a more flexible approach.

HARM OF A TYPE WHICH THE ACT WAS DESIGNED TO PREVENT

In *Donaghey v Boulton & Paul Ltd* (HL, 1968), the plaintiff slipped and fell through an open space in an asbestos roof on which he was working. In breach of their duty the defendants had failed to provide him with adequate crawling boards, but argued that the object of the regulations was to prevent workers from falling through fragile roofing materials, not through holes in the roof. The House of Lords rejected such a narrow interpretation and held the defendants liable. Lord Reid said that if the damage is of a kind which the regulation seeks to prevent, it matters not that it happens in a manner not contemplated by the enactment, though this is not easy to reconcile with the decisions on fencing provisions cited above.

Causation

The burden rests upon the claimant to prove on a balance of probabilities that the breach of statutory duty caused or materially contributed to the damage (*Bonnington Castings Ltd v Wardlaw* (HL, 1956)). In this respect there is no distinction between this tort and a common law negligence action, so that the claimant must show that he would not have sustained injury but for the defendant's breach. That this may present difficulties where, as is often the case with industrial safety legislation, the breach consists of an omission is illustrated in *McWilliams* (below).

CAUSATION IS A RELEVANT FACTOR WHERE A SAFETY PRECAUTION IS NOT PROVIDED

In *McWilliams v Sir William Arrol & Co Ltd* (HL, 1962), an experienced workman fell to his death because he was not wearing a safety harness. Although the employer was in breach of duty for failing to provide a belt he was held not liable since, on the evidence, the deceased would probably not have worn the belt anyway and the accident would still have occurred. See also *Ginty v Belmont Building Supplies Ltd* (below).

At one time it might have been thought that *McGhee v National Coal Board* (HL, 1973) supported the view that the plaintiff need only establish that the breach materially increased the risk of damage, but it has now been held that that case decided no more than that the plaintiff was entitled to succeed upon proof that the breach materially contributed to the damage (see Ch.4).

The claimant must also show that the damage is not too remote and the usual test of reasonable foresight applies. As in an action for negligence at common law, the precise way in which the damage is caused need not be foreseeable, provided that the other elements of the tort are satisfied (*Millard v Serck Tubes Ltd* (CA, 1969)).

On the issue of causation generally, a particular problem arises where it is the claimant's own wrongful act which puts the defendant in breach. In *Ginty v Belmont Building Supplies Ltd* (HC, 1959), a regulation binding upon both parties required the use of crawling boards on fragile roofs. The defendant had provided the boards and given full instructions as to their use to the plaintiff who, although an experienced workman, neglected to use them and fell through a roof. Both parties were clearly in breach of their statutory obligation but it was held that the plaintiff was the sole author of his injury and his action failed.

▌DEFINITION CHECKPOINT

The *Ginty* principle is in the nature of a defence which was explained by Lord Reid in *Boyle v Kodak Ltd* (HL, 1969) in the following terms:

"... once the plaintiff has established that there was a breach of an enactment which made the employer absolutely liable, and that that breach caused the accident, he need do no more. But it is then open to the employer to set up a defence that in fact he was not in any way in fault but that the plaintiff employee was alone to blame".

Even if the claimant is not in breach of his statutory duty he will, for similar reasons, fail in his action if it is his own deliberate act of folly which puts the defendant in breach (*Horne v Lec Refrigeration Ltd* (HC, 1965)). The operation of this principle is, however, confined within narrow limits and it will not avail a defendant who is in some way personally at fault. The employer who, for example, fails to provide adequate instructions or supervision or who acquiesces in the breach will still be liable, though there may be a reduction for contributory negligence (see *Boyle v Kodak Ltd* (above)).

. . . .

DEFENCES

Volenti non fit injuria

As a matter of public policy this defence is not available to an employer who is sued for a breach of her own statutory duty. In *Imperial Chemical Industries Ltd v Shatwell* (HL, 1965), it was held that the defence is available where the plaintiff sues his employer vicariously for the default of a fellow worker, provided that the plaintiff is not of lower rank to, or in the habit of taking orders from, his colleague. In cases other than employer and employee there seems no reason why, in principle, the defence should not be available (see Ch.5).

Contributory negligence

This is clearly available (see Ch.5) but, as far as workmen are concerned, the House of Lords in *Caswell v Powell Duffryn Associated Collieries Ltd* (HL, 1940) said that regard must be had to the conditions in which they work, bearing in mind the noise, fatigue and repetitive nature of the job. All the same, whilst momentary lapses of concentration may not be too harshly penalised, a finding of contributory negligence is by no means uncommon in this type of case. It is to be noted that whilst a breach by the claimant of a statutory duty imposed upon her may well amount to contributory negligence, she is not defeated by the ex turpi principle (*National Coal Board v England* (HL, 1954); and see Ch.5).

Delegation

The general rule is that where a duty is imposed upon the defendant, she does not discharge it by entrusting its performance to another. Where, however, the alleged delegation is to the claimant herself, that is a relevant factor in deciding the issue of causation. In other words it is not so much a question of whether there has been a delegation, but rather whose fault it was that the damage occurred (Pearson J. in *Ginty's* case).

Revision Checklist

You should now understand:

- breach of statutory duty is a tort in its own right independent of any other form of tortious liability;

- whether a claimant can sue depends on whether the statute, upon its proper construction, confers a right of civil action;

- where the statute is silent on the issue, it is then for the courts to interpret the statute and give effect to the intention of Parliament;

- there is considerable inconsistency in judicial approach to interpretation, because, as Lord Browne-Wilkinson observed in *X v Bedfordshire CC* (HL, 1995), although the general principles applicable in determining whether an action lies are well established, the application of those principles in any particular case remains difficult.

QUESTION AND ANSWER

Question

Outline the factors taken into account by the courts in determining whether a claim for breach of statutory duty should be treated at giving rise to a civil claim.

Approach to the answer

The courts would refer to the particular wording of the statute to determine the intention of Parliament as to whether a claim will lie in tort for breach of the duty imposed *(Lonrho Ltd v Shell Petroleum Co Ltd (No.2)* (HL, 1982)). If the statute is silent on the matter, indicators of what Parliament intended are found by looking at whether the statute:

(a) was designed to protect a limited class of the persons and intended to confer upon members of that class a right to sue for breach

(b) provides an alternative method of enforcement—if the Act does contain other provision for enforcing the duty that is an indication of an intention that it was to be enforced by those means alone and not by a civil law action

Once the duty is established the claimant will normally have established that the obligation was imposed for the benefit of a limited class. He must then prove that, on the proper construction of the statutory provision, he is a member of that class *(Hartley v Mayoh & Co* 1954).

The claimant must then prove that the defendant was in breach of this duty and this can only be ascertained by having regard to the precise wording of the Act to determine the nature of the obligation. Some obligations are absolute so that whether reasonable care was taken is irrelevant whereas other safety provisions require measures to be taken "so far as is reasonably practicable", which is similar to the ordinary common law negligence formula. However, the burden is upon the defendant to prove that compliance with the statute was not reasonably practicable.

For the claimant to succeed, the harm suffered must be of a type which the Act was designed to prevent *(Gorris v Scott* (1874)) and, on a balance of probabilities, that the breach of statutory duty caused or materially contributed to the damage *(Bonnington Castings Ltd v Wardlaw* 1956).

Defamation

10

INTRODUCTION

Defamation may be defined as the publication of a statement which tends to lower a person in the estimation of right-thinking people generally or which tends to make them shun or avoid him. The latter part of the definition makes it clear that the words need not bring the claimant into ridicule or contempt, but may arouse only feelings of pity (*Youssoupoff v M.G.M. Pictures Ltd* (CA, 1934)). In *Berkoff v Burchill* (CA, 1996), a majority of the Court of Appeal held that to describe a film actor and director as "hideously ugly" was capable of being defamatory in that it could lower his standing in the public's estimation and make him an object of ridicule. A trading corporation can sue for a defamatory attack upon its commercial reputation (*South Hetton Coal Co Ltd v North Eastern News Association Ltd* (CA, 1894)) but local government, other organs of government and political parties may not sue, because to permit otherwise would be to inhibit freedom of speech and would thus be contrary to the public interest (*Derbyshire CC v Times Newspapers Ltd* (HL, 1993)).

The aim of the law is to strike a balance between freedom of speech and the right of a person not to have their good name sullied so that, whilst liability is strict in the sense that the defendant's intention is generally irrelevant, a number defences are available. However, when considering the role of defamation in protecting reputation, it should be remembered that the competing right to freedom of expression is also increasingly offered protection by the law. Where a conflict between these competing rights arises, the courts must strike a balance between the protection of reputation and freedom of speech. Traditionally, the common law protected freedom of expression through the defences to defamation (it is for this reason that an understanding of the defences to defamation is as important as understanding the elements of liability) but the law of defamation only extends to *un*true statements. Where harm is caused to a claimant by words or images which are true and therefore no remedy in defamation is available, the emerging law of privacy (discussed below) may provide protection in these circumstances.

Although defamation actions are commonly tried before a jury, the court may now, in accordance with s.8 of the Defamation Act 1996, dispose summarily of the claim if either it has no realistic prospect of success or there is no viable defence. In the former case the claim will be dismissed, while in the latter the court may give judgment for the plaintiff and grant summary relief, which by s.9 may include, inter alia, damages not exceeding £10,000.

LEGISLATION HIGHLIGHTER

Free speech is protected under the European Convention on Human Rights and Fundamental Freedoms.

Article 10(1) provides that everyone has the right to freedom of expression and gives individuals the right to hold opinions and receive and impart information and ideas without interference by public authorities.

The Convention acknowledges the potential conflict between freedom of expression and the protection of reputation and in order to strike a balance between freedom of expression and protection of reputation, Art.10(2) places certain restrictions on the exercise of freedom of expression.

LIBEL AND SLANDER

A defamatory statement or representation in permanent form is a libel, but if conveyed by spoken words or gestures, a slander. Apart from the written word, pictures, statues and waxwork effigies are libels. In addition, radio and television broadcasts are treated as publication in permanent form (Broad-casting Act 1990), as are words spoken during a public theatrical performance (Theatres Act 1968).

Reading out a defamatory document to a third party is, on the balance of authority, a libel (*Forrester v Tyrrell* (CA, 1893)). To dictate defamatory material to a typist is clearly a slander, but if it is then put into a letter and sent to a third party the dictator publishes a libel through his agent. As far as defamatory matter on records and recorded tapes and discs is concerned, there is a divergence of opinion among writers as to whether this is libel or potential slander.

DEFINITION CHECKPOINT

An important distinction between libel and slander is that libel is actionable per se, without proof of special damage, whereas slander requires proof of such, except in the following circumstances:

- a direct imputation of a criminal offence punishable in the first instance with imprisonment (words conveying mere suspicion of the offence will not suffice).

- an imputation that the plaintiff is presently suffering from a contagious or infectious disease likely to cause others to shun his society.
- an imputation of unchastity to any woman or girl (**Slander of Women Act 1891**).
- words calculated to disparage the plaintiff in any office, profession, calling, trade or business held or carried on by him at the time of the publication. The common law requirement that the words had to be spoken in the way of the plaintiff's calling has been removed by s.2 of the **Defamation Act 1952**. If, therefore, the natural tendency of the statement is to injure or prejudice the reputation of the plaintiff in his calling the words will be actionable per se.

Aside from the above exceptions slander requires proof of special damage, which means loss of some temporal or material advantage such as loss of one's job or of the hospitality of one's friends (but mere exclusion from their society is not enough). The damage must not be too remote in accordance with general principles (see Ch.4), although illness caused by mental anxiety induced by slander not actionable per se is considered too remote. Where a third party causes loss to the plaintiff as a result of the statement, that may or may not break the chain of causation depending upon what the defendant ought reasonably to have anticipated. Unauthorised repetition makes the damage too remote unless there is a legal or moral duty to repeat, or the defendant intends the repetition or if that is the natural and probable consequence of the original publication (*Speight v Gosnay* (CA, 1891); *Slipper v BBC* (CA, 1991); *McManus v Beckham* (2002)).

WHAT THE CLAIMANT MUST PROVE

Whether the action is for libel or slander the claimant must prove that a defamatory statement referring to him was published.

Statement must be defamatory

The words must be defamatory in accordance with the definition already given, though it need not be proved that anyone who actually heard or read them believed them to be true. Where the statement tends to discredit the claimant only with a special class of persons, she may not succeed unless people generally would take the same view. In *Byrne v Deane* (CA, 1937), for example, it was held not to be defamatory to say of a club member that he had informed the police of an illicit gambling machine on the club premises, because right-thinking persons would not think less well of such a man. *Byrne v Deane* is an example of publication by omission where the golf club's omission in failing to remove a statement from its notice board amounted to publication. In *Godfrey v Demon Internet* (1999) (below), the Internet Service Providers were liable for publication because they had been informed of the libel on the internet and had failed to remove it.

Problems may arise, however, where the general public is divided in its opinion. Thus, to say of another that she went to work during a strike would certainly lower her in the estimation of a considerable number of people and ought perhaps on that basis to be defamatory. The circumstances in which the statement is made may be important; words spoken at the height of a violent quarrel, for example, are not actionable if those who heard them understood them as mere abuse. The question in all cases is what interpretation the reasonable man would put upon the statement. In *Charleston v News Group Newspapers Ltd* (HL, 1995), the defendants published a potentially defamatory headline and photograph, but the text of the accompanying article plainly negated the defamatory meaning. The plaintiff was held to have no cause of action because, in the absence of a legal innuendo, the meaning to be ascribed to the words was the meaning which, taken as a whole, they conveyed to the ordinary, fair-minded reader, not to the limited category of those who only read headlines.

DEFINITION CHECKPOINT

The meaning of words
- It is a question of law for the judge to decide whether the words are capable of a defamatory meaning and, if they are, it is for the jury to decide whether they are in fact. The issue must be left to the jury unless the judge is satisfied that no reasonable person would construe the statement as defamatory (*Capital & Counties Bank Ltd v Henty & Son* (HL, 1882)).
- If the statement is plainly defamatory in its ordinary sense it is actionable (subject to any defence), unless the defendant can successfully explain away the defamatory meaning. Conversely, the words may be prima facie innocent but, in the light of extrinsic facts known to persons to whom the statement is published, bear some secondary defamatory meaning. This is a true, or legal, innuendo and is illustrated in *Tolley v J. S. Fry & Sons Ltd* (HL, 1931). The plaintiff, a well-known amateur golfer, was portrayed in an advertisement for the defendants' chocolate. He successfully pleaded an innuendo that he had received payment for his services and had thereby prostituted his amateur status.
- The extrinsic facts upon which the plaintiff relies in support of the

innuendo must be known to the recipients of the statement at the time of publication and the plaintiff must, as a general rule, specify the persons whom he alleges to have knowledge of those facts (*Grappelli v D. Block (Holdings) Ltd* (CA, 1981)).

- It is plain from *Cassidy v Daily Mirror Newspapers Ltd* (CA, 1929) that it is immaterial that the defendant is unaware of the extrinsic facts.

Where the claimant does not rely upon extrinsic facts but merely contends that a particular meaning is to be attributed to the words themselves, there is said to be a "false" innuendo which, unlike the legal innuendo, does not give rise to a separate cause of action. In *Lewis v Daily Telegraph Ltd* (HL, 1964), the defendants published a statement that the fraud squad was investigating the plaintiffs' affairs. It was held that those words could not mean, as the plaintiffs alleged, that their affairs were conducted fraudulently, but simply meant that there was a suspicion of fraud, which the defendants admitted was prima facie defamatory but which they could justify (see also *Mapp v News Group Newspapers Ltd* (CA, 1998)).

Reference to the plaintiff

There must be a sufficient indication that the claimant is the subject of the statement, and in most cases, at least where the claimant is named, this presents no difficulty. The claimant need not be named, however, nor need there by any key or pointer in the statement to indicate her in particular, provided that people might reasonably draw the inference that it referred to her (*Morgan v Odhams Press Ltd* (HL, 1971)). Where a defamatory statement makes no reference to the claimant, she may rely on a later publication which clearly identifies her with the original statement (*Hayward v Thompson* (CA, 1982)).

DEFINITION CHECKPOINT

It has long been the case that there is no requirement that the defendant must have intended to refer to the claimant (*Hulton & Co v Jones* (HL, 1910)), and even if the statement is true of one person it may still be defamatory of another. Thus, in *Newstead v London Express Newspaper Ltd* (CA, 1940) the defendants were liable for their report that Harold Newstead, a 30-year-old Camberwell man, had been convicted of bigamy, which was true of X but untrue of the plaintiff, who bore the same name, was about the same age, and who also came from Camberwell.

In respect of a defamatory statement directed at a class of persons (e.g. doctors) no individual member of that class may usually sue unless there is some indication in the words, or the circumstances of their publication, which indicates a particular plaintiff. But if the reference is to a sufficiently limited class or group (e.g. the directors of a company) they may all be able to sue if it can be said that the words refer to each of them individually. These principles were established in *Knuppfer v London Express Newspaper Ltd* (HL, 1944).

Publication

There must be publication to at least one person other than the claimant or the defendant's spouse, but there is no publication by a typist or printer merely by handing the statement back to its author (*Eglantine Inn Ltd v Smith* (HC, 1948)). The defendant is liable if he intends further publication, for example by writing a letter to the correspondence editor of a newspaper (*Cutler v McPhail* (HC, 1962)). So, too, is he liable if he is negligent, as where he puts a letter in the wrong envelope or speaks too loudly in a crowded room.

> **DEFINITION CHECKPOINT**
>
> A defendant is not liable if the statement is overheard by one whose presence is not to be expected, or if a letter is read by one who has no authority to do so.
>
> In *Huth v Huth* (CA, 1915), a letter in an unsealed envelope was opened and read by an inquisitive butler in an admitted breach of his duty. There was no publication because it was not part of the butler's duty to open the letter and his conduct was not a direct consequence of the defendant's sending of it.

An unauthorised repetition or republication will break the chain of causation unless the statement is published to one who is under a legal or moral duty to repeat it, or the repetition is foreseeable as a natural and probable consequence of the original publication (*Speight v Gosnay* (CA, 1891); *Slipper v BBC* (CA, 1991)).

Every repetition of a defamatory statement is a fresh publication so that, as regards printed matter, the author, editor and publisher are all liable. At common law a mechanical distributor of print, such as a library or newsagent, is presumptively liable but will have a defence of innocent dissemination if he can prove that he did not know the work contained a libel, and that that lack of knowledge was not due to negligence in the conduct of his business (*Vizetelly v Mudie's Select Library Ltd* (CA, 1900)).

Section 1 of the Defamation Act 1996 now codifies the defence in *Vizetelly* and extends its availability to a wider range of persons, including printers, broadcasters of live programmes containing the statement where there is no effective control over the person making it, and internet service providers.

The defendant must show that he took reasonable care in relation to the publication of the statement and that he did not know, and had no reason to believe, that what he did caused or contributed to the publication of a defamatory statement. For example, in *Godfrey v Demon Internet* (1999) the defendant Internet Service Provider did not dispute the defamatory nature of the statement but claimed that it was not responsible for postings by users on its internet sites. Although the defendant was held not to be the publisher within the meaning of s.1 of the Defamation Act 1996, there was liability in this case because the claimants had notified the defendant of the defamatory content of the message and requested that it be removed. The defendants failed to remove the message and were therefore unable to rely on the defence in s.1 of the Act which required them to show that they had exercised reasonable care in relation to the publication.

A person may be liable for failing to remove defamatory matter placed upon premises by a third party (*Byrne v Deane* (CA, 1937)). The extent of his duty to do so presumably depends upon whether he has control of the premises where the statement is displayed and the ease with which it can be removed. In *Godfrey v Demon Internet* (1999), the Internet Service Providers were liable for publication because they had been informed of the libel on the internet and had failed to remove it.

KEY CASE

SEARCH ENGINE LIABILITY FOR DEFAMATION UNDER UK LAW

In *Metropolitan International Schools Ltd v Designtechnica Corporation, Google UK and Google Inc* (2009), the question was whether Google should be regarded as a "publisher" of the words complained of (whether before or after Google had been notified of their defamatory comments) or whether it was a mere facilitator. The court held that Google was not liable for publication of the statements because it had no control over the search terms entered by users of the search engine or of the material which is placed on the web by its users. This case confirms that mere facilitators, like telephone carriers, are generally not liable for defamatory content.

DEFENCES

Offers to make amends

The Defamation Act 1996 repeals s.4 of the 1952 Act and provides, by ss.2–4, for the similar but modified defence of an offer to make amends. The offer, which must be in writing, must be not only to make a suitable correction of the alleged defamatory statement and a sufficient apology to the claimant, but also to pay such compensation and costs as may be agreed or determined to be payable. If such an offer is accepted no proceedings may be brought or continued in respect of the publication concerned, but if it is not, the defendant has a defence unless he knew or had reason to believe that the statement referred, or was likely to be understood as referring, to the claimant and was both false and defamatory of her. It is presumed that the defendant did not have the requisite knowledge of, or reason to believe, those matters until the claimant proves otherwise. An offer to make amends cannot be made after serving a defence in defamation proceedings and, once made and relied upon by way of defence, no other defence may be raised. The offer may be relied on in mitigation of damages whether or not it was relied on as a defence.

Justification

Justification or truth is generally an absolute defence, though the defendant has the onus of proving the truth of the statement. He need only show that the statement is substantially true and whether the defence is lost through a minor inaccuracy is a matter for the jury.

LEGISLATION HIGHLIGHTER

Section 5 of the Defamation Act 1952 provides that the defence does not fail if the truth of a number of charges cannot be proved, provided that the words not proved to be true do not materially injure the claimant's reputation having regard to the truth of the remaining charges. In such a case, the cautious claimant will plead only the untrue allegation because the defendant cannot then rely on the publication as a whole and will presumably fail to justify. But, if the claimant seeks to adopt this approach, the allegations must be distinct (which is a question of fact and degree) and, if a number of allegations taken together have a common "sting", the defendant is entitled to justify that sting (*Polly Peck (Holdings) Plc v Trelford* (CA, 1986)).

If the defendant seeks to justify the repetition of a defamatory statement made to him he must, as a general rule, prove that the statement is true and cannot simply rely on the fact that another made it (*"Truth" (N.Z.) Ltd v Holloway* (PC, 1960); *Stern v Piper* (CA, 1996)). However, while hearsay and rumour cannot constitute justification for what amounts to an assertion of fact that the rumour is well founded, there may be circumstances in which the existence of a rumour entitles a person to repeat it and to plead in justification that such a rumour is in fact abroad (*Aspro Travel Ltd v Owners Abroad Group plc* (CA, 1995)).

Where the defendant's allegation is that the claimant has been convicted of an offence, s.13 of the Civil Evidence Act 1968 (as amended by s.12 of the Defamation Act 1996) provides that proof that she stands convicted of it is conclusive evidence that she did commit it. The fact that the plaintiff's conviction is "spent" under the Rehabilitation of Offenders Act 1974 does not prevent the defendant from relying upon justification, but in this case the defence is defeated by proof of malice.

Fair comment

It is a defence that the statement is a fair comment upon a matter of public interest. What is in the public interest is a question of law for the judge and, whilst there is no exhaustive category of such matters, it covers the conduct of government and public institutions, works of art and literature produced for public consumption, theatrical productions and the like. A man's private life is not a matter of public interest unless it reflects upon his ability or fitness for public office.

The comment must be an honest expression of opinion based upon true facts existing at the time the comment was made, though the defence is still available where the comment is based upon an untrue statement made by another on a privileged occasion, provided that the defendant can also prove that he gave a fair and accurate report of the occasion on which the privileged statement was made (*Brent Walker Group Plc v Time Out Ltd* (CA, 1991)).

DEFINITION CHECKPOINT

If the statement is one of fact rather than opinion the appropriate defence is justification.
The facts upon which the comment is based need not be expressly stated but may be impliedly indicated in the circumstances of the publication (*Kemsley v Foot* (HL, 1952)). As far as the factual basis for the comment is concerned, the defence does not fail merely because the truth of every allegation of fact is not proved, as long as the expression of opinion is fair comment "having regard to such of the

> facts alleged or referred to in the words complained of as are proved"
> (Defamation Act 1952, s.6).

The comment must be fair and the test is whether the defendant was "an honest man expressing his genuine opinion" (Lord Denning M.R. in *Slim v Daily Telegraph Ltd* (CA, 1968)), though if the factual basis for the comment is untrue the defence fails, no matter how honest the defendant was. It is not for the defendant to prove that the comment was an honest expression of his own views but merely that it was objectively fair (*Telnikoff v Matusevitch* (HL, 1991)).

KEY CASE

WHERE THE WORDS WERE EXPRESSIONS OF OPINION, NO MATTER HOW PARAPHRASED OR EXPRESSED, THE DEFENDANT IS ENTITLED TO RELY ON THE DEFENCE OF FAIR COMMENT.

In *British Chiropractic Association v Dr Singh* (2010), statements about the lack of worthwhile evidence to support the efficacy of treatments were held not to be an assertion of fact but a statement of opinion, protected by the defence of fair comment. It should be noted that Court of Appeal thought the term "fair comment" may have come to: "decay with ... imprecision" and that to describe this defence with the words "honest opinion" would lend greater emphasis to its importance as an essential ingredient of the right to free expression.

Although violent or exaggerated language does not make the comment unfair, if the claimant is charged with base or dishonest motives the defendant must prove that the comment is warranted by the facts in the sense that a fair-minded man might, in the light of those facts, bona fide hold such an opinion (*Peter Walker Ltd v Hodgson* (CA, 1909)).

Comment will not be fair if the defendant is actuated by malice in the sense of improper or evil motive, even though it would have been fair if made by one who genuinely believed it to be true (*Thomas v Bradbury Agnew & Co Ltd* (CA, 1906)). With regard to the defence of qualified privilege (see later) malice on the part of one co-publisher will not "taint" another, and there is support for the view that the same rule applies to fair comment (*Lyon v Daily Telegraph Ltd* (CA, 1943); *Telnikoff v Matusevitch* (HL, 1991)). The burden of proving malice rests upon the claimant (*Telnikoff v Matusevitch* (HL, 1991)).

Figure 14: Absolute privilege

Absolute privilege

Statements made on an occasion of absolute privilege are not actionable regardless of whether the defendant was malicious. They include the following:

(a) Statements made in the course of parliamentary proceedings including reports and papers ordered to be published by either House. Members of Parliament may now, by virtue of s.13 of the Defamation Act 1996, waive Parliamentary privilege for the purpose of bringing proceedings.

(b) Statements made during the course of judicial proceedings, whether by judge, jury, counsel or witnesses, provided they are broadly relevant to the issue before the court. The privilege extends not only to proceedings in an ordinary court of law but to any tribunal recognised by law and acting in a similar manner, even though it is not empowered to take a final decision on the issue (*Trapp v Mackie* (HL, 1979)). This was held in *Addis v Crocker* (HC, 1961) to include the Disciplinary Committee of the Law Society.

(c) Communications between solicitor and client in connection with litigation. It is not clear whether other communications attract absolute or merely qualified privilege, but in any event what passes between them is only protected in so far as it is reasonably referable to the solicitor-client relationship (*Minter v Priest* (HL, 1930)).

(d) Communications by one officer of state to another in the course of his official duty (*Chatterton v Secretary of State for India* (CA, 1895)). It is doubtful whether the privilege extends below communications on a ministerial level, though there may well be a qualified privilege.

(e) By s.14 of the Defamation Act 1996, fair and accurate reports of proceedings in public before any court in the United Kingdom, the European Court of Justice, the European Court of Human Rights or any international criminal tribunal set up by the United Nations. The report must be published contemporaneously with the proceedings.

(f) Statutory protection is given to various reports of the Parliamentary Commissioner for Administration and of Local Commissioners.

Qualified privilege

This defence exists in respect of statements made for the protection of one's private interests or for the protection of the public interest, as where a complaint is laid before the proper authorities to secure the redress of a public grievance. It is also available where the maker of the statement and the recipient have a common interest in the matter, or where the recipient alone has an interest and the maker is under a legal, moral or social duty to communicate as, for instance, where a reference is given to a prospective employer. The common thread in all of these instances is that the defendant has either an interest in making, or a duty (legal, social or moral) to make the statement. But an equally essential requirement is that the person to whom the statement is made must either have a reciprocal interest or be under a corresponding duty to receive it (*Adam v Ward* (HL, 1917)). For the position where an apology tendered in mitigation of a libel is itself defamatory of a person other than the alleged victim of the original libel, see *Watts v Times Newspapers Ltd* (CA, 1996).

KEY CASE

WATT V LONGSDON (CA,1930) provides an illustration of the above principles.

The defendant director of a company received a letter from X, a manager of the company which was defamatory of the plaintiff who was managing director. The defendant replied to X in terms defamatory of the plaintiff and he also published X's letter to the company chairman and to the plaintiff's wife. In a libel action against the defendant, it was held that his letter to X was privileged because both had a common interest in the company's affairs. The communication of X's letter to the chairman was also privileged on the grounds that the defendant was under a duty to report the matter. However, the defendant was held to be under no duty to communicate the letter to the plaintiff's wife notwithstanding the obvious interest which she had in receiving it.

Whether or not there is a duty to communicate is a matter of law for the judge and no satisfactory test has evolved. In relation to the press it has been said that there is no defence of "fair information on a matter of public interest" and there is no duty to report that which is based on mere suspicion or conjecture (*Blackshaw v Lord* (CA, 1984)).

KEY CASES

QUALIFIED PRIVILEGE, PUBLIC INTEREST AND RESPONSIBLE JOURNALISM

- In *Reynolds v Times Newspapers Ltd* (HL, 1999), acknowledging the role of the press in a democratic society, the House of Lords ruled that, notwithstanding the arguments about the freedom of the press and the right to freedom of expression contained in Art.10 of the European Convention on Human Rights, "political information" was not to be adopted as a new category of qualified privilege. The existing tests for the defence were still to be applied as to whether the nature, status and source of the material published, and the circumstances of the publication were such that, in the public interest, the publication should be protected by privilege in the absence of malice. The court was unanimous in the view that it would be unsound in principle to distinguish political discussion from discussion of other matters of public concern. Nevertheless, in emphasising the importance of freedom of expression and in recognition of Art.10, their Lordships held that interference with freedom of speech should be confined to what was necessary in the circumstances of the case. The court should be slow to conclude that a publication was not in the public interest and doubts should be resolved in favour of publication.

- *Jameel v Wall Street Journal Europe* (2006) concerned an article suggesting that the claimants' bank accounts were involved in funding terrorism, which was found to be defamatory. The Court of Appeal rejected the newspaper's defence of qualified privilege but the House of Lords, focusing on the "public interest" aspect of *Reynolds* privilege, allowed the newspaper's appeal and said that the defence was being applied too cautiously by the lower courts. Journalists are under a professional duty to report on matters of public interest and the public has an interest in receiving such information. Where a publication is in the public interest, the duty and interest are taken to exist and, in the context of editorial judgment, the question then is whether responsible steps had been taken to gather and publish the information.

- *Flood v Times Newspapers Ltd* (2010) concerned responsible journalism and whether the steps taken by the journalists to verify the information were adequate to meet the test. An article published by the defendant newspaper that police were investigating an allegation that a senior officer had accepted bribes in exchange for confidential police information. The article named Flood as the officer and set out the details of what had been alleged. Flood appealed against the judge's ruling that the defendant was entitled to rely on the defence of *Reynolds* qualified privilege. In allowing the appeal the Court of Appeal was of the view that the defendant had not acted "responsibly".

In addition to the above, a number of reports are protected, including fair and accurate reports of parliamentary proceedings and of public judicial proceedings. The common law privilege in relation to the latter is wider than the statutory absolute privilege in that it applies to any form of publication made at any time. A number of fair and accurate reports and statements receive qualified privilege by s.15 of the Defamation Act 1996. The reports so protected are to be found in Sch.1 to the Act and are divided into two categories, those in the first being privileged "without explanation or contradiction", and those in the second "subject to explanation or contradiction". The defence is lost as regards those in the second category if the plaintiff requests the defendant to publish a reasonable statement by way of explanation or contradiction and the defendant refuses or neglects to do so. This statutory privilege does not extend to the publication of any matter which is not of public concern and the publication of which is not for the public benefit (s.15(3)). Whether the report is "fair and accurate" and the question of "public concern" and "public benefit", should be left to the jury (*Kingshott v Associated Kent Newspapers Ltd* (CA, 1991)).

Qualified privilege may be lost if the defendant publishes the statement more widely than is necessary for the protection of an interest. However, a publication by the defendant to third persons who have no interest or duty is nevertheless protected if it is reasonable and in the ordinary course of business. If, for example, X sends to Y a letter defamatory of Y which he first dictates to his secretary in the ordinary course of business, Y cannot sue for the publication to the secretary provided that the letter is written to protect or further the aims of the business (*Bryanston Finance Ltd v de Vries* (CA, 1975)).

DEFINITION CHECKPOINT

The defence of qualified privilege is lost upon proof that the defendant was actuated by malice which may either mean lack of honest belief in the truth of the statement or use of the privilege for an improper purpose.

Irrational prejudice or gross or exaggerated language does not amount to malice if the defendant's belief is honest (*Horrocks v Lowe* (HL, 1975)). His honesty is irrelevant, however, if he makes use of the occasion for an improper purpose as, for instance, where his aim is to spite rather than protect a legitimate interest.

The Defamation Bill 2010 aims to amend the law of defamation and encourage the free exchange of ideas and information, whilst providing an effective and proportionate remedy to anyone whose reputation is unfairly damaged. Lord Lester who introduced the Bill said: "It creates a framework of principles rather than a rigid and inflexible code, and it seeks a fair balance between reputation and public information on matters of public interest." However, it should be noted that where a statement contains true facts, no matter how much a person wants them to remain private, the law of defamation offers no protection. A general right of privacy has traditionally not been recognised in English common law.

Privacy

Since the enactment of the **Human Rights Act 1998,** which incorporates the European Convention on Human Rights (ECHR) into English law, privacy is now an emerging area of law. When considering situations where an individual claims a legal right to the protection of personal or private information from misuse or unauthorised disclosure, the courts are required to have regard to the ECHR. Although Art.8 of the ECHR provides an explicit right to respect for a private life for the first time in English law, this must be balanced with Art.10 which protects the right to freedom of expression. One of the concerns of the courts is that if respect for a private life is defined too widely it could lead to an undesirable restriction on the freedom of the press to report and comment on matters of public importance.

DEFINITION CHECKPOINT
Privacy is a difficult concept to clearly define

- The distinction between what constitutes public information and when information is private is not always clear.
- One definition of privacy was provided by American Judge Cooley, in 1888 as: *"the right to be left alone".*
- *The Calcutt Committee, Report on Privacy and Related Matters* (1990) reported: *"nowhere have we found a wholly acceptable statutory definition of privacy."*
- The following working definition of privacy was adopted by the Report: *The right of the individual to be protected against intrusion into his personal life or affairs, or those of his family, by direct physical means or by publication of information.*

Although there is no tort of invasion of privacy in English law, privacy is a value underlying the common law doctrine of breach of confidence, but this is not in itself the recognition of a legal principle. Breach of confidence is a cause of action arising from the breach of a duty to keep confidence arising from a confidential situation, transaction, or relationship. In *Wainwright v Home Office* (2003), a claim that intrusive strip searches amounted to invasion of privacy and a breach of Art.8 was rejected. The House of Lords confirmed that there is no tort of invasion of privacy in English law and doubted that the European Court of Human Rights jurisprudence required a freestanding right of privacy to comply with Art.8. However, In *Von Hannover v*

Germany (2004) the ECHR subsequently confirmed that a positive obligation in respect of privacy rights is imposed by Art.8. In failing to take steps necessary to restrain publication of certain photos of a purely private nature taken in a climate of harassment, the German courts did not strike a fair balance between the competing rights at issue in protecting the private life of Princess Caroline of Monaco. In *McKennitt v Ash* (2006), the English courts followed this decision and held that a pre-existing obligation of confidence gave rise to a reasonable expectation of privacy. Unless the information holds some important public interest value, the right to private and family life under Art.8 will not be outweighed by the Art.10 right to freedom of expression. In upholding McKennitt's right to prevent publication of significant parts of the book on the ground that details of her personal and sexual relationships were intrusive and distressing, the court placed great weight on there being a pre-existing obligation of confidence on Ash, her former close friend. The weight given by the courts to preserving the public interest in employees respecting obligations of confidence that they have assumed is further illustrated by the decision in *HRH Prince of Wales v Associated Newspapers* (2006) where HRH contended that a private leaked travel journal about his 1997 visit to Hong Kong which set out his private and personal thoughts, constituted confidential information. The court examined the balance between protecting confidential information and copyright on the one hand and the extent of press freedom on the other. In upholding HRH's right to keep the information in the journal private, the court found that staff who may have encountered the journal were subject to confidentiality undertakings.

KEY CASES

Before the decision of the ECHR in Ash, the English courts had already concluded that the Human Rights Act 1998 (s.6) required them to act in compatibility with the Convention.

- In *Campbell v MGN Ltd* (2004), the House of Lords held that protection of privacy in England is based not on a distinct tort of infringement of privacy but principally on an action for breach of confidence which takes account of both Art.8 (right to respect to private and family life) and Art.10 (right to freedom of expression) of the ECHR.
- Given Campbell's previous statements, the publication of the fact that she had taken drugs and was receiving treatment was necessary to set the record straight. However, the publication of details of that treatment and a photograph of her leaving the clinic was an unjustified intrusion into her private life.

- In balancing the competing interests under the Human Rights Act 1998, significant weight was given to the photograph and its inclusion in the publication added greatly to the intrusion and Campbell's Art.8 right to privacy was therefore held to outweigh MGN's competing interest in freedom of expression under Art.10.
- In *Mosley v News Group Newspapers* (MGN) (2008), the material and images MGN published in newspapers and on their website were held to be inherently private in nature and infringed Mosley's rights of privacy under Art.8 ECHR. The Court found that the degree of intrusion (which had been done on a massive scale) was not proportionate to the public interest supposed to be served in publishing the information.

In *Douglas v Hello! Ltd* (2005), the couple had entered into an exclusive agreement with a rival magazine for publication of their wedding photographs. They claimed against Hello! Magazine for breach of confidence arising from publication of unauthorised photographs taken at their wedding on the ground that the wedding was a valuable trade asset. Although there was no existing law of privacy under which the claimants were entitled to relief, the photographic representations of the event were held to have the necessary quality of confidence and deserved protection as a trade secret.

Revision Checklist

You should now understand:

- **Defamation requires a claimant to show: (1) a defamatory statement; (2) publication to a third party; and (3) that the statement referred to him;**
- **The function of the defences to defamation in balancing the competing rights of freedom of expression with protection of reputation;**
- **In balancing protection of reputation and free speech, Art.8 and Art.10 of the ECHR are of crucial importance;**
- **The history of the protection of privacy in English law and the impact of the Human Rights Act 1998 on this emerging area of law**

QUESTION AND ANSWER

Question

To what extent does the law of defamation enable the courts to strike the right balance between freedom of expression and protection of reputation?

Approach to answer

When considering the role of defamation in protecting reputation it should be noted that the competing right to freedom of expression is also increasingly offered protection by the law. Traditionally, the common law protected freedom of expression through the defences to defamation but free speech is also protected under the European Convention on Human Rights and Fundamental Freedoms. Article 10(1) provides that everyone has the right to freedom of expression and gives individuals the right to hold opinions and receive and impart information and ideas without interference by public authorities. The Convention acknowledges the potential conflict between freedom of expression and the protection of reputation and in order to strike a balance between freedom of expression and protection of reputation, Art.10(2) places certain restrictions on the exercise of freedom of expression.

The defences should be outlined and the attempts of the courts to strike a balance between the competing rights should be illustrated with case law.

Fair comment: a defence that the statement is a fair comment upon a matter of public interest. The comment must be fair and the test is whether the defendant was "an honest man expressing his genuine opinion" (*Slim v Daily Telegraph Ltd* (1968)). If the factual basis for the comment is untrue the defence fails, no matter how honest the defendant was. It is not for the defendant to prove that the comment was an honest expression of his own views but merely that it was objectively fair (*Telnikoff v Matusevitch* (1991)). Where the words were expressions of opinion, no matter how paraphrased or expressed, the defendant is entitled to rely on the defence of fair comment (*British Chiropractic Association v Dr Singh* (2010)).

Absolute privilege: this covers statements made on an occasion of absolute privilege—they are not actionable regardless of whether the defendant was malicious.

Qualified privilege: exists in respect of statements made for the protection of a private interest or for the protection of the public interest. This defence is also available where the maker of the statement and the recipient have a common interest in the matter, or where the recipient alone has an interest and the maker is under a legal, moral or social duty to communicate as, for instance, where a reference is given to a prospective employer. The common thread in all of these instances is that the defendant has either an interest in making, or a duty (legal, social or moral) to make the statement. But an equally essential requirement is that the person to whom the statement is made must either have a reciprocal interest or be under a corresponding duty to receive it (*Watt v Longsdon* (CA,1930)).

In the context of qualified privilege, in *Reynolds v Times Newspapers Ltd* (1999) the House of Lords acknowledged the role of the press in a democratic society and held that interference with freedom of speech should be confined to what was necessary in the circumstances of the case. The court should be slow to conclude that a publication was not in the public interest and doubts should be resolved in favour of publication. In *Jameel v Wall Street Journal Europe* (2006), the Court of Appeal rejected the newspaper's defence of qualified privilege but the House of Lords, focusing on the "public interest" aspect of *Reynolds* privilege, allowed the newspaper's appeal. However, in *Flood v Times Newspapers Ltd* (2010), the Court of Appeal said it is now accepted that the right to reputation is an Art.8 right and the statement of Lord Nicholls in Reynolds that: "Any lingering doubts should be resolved in favour of publication" no longer applied. Instead the court would have to carry out the balancing exercise between Arts 8 and 10, giving neither precedence.

Nuisance

11

INTRODUCTION

For the purposes of an action in tort a nuisance may be either private or public. In addition, there are a large number of statutory provisions aimed at the control of conduct which is damaging to the environment, some of which impose civil liability in respect of certain hazards. Enforcement of these provisions is in the hands of public bodies, which means that the claimant may save a good deal of time and expense by directing his complaint to the relevant body.

PRIVATE NUISANCE

The claimant may bring an action in private nuisance where the defendant unlawfully interferes with his use or enjoyment of his land or of some right (such as an easement) that he may have in relation to it. What the claimant usually complains of is that there has been an "invasion" of his land as a result of some activity which the defendant has conducted upon his own land. Such activity is often not of itself unlawful, but it becomes a nuisance when the consequences of pursuing it extend to the land of his neighbour.

DEFINITION CHECKPOINT
(a) indirect interference by tangible, physical damage   • To cause an encroachment upon the claimant's land of some tangible thing such as tree roots may be actionable in nuisance (*Davey v Harrow Corp* (CA, 1958)). The distinction between this form of invasion and a trespass is that, in this case, the interference is indirect.   • Causing physical damage to the land, or to the buildings or vegetation upon it, may constitute a nuisance, as where a drain becomes blocked and floods the claimant's land (*Sedleigh-Denfield v O'Callaghan* (HL, 1940)), or a building is allowed to fall into disrepair with the result that parts of it fall on the claimant's land (*Wringe v Cohen* (CA, 1940)

Hunter v Canary Wharf Ltd (HL, 1997) makes it clear that private nuisance is a tort which concerns injury to land, regardless of the nature of the alleged damage. This means that the claimant must show that the land itself has been adversely affected, one consequence of which is that no action should lie in respect of personal injury (see, e.g. Lord Lloyd in Hunter). In *Hunter* itself a unanimous House of Lords held that no action lay for interference with television reception caused by the erection of a large building.

The law, it is said, seeks to achieve a balance between two competing interests, namely that of the defendant to use his land as he wishes and that of his neighbour not to be seriously inconvenienced by this. Not every interference is actionable, therefore, because people must be expected to tolerate some degree of inconvenience in the interests of peaceful co-existence. An interference becomes unlawful only where the defendant has put his land to an unreasonable use. Where, however, the alleged nuisance causes tangible damage the claimant will usually have little difficulty in establishing an unlawful interference with his rights (though see, e.g. *Ellison v Ministry of Defence* (HC, 1997)); this is either because, in the case of such damage, many of the factors involved in the balancing exercise to determine whether the defendant's user of land is reasonable are irrelevant, or because such damage usually tips the balance irreversibly in the claimant's favour. On the other hand, in the case of amenity damage the claimant must prove a substantial interference with the ordinary comfort and convenience of living such as would adversely affect the average person, and it is in this context that the balancing exercise becomes more critical.

Where the action is for interference with a servitude, such as an easement, the claimant need only show a substantial degree of interference. It will then be treated in the same way as a claim for physical damage to property, so that no balancing exercise is necessary and the defendant's conduct is irrelevant, i.e. liability is strict.

Unreasonable interference

"The very essence of a private nuisance ... is the unreasonable use by a man of his land to the detriment of his neighbour" (Lord Denning M.R. in *Miller v Jackson* (CA, 1977)). The defendant's actual or constructive knowledge of that detriment is a factor in determining whether the interference is unreasonable, but a number of other factors, including the character and duration of the interference, must also be considered.

DEFINITION CHECKPOINT

Whether the defendant has unreasonably used his land cannot be gauged solely by reference to the nature of his conduct, because some foreseeable harm may be done which the law does not regard as excessive between neighbours under a principle of "give and take, or live and let live" (*Kennaway v Thompson* (CA, 1980)).

In deciding the issue of reasonable user, the court may have regard to the following matters.

1. Degree of interference

Where physical damage to property has been done, a relatively small interference may amount to a nuisance, but in other cases the interference must be substantial, something more than ordinary everyday inconveniences, such as the claimant will be expected to put up with.

DEFINITION CHECKPOINT

In *Walter v Selfe* (HC, 1851), the test was said to be whether there was:

> "an inconvenience materially interfering with the ordinary comfort physically of human existence, not merely according to elegant or dainty modes and habits of living, but according to plain and sober and simple notions among the English people".

It is therefore a question of degree as to whether the interference is sufficiently serious, and a good illustration is *Halsey v Esso Petroleum Co Ltd* (HC, 1961) where the defendants were held liable for, inter alia, nuisance caused by a nauseating smell emanating from their factory and by the noise at night both from the plant at their depot and from the arrival and departure of petrol tankers.

2. Nature of the locality

A person living in an industrial town cannot expect the same freedom from noise and pollution as one who lives in the country, but this is not a relevant consideration where there is physical injury to property.

THE NATURE OF THE LOCALITY IS IRRELEVANT WHERE THE INTERFERENCE CAUSES PHYSICAL DAMAGE

- In *St Helen's Smelting Co v Tipping* (HL, 1865), the defendants were held liable for the emission of fumes from their factory in a manufacturing area which proved injurious to the plaintiff's shrubs.

Conversely, in *Murdoch v Glacier Metal Co Ltd* (CA, 1998) night time factory noise was held not to constitute an actionable nuisance having regard to all the circumstances including, inter alia, the proximity of the plaintiff to a busy bypass, notwithstanding that the level of noise was marginally greater than the World Health Organisation's recommended level, above which the restorative value of sleep could be affected.

A grant of planning permission is not a licence to commit a nuisance, but where the effect of such is to alter the character of the neighbourhood; the question of whether a nuisance arises must be decided by reference to that character as altered and not as it was previously (*Gillingham BC v Medway (Chatham) Dock Co Ltd* (HC, 1992)). On the other hand, if the effect of the grant cannot be regarded as changing the character of the neighbourhood, there may be an actionable nuisance even though the interference inevitably results from the authorised use (*Wheeler v J.J. Saunders Ltd* (CA, 1995)). *Watson v Croft Promo-Sport Ltd* (2009) applied the principle in *Wheeler* where owners of a home located close to a motor racing circuit were awarded damages for the diminution in value of their property and loss of amenity. The Court of Appeal rejected the argument put forward by the motor circuit operator that there was no actionable nuisance because the nature and character of the locality had been changed by the planning permission.

3. Social utility

The mere fact that the defendant's act is of benefit to the community will not in itself relieve the defendant of liability. Since nuisance is concerned with a balancing of conflicting interests, however, it may be that the claimant will have to bear minor disturbances. Once again it is a question of degree and if there is physical damage or the interference is substantial, the public interest should not be allowed to prevail over private rights (*Kennaway v Thompson* (CA, 1981); cf. *Miller v Jackson* (CA, 1977)). In *Adams v Ursell* (HC, 1913), the smell from a fried-fish shop was held to constitute a nuisance to nearby residents, notwithstanding the defendant's argument that he was providing a valuable service to poor people in the neighbourhood.

4. Abnormal sensitivity

A man cannot increase the liabilities of his neighbour by applying his own property to special uses, whether for business or for pleasure (*Eastern and South African Telegraph Co Ltd v Cape Town Tramways Co Ltd* (PC, 1902)).

KEY CASES

SENSITIVITY OF THE CLAIMANT AND THE NOTION OF "GIVE AND TAKE"

- In *Robinson v Kilvert* (CA, 1889), warm air from the defendant's premises increased the temperature in an upper part of the building and caused damage to stocks of brown paper which the plaintiff stored there. The amount of heat was not such as to cause annoyance or inconvenience to those working for the plaintiff, nor was it harmful to paper generally, so the action failed. The same principle applies to sensitive persons, and no regard is had to the particular needs of individuals such as those with an acute sense of smell or hearing (*Heath v Brighton Corp* (HC, 1908)).

- Once a nuisance is established, however, the claimant can recover even in respect of delicate operations, such as the cultivation of orchids (*McKinnon Industries Ltd v Walker* (PC, 1951)).

---

5. State of affairs

It is often said that the interference must be continuous or recurrent rather than merely temporary or occasional. An injunction will not normally be granted unless there is some degree of permanence in the defendant's activities, except in extreme cases (see, e.g. *De Keyser's Royal Hotel Ltd v Spicer Bros Ltd* (HC, 1914); cf. *Murdoch v Glacier Metal Co Ltd* (CA, 1998)). The duration of the interference, and the times at which it occurs, are important in determining whether the defendant is liable. A man who builds an extension on to the back of his house no doubt causes inconvenience to his neighbour, but he is not liable for nuisance if he takes all reasonable care to see that no undue annoyance is caused (*Harrison v Southwark and Vauxhall Water Co* (HC, 1891)). If, on the other hand, he conducts his operations at unreasonable hours, or takes an inordinately long time, or uses antiquated methods and thereby increases the level of interference, he may be liable (*Andreae v Selfridge & Co Ltd* (CA, 1938)).

An isolated escape is probably not actionable as a nuisance (*S.C.M. (United Kingdom) Ltd v Whittall & Son Ltd* (HC, 1970)), though it may afford evidence of the existence of a dangerous state of affairs upon the defendant's land. In *Spicer v Smee* (HC, 1946), for example, defective electrical wiring which started a fire and caused damage to adjacent property was held to constitute a nuisance. In *Crown River Cruises Ltd v Kimbolton Fireworks Ltd* (HC, 1996), the holding of a firework display in circumstances where it was inevitable that for 15–20 minutes burning debris would fall upon nearby property of a potentially flammable nature was held to constitute a nuisance. Furthermore, there may be liability in negligence or under the rule in *Rylands v Fletcher* (see Ch.12) in respect of a single escape.

6. Intentional annoyance

KEY CASES

MALICE: AN ACTIVITY WHICH IS NOT OF ITSELF UNLAWFUL MAY BECOME A NUISANCE WHEN THE DEFENDANT'S ACTIVITIES ARE MOTIVATED BY MALICE

- If the defendant carries out his activity with the express purpose of annoying his neighbour, he will be liable, even though the degree of interference would not constitute a nuisance if done in the ordinary and reasonable use of property (*Christie v Davey* (HC, 1893)).
- In *Hollywood Silver Fox Farm Ltd v Emmett* (HC, 1936), the defendant deliberately fired his gun near the boundary of the plaintiff's land in order to disturb the breeding of the plaintiff's silver foxes. Many of the vixens aborted, for which damage the defendant was held liable.

An anomalous case is *Bradford Corp v Pickles* (HL, 1895) where, in order to induce the plaintiffs to buy his land, the defendant abstracted percolating water, which flowed in undefined channels beneath his land and which fed the plaintiffs' reservoir. His motive was held to be irrelevant and he was therefore not liable. This is distinguishable from *Emmett* on the ground that the plaintiff had no right to receive the water, so that there was no interest to be protected. The right to make noise on one's land, however, is qualified by the right of one's neighbour to the quiet enjoyment of his land. A landowner's right to abstract subterranean water flowing in undefined channels, regardless of the consequences to his neighbour and of his motive, was affirmed in *Stephens v Anglian Water Authority* (CA, 1987).

Damage

Damage must usually be proved, either in the form of tangible injury to land or to property upon it, or in the form of amenity damage as evidenced by substantial personal discomfort, though nuisance to a servitude may be actionable per se (*Nicholls v Ely Beet Sugar Factory Ltd* (HC, 1936)). In the light of *Hunter v Canary Wharf Ltd* (HL, 1997), it seems that no claim will lie in respect of personal injury or for damage to personal property where the land itself is not adversely affected.

Who can sue?
It is now clear that only a person with a proprietary or possessory interest in the land can sue, as originally established in *Malone v Laskey* (CA, 1907). A majority of the House of Lords so held in *Hunter v Canary Wharf Ltd* (HL, 1997), overruling the Court of Appeal on this point in *Khorasandjian v Bush* (CA, 1993) and in *Hunter* itself. Thus, a freeholder, a tenant in possession and a licensee with exclusive possession may sue, as may a landlord out of possession whose reversionary interest is adversely affected.

DEFINITION CHECKPOINT
Malone v Laskey (CA, 1907) established that a person in exclusive possession of the land but who cannot prove title to it has a right to sue. However, mere licensees, such as a lodger, hotel guest or, in some cases, a non-owning spouse have no sufficient interest and are thereby precluded from maintaining an action.

If the claimant does have the requisite interest he can recover in respect of a continuing nuisance even though the damage occurs before he acquires his interest and he is aware of it (*Masters v Brent London BC* (HC, 1978); *Delaware Mansions Ltd v Westminster City Council* (2001)).

Who is liable?

1. The creator
The creator of the nuisance is liable whether or not he occupies the land whence the interference emanates (*Hall v Beckenham Corp* (HC, 1949)). He remains liable even if he parts with possession and is no longer able to stop the nuisance without committing trespass.

2. The occupier
The occupier will be liable if he creates the nuisance, but, apart from this, he may incur liability either in respect of the acts of others upon his land or where the nuisance existed before he became the occupier. He may, for example, be answerable for those whom he allows on to his land as guests (*Att Gen v Stone* (HC, 1895)), at least if he knew or should have known of the interference.

DEFINITION CHECKPOINT

Although the general rule is that an employer is not liable for the defaults of his contractor, he will be liable if he is under a non-delegable duty where:

- there is a withdrawal of support from neighbouring land (*Bower v Peate* (HC, 1876),
- operations are conducted on or adjoining the highway (*Tarry v Ashton* (HC, 1876); see Ch.14).

It seems that he will also be liable whenever the work that the contractor is employed to do creates a foreseeable risk of nuisance. In *Matania v National Provincial Bank Ltd* (CA, 1936), the occupier of premises who employed contractors to carry out alterations was held liable for nuisance by dust and noise caused to other occupants in the building. In *Spicer v Smee* (HC, 1946), it was said that "where danger is likely to arise unless the work is properly done, there is a duty to see that it is properly done", but this proposition is probably too wide (*Salsbury v Woodland* (CA, 1970)).

Nuisance created by a trespasser

If a nuisance is created by a trespasser, the occupier is liable not only if he adopts the nuisance for his own purposes (*Page Motors Ltd v Epsom and Ewell BC* (HC, 1982)) but also if, with actual or constructive knowledge of its existence, he fails to take reasonable steps to abate it (in which case he is said to "continue" the nuisance). This principle was laid down in *Sedleigh-Denfield v O'Callaghan* (HL, 1940) and has since been extended to dangerous states of affairs which arise naturally upon the land.

KEY CASE

LIABILITY FOR A DANGEROUS STATE OF AFFAIRS ARISING NATURALLY ON THE LAND

In *Goldman v Hargrave* (PC, 1967), a tree on the defendant's land was struck by lightning and caught fire. The defendant had the tree felled and decided to let the fire burn itself out, but it eventually spread to and damaged the plaintiff's land. The defendant was held liable because, with actual knowledge of the danger, he failed to take rea-sonable steps to abate it (followed in *Leakey v National Trust* (CA, 1980)).

NUISANCE

159

Nuisance created by a natural occurrence

In *Holbeck Hall Hotel v Scarborough BC* (CA, 2000), natural coastal erosion caused a catastrophic land slip and as a result the claimant's hotel was damaged by lack of support and had to be demolished. The Court of Appeal held that a "measured" duty of care to a neighbouring landowner arose out of a danger due to lack of support caused by a land slip in just the same way as it arose out of an escape or encroachment of a noxious thing. The scope of the defendant's duty, however, was to avoid damage to the claimant's land which they ought to have foreseen. They were not liable for a catastrophic collapse which they could only have discovered by further geological investigation. However, it was held in *Home Brewery Co Ltd v William Davis & Co (Leicester) Ltd* (HC, 1987) that a lower occupier cannot sue a higher occupier for permitting the natural flow of water to pass to the lower ground, but that the lower occupier can erect barriers to prevent the flow provided that, in so doing, he does not put his land to an unreasonable use. In this type of case liability is based essentially upon proof of negligence with one important difference, namely that, since the danger is not of the occupier's own making, his individual circumstances should be taken into account, including his financial resources. The test of reasonableness therefore imports a subjective element. As far as the encroachment of tree roots is concerned, liability was imposed without qualification in *Davey v Harrow Corp* (CA, 1958). This was approved in Leakey's case subject to the proviso that actual or constructive knowledge of the defect was required in accordance with the *Goldman* formula, and it is now clear from *Solloway v Hampshire CC* (CA, 1981) that the defendant is only liable if there was a foreseeable risk of damage by encroachment which he could reasonably be expected to take steps to guard against.

Where a nuisance has been created by the occupier's predecessor the claimant must prove that he knew, or ought to have known, of its existence (*St Anne's Well Brewery Co v Roberts* (CA, 1928)).

3. The landlord

Where the premises are let the usual person to sue is the tenant. The landlord will, however, be liable in the following circumstances.

First, if he expressly or impliedly authorises the nuisance, as where the interference arises as a result of using the land for the very purpose for which it was let (*Harris v James* (HC, 1876); *Tetley v Chitty* (HC, 1986)). In *Smith v Scott* (HC, 1973), a local authority was held not to have authorised the commission of a nuisance by a "problem" family which it had housed next to the plaintiff.

LIABILITY OF LANDLORDS

- In *Hussain v Lancaster City Council* (CA, 1999), the council was not liable in respect of a long term campaign of racial harassment on a shopkeeper by the local authority's tenants because the acts complained of did not involve the use of the tenants' land.
- *Hussain* was distinguished in *Lippiatt v South Gloucestershire Council* (1999), where the council allowed trespassers to park their caravans on a piece of its land bordering the claimant's farm. The council could have evicted the travellers from its land but had failed to so and was therefore held liable for the travellers' repeated acts of interference.

Secondly, the landlord is liable if he either knew or ought to have known of the nuisance before letting the premises.

Thirdly, if the premises fall into disrepair during the period of the lease, he is liable if he has reserved the right to enter and repair (*Heap v Ind Coope & Allsopp Ltd* (CA, 1940)), and such a right will readily be implied in a short-term tenancy (*Mint v Good* (CA, 1951); but the significance of this decision is greatly reduced by the **Landlord and Tenant Act 1985** which provides that, where a dwelling-house is let for less than seven years, there is an implied covenant by the landlord to keep in repair the structure and exterior of the premises, and certain installations for the supply of essential services). The landlord is clearly liable where he is under an express covenant to repair, but it was held in *Brew Bros Ltd v Snax (Ross) Ltd* (CA, 1970) that he does not escape responsibility by extracting that obligation from his tenants, provided that he knows or ought to know of the nuisance.

DEFINITION CHECKPOINT
Liability for premises adjoining a highway In one particular case, that is where premises adjoining a highway collapse and cause injury to a passer-by or to an adjoining owner, liability is, according to *Wringe v Cohen* (CA, 1940), strict, subject to a defence either that the defect was due to a secret and unobservable process of nature or to the act of a trespasser (but in the latter case see *Sedleigh-Denfield v O'Callaghan* (above)).

Apart from these common law obligations the landlord may also be liable under the **Defective Premises Act 1972**, s.4. This provides that if the landlord is under an obligation to his tenant to repair, or has an express or implied power to enter and repair, he owes a duty to take reasonable care to see that all who might reasonably be expected to be affected by defects in the state of the premises are reasonably safe from personal injury or damage to their property. A right to repair will be implied where the landlord could, if necessary, obtain an injunction to enter and effect repairs (*McAuley v Bristol City Council* (CA, 1992)).

The Human Rights Act 1998

A common law nuisance may further constitute an interference with a claimant's rights under Art.8 of the European Convention on Human Rights (respect for private and family life) and/or Protocol 1, Art.1 (protection of property). Since the Human Rights Act 1998 came into force such rights may be relied on in domestic courts but Human Rights principles require a fair balance between competing interests.

KEY CASE

HUMAN RIGHTS

In *Marcic v Thames Water Authorities* (HL 2003), sewers provided by Thames Water had caused flooding which discharged both surface water and foul water on to the claimant's garden. Many thousands of other householders were at a similar risk of flooding as a consequence of the discharge from overburdened sewers in the Thames area. Thames Water claimed that the cost of work required to alleviate the flooding would result in a total expenditure in excess of £1000 million and they sought to rely on lack of resources to justify their decision to take no steps to abate the nuisance. At first instance the judge held that he was bound by authority to dismiss the claims founded in *Rylands v Fletcher*, nuisance and negligence. He further concluded that the failure by Thames Water to carry out suitable work to repair the sewer gave no action for a breach of statutory duty (see Ch.9). Nevertheless, he held that the failure of Thames Water to repair the sewer constituted an interference with the claimant's rights under Art.8 and Protocol 1, Art.1, of the European Convention on Human Rights. Although the Court of Appeal held that this was not, in fact, a human rights case at all, it did state that the claimant was entitled to succeed under the common law of nuisance and agreed with the judge's conclusion that the defendant had acted incompatibly with the claimant's Convention rights. When *Marcic* reached the House of Lords, their Lordships allowed an appeal and held that Mr Marcic did not have a common law action in nuisance and further held his claim under the Human Rights Act 1998 to be ill-founded as there had been no infringement of his rights under the European Convention on Human Rights.

The decision of the Grand Chamber of the European Court of Human Rights in *Hatton v United Kingdom* (2003) makes clear that the Convention does not accord absolute protection to property or even to residential premises. It requires a fair balance to be struck between the competing interests of the parties involved and Parliament had achieved this balance in *Marcic* through a statutory regulatory scheme and an independent regulator under the Water Industry Act 1991. Before the House of Lords ruling, the Court of Appeal decision in *Marcic* was applied in *Dennis v Ministry of Defence* where the flying of RAF Harrier jets caused severe and frightening noise disturbance which resulted in a reduction in the capital value of the claimants' property. The Court found nuisance at common law but also held that claimants' rights under Art.8 and Art.1 of Protocol 1 had been breached and awarded substantial damages.

Defences

1. Prescription

A right to commit a private nuisance may be acquired by 20 years' continuance thereof, though it may be that this is only so where the right is capable of existing as an easement. It has been doubted whether the defendant can acquire a prescriptive right to cause unlawful interference by such things as noise, smoke, smell or vibration in which the degree of inconvenience is variable and may at times cease altogether. The claimant must have full knowledge of the nuisance before the period begins to run, and there must have been an actionable nuisance during the 20 years.

KEY CASE

PRESCRIPTION: 20 YEARS' CONTINUANCE
In *Sturges v Bridgman* (CA, 1879), the plaintiff built a consulting room at the end of his garden and complained of noise from the defendant's premises. The defendant's argument that he had been pursuing his trade for more than 20 years failed, because the interference did not become actionable as a nuisance until the plaintiff extended his premises.

2. Statutory authority

Many nuisance actions arise out of the activities of bodies authorised by statute to conduct those operations. It is generally a defence to prove that the interference is an inevitable result of what they were obliged or empowered to do, so that there will be no liability without negligence (*Manchester Corp v Farnworth* (HL, 1930)). The following principles were laid down in *Department of Transport v North West Water Authority* (HL, 1984). First, in fulfilling a statutory duty there is no liability without negligence, whether or not liability for nuisance is expressly preserved in the Act. Secondly, in exercising a statutory power, liability depends upon whether nuisance is expressly preserved; if it is, negligence need not be proved, but if it is not, there is no liability in the absence of negligence (see also Ch.12).

Precisely what a body is authorised or obliged to do depends upon the provisions of the Act.

KEY CASE

ACTIVITIES AUTHORISED BY STATUTE

A liberal interpretation was given in *Allen v Gulf Oil Refining Ltd* (HL, 1981), where authority to acquire land and build a refinery was held to confer, by necessary implication, the right to operate the refinery. Since there was no express provision for liability in nuisance, the defendants were held not liable for the inevitable consequences of working the refinery.

3. Coming to nuisance

It is no defence that the claimant moved into the area of the nuisance (*Sturges v Bridgman* (CA, 1879); *Miller v Jackson* (CA, 1977)).

4. Other defences

Consent and contributory negligence are valid defences, although not likely in nuisance actions. Necessity, act of God, and act of a stranger are defences provided that there is no negligence. It is no defence, however, that the nuisance was the product of the combined acts of two or more persons, though the act of any one individual would not be unlawful (*Lambton v Mellish* (HC, 1894)).

Remedies

The claimant may recover damages for any resulting loss which is of a reasonably foreseeable kind (*The Wagon Mound (No.2)* (PC, 1967)).

The remedy of an injunction is an equitable one and will therefore only be granted where damages would be inadequate. If the interference is trivial or temporary it is unlikely to be granted, but it should not be refused simply on the ground that the defendant's activity is in the public interest. For the factors to be considered in determining whether damages should be awarded in lieu of an injunction see *Shelfer v City of London Electric Lighting Co* (CA, 1895). The principles laid down in that case were applied in *Jaggard v Sawyer* (CA, 1995) where the fact that the defendants had acted openly and in good faith, and that the plaintiff had delayed in seeking interlocutory relief, were considered to be relevant (though not conclusive) factors in deciding that the grant of an injunction would be oppressive.

> ### DEFINITION CHECKPOINT
> *Injunction an equitable remedy*
> - The majority decision in *Miller v Jackson* (CA, 1977) not to grant an injunction in respect of the frequent escape of cricket balls from the defendant's land because the cricket club was a valuable local amenity, was held to be wrong in *Kennaway v Thompson* (CA, 1981).
> - An injunction is a flexible remedy and terms may be imposed, for example as to the types of activity permitted and the times at which it may be conducted. This was done in *Kennaway* (above) but the court refused to do so in *Tetley v Chitty* (HC, 1986), distinguishing *Kennaway* on the ground that, in that case, the defendants had been pursuing their activities before the plaintiff moved into the area.

The standard of liability

A question of some considerable difficulty is the extent to which fault (i.e. negligence) is relevant to an action in nuisance. According to the House of Lords in *Cambridge Water Co v Eastern Counties Leather Plc* (HL, 1994), subject to the concept of reasonable user liability is generally regarded as strict; that is to say that if the defendant's user is unreasonable it matters not that he took all reasonable care to avoid the interference. This at least is the position where the defendant actively created the dangerous state of affairs which caused the damage; in other cases, as has been noted, the claimant will generally have to prove fault.

> ### DEFINITION CHECKPOINT
> A distinction must be drawn between a claim for damages and an application for an injunction to restrain future harm. In the latter case the defendant will inevitably become aware of the interference at the latest when the claimant institutes proceedings, so the question of fault is then largely irrelevant; the defendant's conduct is deliberate as soon as he has knowledge of the interference, and the court is simply concerned with whether the degree of interference exceeds that which the claimant can reasonably be expected to tolerate.

Where the defendant could not reasonably have foreseen the possibility of interference of the type which in fact occurs he is not liable. If he later acquires actual or constructive knowledge of a potential danger he may be liable in negligence if he fails to take steps to abate it, but it seems he cannot be liable once that danger has passed out of his control. What is not clear from *Cambridge Water* is the position where the defendant knows that his activity creates a possible risk and takes all reasonable care to avoid it. To suggest that the defendant would not be liable in the absence of fault seems to run counter to dicta in Lord Goff's judgment that the defendant would be strictly liable if the risk materialised. On the other hand it is not easy to see how the defendant can be said to have put his land to an unreasonable use for so long as the activity is conducted with reasonable care without causing any interference to his neighbours. It would appear that the question of the extent to which liability is truly strict therefore requires further elucidation.

PUBLIC NUISANCE

A public nuisance may be defined as an unlawful act or omission which materially affects the comfort and convenience of a class of Her Majesty's subjects who come within the sphere of its operation; whether the number of persons affected is sufficiently large to warrant the epithet "public" is a question of fact (*Att Gen v PYA Quarries Ltd* (CA, 1957)). At common law, public nuisances cover a wide variety of activities such as carrying on an offensive trade, selling food unfit for human consumption and obstructing the highway.

Public and private nuisance

Public nuisance is a crime in respect of which the Attorney-General may, if a criminal prosecution is felt to be inadequate, bring a "relator" action for an injunction to restrain the offending activity.

DEFINITION CHECKPOINT
The same conduct may amount to both a private and a public nuisance. However, an individual may only sue in tort in respect of the latter if he has suffered "particular" damage, which means loss or damage over and above that suffered by the rest of the class affected. This encompasses personal injury, and there is clearly no requirement that the claimant must have an interest in the land.

In *Halsey v Esso Petroleum Co Ltd* (HC, 1961), the plaintiff's washing was damaged by the emission of acid smuts from the defendants' factory, as was the paintwork of his car which was parked in the road outside his house. The damage to the washing was actionable as a private nuisance, whilst that to the car amounted to particular damage for the purposes of an action in public nuisance. The term "particular damage" may also include loss of an economic nature consequential upon the interference. In *Tate & Lyle Industries Ltd v GLC* (HL, 1983), the plaintiffs were held entitled to recover the cost of dredging to facilitate access to their jetty, which had been obstructed by the defendants' building works (see also *Lyons, Sons & Co v Gulliver*, below).

Nuisance on the highway

Perhaps the most common instance of public nuisance is an unlawful obstruction or interference with the public's right of passage along the highway. In *Castle v St Augustine's Links* (HC, 1922), for example, the defendant golf club was held liable for so siting one of its fairways that golf balls were frequently sliced on to the highway, with the result that the plaintiff was injured while driving along the road when a ball crashed through the windscreen of his car. In *Wandsworth London BC v Railtrack Plc* (CA, 2001), droppings from feral pigeons roosting under a railway bridge created a hazard over the footpath and to pedestrians and therefore constituted a public nuisance.

DEFINITION CHECKPOINT

In relation to obstructions, the defendant is liable only if he creates an unreasonable risk, but he is generally liable for the defaults of his contractor because of the non-delegable nature of the duty (see Ch.14). If the obstruction is reasonable in terms of duration and degree, such as a van delivering goods to a shop, it is generally not actionable.

To conduct one's trade in such a manner as to cause a foreseeable obstruction is actionable, and if such obstruction causes loss of custom to other traders, that is special damage (*Lyons, Sons & Co v Gulliver* (CA, 1914)). But the defendant is not liable for an obstruction, such as a queue outside his shop, which is beyond his control. The claimant must in all cases prove damage.

Where damage is done by a projection over the highway, there may be a distinction between artificial and natural things. In the case of the former, liability may be strict (*Tarry v Ashton* (HC, 1876)), whereas in the case of natural projections (for example, trees) it seems that negligence must be proved and, even though the source of the nuisance is plain to see, the occupier will not be liable until he has actual or constructive knowledge that it is a danger (*British Road Services Ltd v Slater* (HC, 1964)). With regard to premises adjoining the highway, the nature of the liability imposed by *Wringe v Cohen* (CA, 1940) has already been mentioned.

A highway authority is under a duty to maintain the highway and may be liable in negligence, nuisance or for breach of statutory duty under the

NUISANCE

Highways Act 1980. This right of action for non-repair does not, however, extend to claims for pure economic loss (*Wentworth v Wiltshire CC* (CA, 1993)). The Act provides that it shall be a defence to prove that the authority had taken such care as in all the circumstances was reasonably required to make sure that the part of the highway to which the action relates was not dangerous for traffic. Nor does the authority owe a duty of care to exercise its statutory powers for the benefit of road users (*Stovin v Wise* (HL, 1996)).

Revision Checklist

By the end of this chapter you should know:

- Nuisance covers *indirect* interferences with use or enjoyment of land and it differs from the tort of trespass which protects against *direct* interferences;

- Although public nuisance is a crime as well as a tort, private nuisance is only a tort;

- A claimant in private nuisance must have an interest in land to sue; public nuisance is not linked to the claimant's interest in land and it protects against personal injury which is not recoverable in private nuisance;

- In certain respects nuisance and negligence are similar because they both use the concept of reasonableness.

QUESTION AND ANSWER

Question

Kofi's next door neighbour, Soo, manufactures "natural herbal remedies" in a room she had specially built on to her house. Soo uses plants she grows in her garden for the products she manufactures and she fertilises the plants with manure from the local stables. Kofi has told Soo that the manure stored in her garden attracts flies and the smell coming into his property from her manufacturing has become unbearable, even with the windows closed. Soo was quite unsympathetic towards Kofi's complaint and replied that she had been granted planning permission for the extension where the manufacturing is taking place and she suggested that if Kofi does not like the smell then he should move elsewhere. Angered by Soo's attitude, Kofi decided to hold a pop concert on his land in order to "teach her a lesson". He sold five hundred tickets and the loud music and fireworks display from Kofi's land kept all the villagers awake through the night.

Advise Kofi of his rights and liabilities in respect of the above situations.

Approach to the answer

Kofi would complain that the emission of smells and the flies coming from Soo's garden constitute an unreasonable interference with his use and enjoyment of land which gives rise to a claim in private nuisance. The distinction between this form of interference and a trespass is that, in nuisance, the interference is indirect. *Thompson-Schwab v Costaki* (1956) and (*Laws v Florinplace* (1981).

The law would seek to achieve a balance between the right of Soo to use her land as she wishes and the right of Kofi not to be seriously inconvenienced by this. Therefore, not every interference amounts to an actionable tort because people must be expected to tolerate some degree of inconvenience in the interests of peaceful co-existence. *Miller v Jackson* (1977) (*Kennaway v Thompson* (CA, 1980)).

The interference from Soo's land is causing "amenity" (i.e. intangible) damage which would become unlawful only if the court found that she put her land to an unreasonable use. If, however, the alleged nuisance caused tangible damage then Kofi would have little difficulty in establishing an unlawful interference with his rights. *Halsey v Esso Petroleum Co Ltd* (1961).

In carrying out the balancing exercise, the court takes account of the nature of the locality. A person living in an industrial town cannot expect the same freedom from noise and pollution as one who lives in the country, but this is not a relevant consideration where there is physical injury to property. However, an important factor in Kofi's favour is that the grant of planning permission is not a licence to commit a nuisance. In *Wheeler v J.J. Saunders Ltd* (1995), approved by *Watson v Croft Promo-Sport Ltd* (2009), an actionable nuisance was established even though the interference inevitably resulted from the authorised use.

Kofi may find himself liable in nuisance by holding a pop concert on his land with the express purpose of annoying Soo, even if the degree of interference would not constitute a nuisance if done in the ordinary and reasonable use of property (*Christie v Davey* (1893); *Hollywood Silver Fox Farm Ltd v Emmett* (1936)).

The same conduct may amount to both a private and a public nuisance because the loud music and fireworks at the pop concert materially affected the comfort and convenience of the villagers (as a class of Her Majesty's subjects) and Kofi may be liable in public nuisance for this interference (*Att Gen v PYA Quarries Ltd* (CA, 1957). However, an individual villager would only be able to sue in public nuisance if he had suffered "particular" damage, which means loss or damage over and above that suffered by the rest of the villagers (the class affected). *Tate & Lyle Industries Ltd v GLC* (1983).

Strict Liability

12

INTRODUCTION

Although the law of tort is predominantly fault-based there are instances in which liability may be imposed without negligence on the defendant's part. Thus, there may be strict liability for damage caused by defective products (see Ch.6) and animals (see Ch.13), and an employer's vicarious liability for the torts of its employees is similarly not dependent on fault on the part of the employer (see Ch.14). It has also been seen that liability in nuisance may be strict where the defendant created the source of the interference, in the sense that, if the defendant's user is unreasonable, it is irrelevant that he took all reasonable care to avoid it. Strict civil liability is also imposed by certain statutes; see, e.g. Nuclear Installations Act 1965.

Apart from the above instances a form of strict liability may arise under the rule in *Rylands v Fletcher* (HL, 1868) and in respect of the escape of fire. The incidence of such liability is the subject of this chapter.

THE RULE IN RYLANDS V FLETCHER

Although the rule had its origins in nuisance it had, until recently, come to be regarded as having evolved into a distinct principle governing liability for the escape of dangerous things. However, in *Cambridge Water Co Ltd v Eastern Counties Leather Plc* (HL, 1994), it was said that it would lead to a more coherent body of common law principles if the rule were to be regarded as an extension of the law of nuisance to cases of isolated escapes from land (even though the rule is not limited to escapes which are in fact isolated). The Rylands principle has recently been restated with certainty in *Transco v Stockport Metropolitan BC* (2003), where the House of Lords held that the strict liability rule, which had stood for nearly 150 years, should not be discarded.

DEFINITION CHECKPOINT

The rule in *Rylands v Fletcher* was stated by Blackburn J. as follows

> "We think that the true rule of law is, that the person who for his own purposes brings on his lands and collects and keeps there anything likely to do mischief if it escapes must keep it in at his peril, and, if he does not do so, is prima facie answerable for all the damage which is the natural consequence of its escape."

The House of Lords added the qualification that the defendant must have put his land to a non-natural use.

Things brought on to the land

There is no liability for an escape of things naturally upon the land such as self-sown vegetation (*Giles v Walker* (CA, 1890)), or an outcrop of rock which falls by the process of weathering (*Pontardawe RDC v Moore-Gwyn* (HC, 1929)). The defendant may however be liable in nuisance or negligence in accordance with *Goldman v Hargrave* (see Ch.11), and will also be liable if he is instrumental in causing the escape of something naturally upon his land, as where the blasting of explosives caused an escape of rock (*Miles v Forest Rock Granite Co Ltd* (CA, 1918)). It must now be taken as clear that forseeability is an element necessary to establish liability under *Rylands v Fletcher* as under nuisance.

Likely to do mischief

The rule has over the years been applied to a wide variety of things including water, gas, electricity, fire, explosions, vibrations, noxious fumes, flag-poles and fairground swings.

KEY CASE

In *Cambridge Water* the House of Lords rejected any rationalisation of the rule in *Rylands v Fletcher* into a broad principle of liability for damage caused by extra hazardous activities, inclining to the view that this was a matter best left to Parliament. It was also held that, by analogy with nuisance, the rule did not apply unless damage of the relevant type was foreseeable as the result of an escape, though it was made clear that liability was strict notwithstanding that the defendant had exercised all reasonable care and skill to prevent the escape.

Escape

There must be an "escape from a place where the defendant has occupation or control over land to a place which is outside his occupation or control" (*Read v J. Lyons & Co Ltd* (HL, 1947). In Transco (2003) (above), the House of Lords held that there had been no "escape" when the water which leaked from the council's service pipe remained on its land. Provided there has been a non-natural user, the thing which escapes need not be the subject-matter of the accumulation (*Miles v Forest Rock Granite Co Ltd* (CA, 1918)).

DEFINITION CHECKPOINT

The defendant need not have any interest in the land from which the thing escapes; in *Rigby v Chief Constable of Northamptonshire* (HC 1985), it was considered that the rule applied where a dangerous thing was brought on to the highway whence it escaped and caused damage.

Whether the claimant needed to be an occupier was unclear but an affirmative answer was given in *Weller v Foot and Mouth Disease Research Institute* (HC, 1966), and dicta in *Read v Lyons* support that view. There are also a number of authorities to the contrary (see, e.g. *Shiffman v Order of St John* (HC, 1936); *Perry v Kendrick's Transport Ltd* (CA, 1956)). However, in *Transco* (2003) (above), the House of Lords has reaffirmed the approach taken in Cambridge Water, that only those with rights over land may sue under *Rylands v Fletcher.*

It is doubtful if the rule applies to the intentional projection of things on to the plaintiff's land. In this case trespass is the more appropriate cause of action (*Rigby v Chief Constable of Northamptonshire*), although the view was expressed obiter in *Crown River Cruises Ltd v Kimbolton Fireworks Ltd* (HC, 1996) that liability could extend to an intentional release which was not deliberately directed towards the claimant.

Non-natural user

It has already been noted that the defendant is not liable under the rule for an escape of something naturally upon the land. In Cambridge Water it was said that the concept of non-natural user limits liability under the rule just as the concept of reasonable user does in a nuisance action, though the relationship, if any, between the two was not discussed.

KEY CASE

It is clear from *Cambridge Water* that there is no liability for deliberate accumulations unless there has been a non-natural user by the defendant, which was defined in *Rickards v Lothian* (PC, 1913), in the following terms:

"It must be some special use bringing with it increased danger to others, and must not merely be the ordinary use of land or such a use as is proper for the general benefit of the community."

A distinction must therefore be drawn between an "ordinary" and an "extraordinary" use of land, though the concept of non-natural user has enabled the courts to adopt a flexible approach and to adapt the application of the rule to changing circumstances of time and place (see *Read v Lyons*, where there are dicta to the effect that a munitions factory in time of war was a normal use of land). In the past, domestic water supplies, household fires, electric wiring in houses and shops, the ordinary working of mines and minerals and the keeping of trees and shrubs (unless, perhaps, poisonous: *Crowhurst v Amersham Burial Board* (Ex., 1878)) have been held to be natural uses. In *Transco* (2003) (above), the piping of a water supply to flats in a tower block constituted an ordinary use of the council's land.

DEFINITION CHECKPOINT

It should be noted that the bulk storage of water, gas or electricity and the collection of sewage by a local authority have at various times been held non-natural.

- The approach adopted in *Mason v Levy Auto Parts of England Ltd* (HC, 1967) was to equate the concept of non-natural user with that of abnormal risk, so that the court took account of the quantity of the accumulation of combustible material, the manner in which it was stored, and the character of the neighbourhood, and conceded that those considerations might equally have justified a finding of negligence.
- This approach was adopted more recently in *LMS International Ltd v Styrene Packaging and Insulation Ltd* (2005), where the defendant's means of storing large quantities of flammable polystyrene "involved a very real risk" that a fire would spread to adjoining premises.

Although, according to the original formulation of the rule, the defendant must have collected the thing "for his own purpose," this did not at one time necessarily mean that she should derive any personal benefit (*Smeaton v*

Ilford Corp (HC, 1954)). Where, however, the accumulation is for the public benefit pursuant, for example, to the provision of a public service (*Dunne v North Western Gas Board* (CA, 1964)) or indeed to ordinary manufacturing processes (*British Celanese Ltd v A. H. Hunt (Capacitors) Ltd* (HC, 1969)) the more modern tendency has been to deny the application of the rule.

The status of the above authorities will now have to be reconsidered in the light of Cambridge Water and in that case it was said that the storage of large quantities of chemicals on industrial premises was "an almost classic case of non-natural use" even in an industrial area. Furthermore, the fact that the chemical in question was commonly used in the particular industry, and that the defendants' operations served to support a local industrial community, was not sufficient to render the use natural. Unfortunately there was no real discussion of the relationship between public benefit and non-natural user, so the matter awaits further clarification.

Personal injury

It was unclear whether the claimant could succeed in a claim for personal injuries, and there was no discussion of this point in Cambridge Water. The view of Lord Macmillan in *Read v Lyons* was that the claimant would have to prove negligence, at least if he is a non-occupier, but there is authority to the contrary (*Shiffman v Order of St John*; *Perry v Kendrick's Transport Ltd* (see earlier in this Chapter)).

DEFINITION CHECKPOINT
Although claims for personal injury had been admitted in the past, in *Transco* (above), Lord Hoffman expressed the view that, damages for personal injuries are not recoverable under *Rylands v Fletcher*.

Remoteness of damage

KEY CASE

Following *Cambridge Water* the test for remoteness would appear to be reasonable foreseeability, as it is in nuisance, although the case does not speak in terms of remoteness as such.

In referring to the phrase "likely to do mischief if it escapes" taken from the original formulation of the rule, it was said that the general tenor of the statement was that:

"knowledge, or at least foreseeability of the risk, is a prerequisite of the recovery of damages ...".

It is not entirely clear from this whether both the escape and the consequences thereof must be foreseeable or merely whether, given that an
escape has occurred, the consequences alone must be foreseeable, though
the actual decision seems to support the former analysis.

Defences
There are a number of defences, the first three of which mentioned below,
together with the concept of non-natural user, have gone a long way towards
introducing elements of fault into this area of the law.

1. Act of God
An act of God is an operation of natural forces "which no human foresight
can provide against, and of which human prudence is not bound to recognise
the possibility". But this is not to say that the defendant will escape liability
merely because the event is not reasonably foreseeable.

DEFINITION CHECKPOINT

Two cases may be contrasted
- In *Nichols v Marsland* (CA, 1876), the defendant was held not liable
  when an exceptionally violent rainfall caused his artificial orna-
  mental lakes to flood his neighbour's land.
- This decision was criticised in *Greenock Corp v Caledonian Ry* (HL,
  1917) where, on similar facts, the defendant was held liable on the
  ground that it is insufficient for him to show that the occurrence
  was one which could not reasonably be anticipated. He must go
  further and prove that no human foresight could have recognised
  the possibility of such an event. For practical purposes the defence
  is therefore of very limited application.

---

2. Act of a stranger
The defendant is not liable if the escape is due to the unforeseeable act of a
third party over whom she has no control. In *Rickards v Lothian* (PC, 1913), the
occupier of a lavatory was not liable when an unknown person deliberately
blocked up the overflow pipe and caused flooding on the plaintiff's premises.
The defence is not available, however, if the act is one which the defendant
ought reasonably to have foreseen and guarded against. In *Northwestern
Utilities Ltd v London Guarantee and Accident Co* (PC, 1936), the defendants'
gas main was fractured by a local authority in the course of constructing a
sewer. The defendants were held liable in negligence for damage caused by
an explosion of the gas because they knew of the work being carried out and,
in view of the risks involved, should have checked to make sure that no

damage had been done to their mains. In cases such as this a claim based on *Rylands v Fletcher* merges into a claim for negligence, though according to Goddard L.J. in *Hanson v Wearmouth Coal Co* (CA, 1939), the onus is upon the defendant to prove both that the escape was caused by the independent act of a third party and that she could not reasonably have anticipated and guarded against it.

For the purposes of this defence a trespasser is a stranger but employees within the course of their employment and independent contractors are not. The defendant is probably responsible for the acts of her family and guests, although the issue is not entirely free from doubt and may depend upon the degree of control which she can be expected to exercise over them. In *Hale v Jennings Bros* (CA, 1938), the defendant was held liable for the deliberate act of a lawful visitor in tampering with a potentially dangerous machine.

3. Consent of the plaintiff

Express or implied consent to the presence of the dangerous thing is a defence unless the defendant was negligent (*Att Gen v Cory Bros & Co Ltd* (HL, 1921)). Consent may be implied where a thing is brought on to the land for the common benefit of the claimant and defendant as, for example, where one cistern supplies water to several flats. A further aspect of implied consent is that a person who enters into occupation of property as a tenant takes it as he finds it in so far as she knows of the presence of the dangerous thing (*Peters v Prince of Wales Theatre (Birmingham) Ltd* (CA, 1943)). In *North-western Utilities Ltd v London Guarantee & Accident Co Ltd* (PC, 1936), the issue of common benefit was held not to be relevant as between the consumer of a product such as gas or electricity, and the supplier and, notwithstanding dicta in *Dunne v North Western Gas Board* (CA, 1964) to the contrary, such a view would seem to accord with Cambridge Water.

4. Default of the claimant

If the claimant's own act or default causes the damage, no action will lie. In *Dunn v Birmingham Canal Navigation Co* (EC, 1872), the claimants persisted in working their mine beneath the defendant's canal and failed in their action when water flooded the mine. Where the claimant is partly at fault the defence of contributory negligence will apply.

DEFINITION CHECKPOINT
If damage is caused only by reason of the extra-sensitive nature of the claimant 's property he may not, by analogy with nuisance (see Ch.11), be able to recover (*Eastern and South African Telegraph Co Ltd v Cape Town Tramways Co Ltd* (PC, 1902)).

However, in *Hoare & Co v McAlpine* (HC, 1923) it was thought not to be a good defence that a building damaged by vibrations was exceptionally unstable.

5. Statutory authority

This may afford a defence as in nuisance and the same principles of law apply (see Ch.11).

THE ESCAPE OF FIRE

Common law

At common law a person was liable if a fire spread from his premises and did damage to adjoining premises, though there is some doubt as to whether or not liability was strict. He is now liable where the fire is caused by negligence or nuisance, or where it starts or spreads as a result of a non-natural user of land, in which case negligence need not be proved. The latter instance is simply an application of the rule in *Rylands v Fletcher* except that it is not the thing accumulated that escapes, and the test, according to *Mason v Levy Auto Parts of England Ltd* (HC, 1967), is whether the defendant brought to her land things likely to catch fire and kept them there in such conditions that if they did ignite the fire would be likely to spread. Although liability under *Rylands v Fletcher* is supposedly strict there seems to be little difference between this formulation and ordinary negligence.

There is a defence in respect of a fire started by an act of God or a stranger, though the defendant may be under a duty to abate a known danger upon his land in accordance with the principle in *Goldman v Hargrave* (PC, 1967).

DEFINITION CHECKPOINT
The term "stranger" applies only to those over whom the defendant has no control, so that there is liability for: • fires started by the default of a servant (*Musgrove v Pandelis* (CA, 1919); • an independent contractor (*Balfour v Barty-King* (CA, 1957)); and • a guest (*Crogate v Morris* (1617)).

Statute

The Fires Prevention (Metropolis) Act 1774 provides that no action shall lie against a person upon whose land a fire accidentally begins. This provision only applies to fires produced by mere chance or incapable of being traced to any cause. It therefore affords no protection where the fire is caused by negligence or is due to a nuisance or arises from a non-natural user of land.

Nor will the defendant escape liability if there is negligence in permitting an accidental fire to spread.

WHERE A FIRE ACCIDENTALLY BEGINS
In *Musgrove v Pandelis* (CA, 1919), the defendant was held liable when a fire started in the carburettor of his car in a garage without fault on anyone's part and his chauffeur negligently failed to extinguish it. It was also held that the 1774 Act was no defence to an action brought under *Rylands v Fletcher*.

However, if a domestic fire, intentionally lit, spreads without negligence the defendant is not liable (*Sochaki v Sas* (HC, 1947)). The Act also provided a defence in *Collingwood v Home and Colonial Stores Ltd* (CA, 1936), where a fire broke out on the defendants' premises due to faulty electrical wiring but without negligence. In neither of these last two cases could *Rylands v Fletcher* be invoked because there was no non-natural user of land.

Revision Checklist

You should now understand:

- the law of tort is predominantly fault based but there are instances in which liability may be imposed without negligence on the defendant's part;

- application of the principle in *Rylands v Fletcher* governing liability for the escape of dangerous things;

- the defences under *Rylands v Fletcher* which, together with the concept of non-natural user, have introduced elements of fault into this area of the law;

- in nuisance, liability may be strict where the defendant created the source of the interference even if he took all reasonable care to avoid it.

QUESTION AND ANSWER

Question

The concept of non-natural user under *Rylands v Fletcher* is said to limit liability under the rule just as the concept of reasonable user does in a nuisance action. Using case law to illustrate your answer, consider the approach of the courts to "non-natural" use of land.

Approach to the answer

This answer requires an outline of the meaning of non-natural user as formulated under *Rylands v Fletcher* and an illustration of how the concept of non-natural user has enabled the courts to adopt a flexible approach and to adapt the application of the rule to changing circumstances time and place (*Read v Lyons*, where there are dicta to the effect that a munitions factory in time of war was a normal use of land).

In the past, domestic water supplies, household fires, electric wiring in houses and shops, the ordinary working of mines and minerals and the keeping of trees and shrubs (unless, perhaps, poisonous: *Crowhurst v Amersham Burial Board* (Ex., 1878)) have been held to be natural uses. In *Transco* (2003), the piping of a water supply to flats in a tower block constituted an ordinary use of the council's land.

There is no liability under the rule for an escape of something naturally upon the land. *Cambridge Water* made it clear that there is no liability for deliberate accumulations unless there has been a non-natural user by the defendant, which was defined in *Rickards v Lothian* (PC, 1913), in the following terms:

> "It must be some special use bringing with it increased danger to others, and must not merely be the ordinary use of land or such a use as is proper for the general benefit of the community."

The bulk storage of water, gas or electricity and the collection of sewage by a local authority have at various times been held non-natural. In *Mason v Levy Auto Parts of England Ltd* (HC, 1967), the concept of non-natural user was equated with that of abnormal risk, so that the court took account of the quantity of the accumulation of combustible material, the manner in which it was stored, and the character of the neighbourhood, and conceded that those considerations might equally have justified a finding of negligence. This approach was adopted in *LMS International Ltd v Styrene Packaging and Insulation Ltd* (2005) where the defendant's means of storing large quantities of flammable polystyrene "involved a very real risk" that a fire would spread to adjoining premises.

According to the original formulation of the rule, the defendant must have collected the thing "for his own purpose", but where the accumulation is for the public benefit for example, provision of a public service (*Dunne v North Western Gas Board* (CA, 1964)) or for ordinary manufacturing processes (*British Celanese Ltd v A. H. Hunt (Capacitors) Ltd* (HC, 1969)) the more modern tendency has been to deny the application of the rule.

The status of the above authorities will now have to be reconsidered in the light of Cambridge Water and in that case it was said that the storage of large quantities of chemicals on industrial premises was "an almost classic case of non-natural use" even in an industrial area. Furthermore, the fact that the chemical in question was commonly used in the particular industry, and that the defendants' operations served to support a local industrial community, was not sufficient to render the use natural.

Liability for Animals

. . . .

13

INTRODUCTION

Common law

A person may incur liability for damage caused by his animals in accordance with ordinary tort principles. Thus the crowing of cockerels may be actionable in nuisance (*Leeman v Montagu* (HC, 1936)), fox hunters may be liable in trespass if they cause their hounds to enter prohibited land (*League Against Cruel Sports Ltd v Scott* (HC, 1985)), and there have been numerous cases in which a person has been held liable in negligence because he owes the ordinary duty to take care that his animal is not put to such a use as is likely to injure his neighbour (*Lord Atkin in Fardon v Harcourt-Rivington* (HL, 1932)).

KEY CASE

LIABILITY FOR DAMAGE CAUSED BY ANIMALS
Draper v Hodder (CA, 1972) is a modern example of liability for animals where the defendant, whose terriers savaged the infant plaintiff, was held liable for failing to confine them. A defendant is generally not liable if animals naturally upon his land escape and do damage to his neighbour unless he was at fault in permitting their accumulation. However, since the decision in *Goldman v Hargrave* (PC, 1967) a defendant may be liable if, with knowledge of a potential threat (albeit not of his making), he fails to take reasonable steps to avert it.

Apart from the above, special rules relating to animals were developed at common law and these were modified by the Animals Act 1971. It should be noted that the Act, with which the remainder of this chapter is concerned, does not affect the availability of common law actions.

. . . .

STRICT LIABILITY FOR DANGEROUS ANIMALS

The keeper of an animal was strictly liable at common law for damage done by the animal if either it belonged to a dangerous species or it did not so belong but he knew of its vicious characteristics. The 1971 Act preserves the distinction between dangerous and non-dangerous species.

Animals belonging to a dangerous species

By s.2(1) of the Act the keeper of an animal belonging to a dangerous species is liable for any damage caused by it. A dangerous species (which, by s.11, includes sub-species and variety) is one which is not commonly domesticated in the British Islands and whose fully-grown animals normally have such characteristics that they are likely, unless restrained, to cause severe damage or that any damage they may cause is likely to be severe (s.6(2)). With regard to the first part of this definition, the fact that an animal may be commonly domesticated in some other part of the world where it is indigenous, such as a camel, does not affect its classification as a dangerous species (*Tutin v Chipperfield Promotions Ltd* (HC, 1980)). Furthermore, once a species has been so classified, the law takes no account of the fact that an individual animal within that species may in truth be harmless, so that the trained circus elephant is treated no differently to the wild elephant in the bush (*Behrens v Bertram Mills Circus* (HC, 1957)).

DEFINITION CHECKPOINT

As far as the latter part of the above definition is concerned, the species envisaged fall into two categories:

(1) Those animals which are by natural disposition ferocious.

(2) Those animals which although normally peaceful have a potential for causing severe damage. There is no definition of "severe" and, by s.11, "damage" includes the death of, or injury to, any person (including any disease and any impairment of physical or mental condition). Since this is not an exhaustive definition the generally accepted view is that "damage" should be given its normal meaning which is wide enough to include damage to property.

Strict liability is thus imposed by s.2(1) but there is no indication in the Act as to what the test for remoteness should be. It has been suggested that, as long as a causal link is established between the animal and the damage, there is no need for the damage to be of a kind normally associated with the animal's characteristics. Support for this view is to be found in *Tutin v Chipperfield Promotions Ltd* (HC, 1980) where the defendant was held liable for injuries suffered as a result of a fall from a swaying camel. It would therefore seem that the test is one of direct consequence rather than reasonable foresight.

LEGISLATION HIGHLIGHTER

Animals not belonging to a dangerous species

Strict liability is imposed by s.2(2) for harm done by animals not belonging to a dangerous species. Any animal not coming within the definition of dangerous species in s.6(2) falls into this category. The keeper is liable for damage caused by such an animal if:

(a) the damage is of a kind which the animal, unless restrained, was likely to cause or which, if caused by the animal, was likely to be severe; and

(b) the likelihood of the damage or of its being severe was due to characteristics of the animal which are not normally found in animals of the same species, or are not normally so found except at particular times or in particular circumstances; and

(c) those characteristics were known to the keeper or to any person in charge of the animal at the time as the keeper's servant or, where that keeper is the head of a household, were known to another keeper who is a member of that household and under the age of 16.

The operation of this section may be illustrated in the context of *Curtis v Betts* (CA, 1990), where the plaintiff was attacked and bitten by the defendant's bull mastiff (which was generally docile and indolent) as it was being transferred into the rear of the family car. With respect to (a) it was found that although the damage in question was not of a kind which this dog, unless restrained, was likely to cause, a bite from a bull mastiff was likely to be severe, thus satisfying the second limb of the paragraph. In relation to (b) it was found that the dog, in common with its breed generally, was territorially defensive, and that the likelihood of damage being severe was thus due to characteristics which would not normally be found in bull mastiffs except in particular circumstances (i.e. when defending what they regarded as their territory). The second limb of (b) was therefore satisfied and, since on the evidence the defendant knew of his dog's characteristics, he was liable under the Act even though not negligent. The earlier case of *Cummings v Granger* (CA, 1977) had similarly held that injuries suffered by a person who entered the domain of an Alsatian kept to guard premises fell within the second limb of (b).

INTERPRETATION OF S.2(2)(B)

In *Mirvahedy v Henleys* (2003), the House of Lords affirmed the interpretation of s.2(2)(b) adopted in *Curtis v Best* and *Cummings v Grainger* and held that horses which were inexplicably terrified and stampeded onto a busy road causing an accident were behaving in the usual way because of their panic and the owners were strictly liable.

In *Shirley McKaskie v John Cameron* (2009) (Unreported), the claimant suffered serious injuries when she was attacked by a herd of cows as she was walking close to the defendant farmer's footpath with her dog. At the time of the incident she had not appreciated the enhanced risk presented by cows with young calves or that they would act aggressively if they became stressed. The defendant was liable under s.2(2)(b) of the Act because the cows had calves at foot, which meant that they had unusual characteristics.

In *Smith v Ainger* (CA, 1990), the keeper of a dog with a known propensity to attack other dogs was held liable to a plaintiff who was knocked over and injured by the dog in the course of its attack upon the plaintiff's dog. In reaching this conclusion it was said that the word "likely" in (a) did not mean "more probable than not" but simply that there was a "material risk" that it would happen. Since there was a material risk that the owner of a dog being attacked would intervene to protect it, it followed that personal injury was likely to be caused within the meaning of the first limb of (a), and it was "unrealistic to distinguish between a bite and a buffet".

It is clear that the abnormal characteristics referred to in (b) do not mean that the animal must have a propensity to attack; nor need it escape from control (*Wallace v Newton* (HC, 1982)).

DEFINITION CHECKPOINT

The statutory provision also requires a comparison between the characteristics of the animal in question and those of animals of the same species (which includes sub-species and variety) thus:

- in considering the characteristics of an Alsatian dog the relevant comparison is with other Alsatians, not dogs generally (*Hunt v Wallis* (HC, 1991).
- in *Gloster v Chief Constable of Greater Manchester Police* (CA, 2000), the ability of the dog to respond to specific training and instruction was held to be the relevant characteristic and, since this is a characteristic of Alsatian dogs generally, there was no liability when an Alsatian dog, reacting to instructions, mistakenly attacked the claimant.

For the purposes of (c) the keeper must have actual, not merely constructive, knowledge of her animal's characteristics. Knowledge is however imputed to her where she is the head of a household and another keeper under the age of 16, being a member of that household, knew of those characteristics, or where a person in charge of the animal as the keeper's employee knew of them.

The keeper

Liability under s.2 is imposed upon the keeper who, by s.6(3), is the person who owns the animal or has it in her possession, or is the head of a household of which a member under the age of 16 owns it or has it in her possession. If a person ceases to own or have possession of the animal she will remain the keeper until such time as another person becomes the keeper. Thus, those who abandon unwanted pets do not thereby divest themselves of responsibility. A person who takes possession of an animal to prevent it from causing damage or to return it to its owner does not, merely by so doing, become a keeper.

Defences to liability under s.2

Apart from contributory negligence, which is preserved by s.10, s.5 of the Act contains a number of defences. Thus, there is no liability if the damage is wholly due to the claimant's fault (s.5(1)) or she voluntarily assumes the risk thereof (s.5(2)). The first of these defences will apply where, for example, the claimant deliberately provokes or teases the animal, or if she goes too close to its cage knowing that it is dangerous (*Marlor v Ball* (CA, 1900)). As far as the second is concerned, it should be noted that the Unfair Contract Terms Act 1977 does not apply to strict liability under the Animals Act so that a suitably worded notice may be sufficient to exclude liability. An important limitation upon the defence is that, by s.6(5), a keeper's employee is not to be treated as voluntarily accepting risks incidental to her employment. Section 5(3) applies to trespassers and provides that the keeper is not liable for damage done by an animal to persons trespassing upon the premises if either the animal was not kept there to protect persons or property or, if it was kept for that purpose, it was not unreasonable to do so. This does not affect the liability which a person may incur as an occupier under the Occupiers' Liability Act 1984 (see Ch.8).

The **Guard Dogs Act 1975** makes it a criminal offence to keep a guard dog on business premises (but not on agricultural land or land surrounding a private dwelling) unless either it is secured or under the control of a handler.

In *Cummings v Granger* (CA, 1977), Lord Denning said that a keeper who contravenes the 1975 Act is therefore unlikely to be able to claim the protection of s.5(3) since it is doubtful whether he could then be said to be acting reasonably. In that case the plaintiff had entered the defendant's scrap-yard as a trespasser knowing that an Alsatian roamed the premises as a guard dog. It was held that, although the damage was not wholly due to the plaintiff's fault, she had nevertheless voluntarily assumed the risk and was also defeated by the defence in s.5(3) (the cause of action arose before the passing of the Guard Dogs Act, so there was no question of the defendant's having committed an offence).

No mention is made in the Act of act of a stranger or act of God, so that these are not available defences

DOGS ATTACKING LIVESTOCK

Section 3 of the Animals Act imposes strict liability upon the keeper of a dog which causes damage by killing or injuring livestock. As well as the more common types of farm animal, "livestock" includes the domestic varieties of geese, ducks, guinea-fowl, pigeons, peacocks and quails, deer not in the wild state, and pheasants, partridges and grouse in captivity. As well as the defences in ss.10 and 5(1), it is a defence under s.5(4) that the livestock was killed or injured on land on to which it had strayed and the dog belonged to the occupier or its presence was authorised by him.

There is a defence in s.9 of the Act to an action for killing or injuring a dog. The defendant must prove that he acted for the protection of livestock and was entitled to do so, and that within 48 hours he notified the police. A person is entitled to act for the protection of either the livestock or the land on which it is belongs to him, or if he is acting under the express or implied authority of such a person.

DEFINITION CHECKPOINT

A person acts for their protection only if either of the following conditions (satisfied by reasonable belief on her part (s.9(4)) applies:

(a) the dog is worrying or is about to worry the livestock and there are no other reasonable means of ending or preventing the worrying; or

(b) the dog has been worrying livestock, has not left the vicinity, is not under anyone's control, and there are no practicable means of ascertaining to whom it belongs.

For the purpose of this section, the Act provides that livestock belongs to a person who owns or has it in his possession and land belongs to the occupier thereof (s.9(5)).

The defence in s.9 applies only to the protection of livestock from marauding dogs, so that if damage is caused to property by other animals (for example homing pigeons eating crops as in *Hamps v Darby* (CA, 1948)), or if for some reason the statutory provisions are not satisfied, the defendant may fall back on the common law as laid down in *Cresswell v Sirl* (CA, 1948). This entitles the defendant to take punitive action if the animal is actually attacking her property or there is imminent danger that it will renew an attack already made, and it is reasonable in the circumstances for the protection of that property to kill it.

STRAYING LIVESTOCK

Livestock straying on to another's land

By s.4(1) of the Act, where livestock belonging to any person strays on to land owned or occupied by another and causes damage to the land or property in the ownership or possession of the other person, the person to whom the livestock belongs is liable for the damage. She is also liable for reasonable expenses incurred by the other person in keeping the livestock while it cannot be restored to the person to whom it belongs or while it is detained in pursuance of s.7 (see below), or in ascertaining to whom it belongs.

DEFINITION CHECKPOINT

The definition of livestock in s.11 is slightly narrower than for the purposes of s.3 and s.9 since it does not include captive pheasants, partridges or grouse.

Livestock belongs to the possessor thereof, so that the owner out of possession, such as a finance company which has bailed the beasts under a hire-purchase agreement, is not liable. There is no liability under this section for personal injuries or third party property damage, which means that if such damage is caused the action must be brought either in negligence or, if appropriate, under s.2(2) of the Act.

Defences

The defences laid down in ss.10 and 5(1) apply but, so far as the latter is concerned, s.5(6) provides that damage is not to be treated as due to the fault of the person suffering it by reason only that he could have prevented it by fencing. If, however, any person having an interest in the land is in breach of a duty to fence, the defendant is not liable if the livestock would not have strayed but for that breach. It is plain from the statutory wording that the duty, if such there be, need not be owed by the claimant, nor need it be owed to the defendant. A final common law defence is preserved by s.5(5), which states that there is no liability for damage done by livestock which strays from the highway so long as its presence on the highway was lawful. This is not to say that a defendant may not be liable for negligence in such circumstances (*Gayler and Pope Ltd v B. Davies & Son Ltd* (HC, 1924)).

Detention and sale of straying livestock

An occupier on to whose land livestock has strayed has a right under, and subject to the conditions of, s.7 to detain, and ultimately to sell, the livestock to recover the cost of damage done to his property.

. . . .

STRAYING ON THE HIGHWAY

The common law immunity in respect of damage caused by animals straying on to the highway from adjacent land is abolished by s.8(1) of the Animals Act with the result that liability is now determined in accordance with ordinary negligence principles.

▊ DEFINITION CHECKPOINT
A landowner is not necessarily obliged to fence his land, and if he does not, important factors in deciding whether he has been negligent are the prevailing traffic conditions, whether any warning has been given, and what users of the highway ought reasonably to expect.

In particular, by s.8(2), if he has a right to place his animals on unfenced land a defendant will not be in breach of a duty of care merely by placing them there, so long as the land is in an area where fencing is not customary or is common land or is a town or village green.

Revision Checklist

By the end of this chapter you should understand:

- a person may incur liability for damage caused by his animals in accordance with ordinary tort principles;

- a defendant is generally not liable if animals naturally upon his land escape and do damage to his neighbour unless he was at fault in permitting their accumulation;

- the Animals Act 1971 provides that the keeper of an animal belonging to a dangerous species is liable for any damage caused by it;

- a dangerous species is one which is not commonly domesticated in the British Islands and whose fully-grown animals normally have such characteristics that they are likely, unless restrained, to cause severe damage or that any damage they may cause is likely to be severe.

QUESTION AND ANSWER

Consider the approach of the courts to claims for damage caused by an animal of a non-dangerous species.

The Animals Act 1971 s.2(2) imposes strict liability for harm done by animals not belonging to a dangerous species. The factors taken into account are:

(a) whether the damage is of a kind which the animal, unless restrained, was likely to cause;

(b) whether the damage, if caused, is likely to be severe;

(c) whether the likelihood of the damage being caused or being severe was due to characteristics of the animal not normally found in animals of the same species or not normally found except at particular times or in particular circumstances;

(d) whether those characteristics were known to the keeper or were at any time known to a person who at that time had charge of the animal as that keeper's servant or were known to another keeper of the animal who is a member of that household and under 16 years of age. In *Mirvahedy v Henleys* (2003), the House of Lords interpreted s.2(2)(b) and held the keeper liable for the behaviour of a horse that bolted and exhibited a characteristic which is not normal for an animal of that species, but which was normal in the circumstances because of horse's panic.

Vicarious Liability

14

INTRODUCTION

The general rule is that one who expressly authorises or ratifies a tort is personally liable, but there are circumstances in which a person is liable for the torts of another even in the absence of such authorisation or ratification. The liability which thus arises is known as vicarious liability and the most common example of it is the liability of an employer/master for the torts of its employees committed in the course of their employment.

EMPLOYER AND EMPLOYEE (FORMERLY MASTER AND SERVANT)

It is not necessary, for the purposes of the doctrine, that the employer be in breach of any duty owed to the injured party (who may himself be either a fellow-employee or a stranger). What is required is that the wrongdoer be an employee and the wrong done in connection with what he is employed to do. The modern justification for the doctrine is that the employer is better able to pay because he will insure against such liability, the cost of which is reflected in the price charged for his goods and services. It is also said to act as an inducement to the employer to promote high standards of safety within his organisation.

The meaning of employee (servant)
An employee is employed under a contract of service, an independent contractor under a contract for services, but this does not explain the essential distinction between the two types of contract.

DEFINITION CHECKPOINT

No single test has yet been devised which is capable of application in all cases, and even the express declaration of the parties as to the nature of their contract is simply one factor to be taken into account (*Ferguson v John Dawson & Partners (Contractors) Ltd* (CA, 1976).

- If the employer controls not only the type of work to be done but also the manner in which it is to be done, that points to a contract of service; but this so-called "control" test has, especially where the task to be performed requires a high degree of skill or expertise, lost much of its use, for the employee will in practice frequently be left to decide for himself how best to carry out the job.
- In *Stevenson, Jordan and Harrison Ltd v Macdonald and Evans* (CA, 1952), Denning L.J. suggested that, under a contract of service, the employee's work is done as an integral part of the business, whereas under a contract for services his work is not integrated into the business but is merely accessory to it.

In *Ready Mixed Concrete (South East) Ltd v Minister of Pensions and National Insurance* (HC, 1968), it was held that three conditions must be fulfilled for a contract of service to exist. First, the servant agrees, in consideration of a wage or other remuneration, to provide his own work and skill in the performance of some service for his master; secondly, he agrees to be subject to the other's control to such degree as to make that other the master; thirdly, the other provisions of the contract are consistent with its being a contract of service. A different approach was adopted in *Market Investigations Ltd v Minister of Social Security* (HC, 1969), where it was suggested that the basic test is whether the worker is performing the service as a person in business on his own account. In answering this question it is relevant to consider whether the person uses his own premises and equipment, whether he hires his own helpers, the degree of financial risk he takes and the degree of responsibility, if any, which he has for investment and management. Although this approach has been followed in later cases, judicial warnings have been given that the test is not of itself to be regarded as conclusive of the question. All that can be said is that there is no exhaustive category of matters relevant in deciding the issue, and what is regarded as the crucial factor in one case may well be outweighed by different considerations in another.

Lending an employee

A particular problem is that of lending an employee, for the difficulty then arises as to who is the employer for the purposes of vicarious liability. In *Mersey Docks and Harbour Board v Coggins and Griffith (Liverpool) Ltd* (HL,

1947), the Board hired a crane driver, together with his crane, to X, under a contract which provided that the driver was to be the servant of X. In the course of working the crane the driver negligently injured a third party. Although X had, at the time, the immediate direction and control of what was to be done, they had no power to direct how the crane should be worked. Furthermore, the driver continued to be paid by the Board, which alone had the right to dismiss him. It was held that, notwithstanding the terms of the hire contract, the Board had failed to discharge the heavy burden of proof to shift responsibility for the driver's negligence onto X. This case establishes no universal test but Lord Porter said that factors for consideration are who is paymaster, who can dismiss, how long the alternative service lasts and what machinery is employed.

DEFINITION CHECKPOINT
Where an employee was lent by one employer to another
<ul><li>*Mersey Docks* shows that the degree of control exercised by the respective employers is clearly important and that the right to control is more readily transferred in the case of an unskilled servant.</li><li>In *Viasystems Ltd v Thermal Transfer Ltd* (2005), however, where both employers were vicariously liable, the Court of Appeal held that entire and absolute control of the employee was not a precondition of vicarious liability. It had previously been assumed that where an employee was lent by one employer to another, vicarious liability for the employee's negligence had to rest with one employer or the other, but not both.</li></ul>

The course of employment

For the employer to be liable, the wrong must be committed in the course of the employee's employment. This will be the case where what the employee does is authorised by the employer, or is an unauthorised way of doing that which he is employed to do. Whether or not the act is done in the course of employment is a question of fact, and the modern trend has been to adopt a liberal approach. Thus, a tanker driver who, whilst delivering petrol, lit a cigarette and carelessly discarded a match causing a fire, was held to be acting within the course of his employment. It was said that the act of lighting the cigarette, whilst not in itself connected with his job, could not be looked at in isolation from the surrounding circumstances (*Century Insurance Co Ltd v Northern Ireland Road Transport Board* (HL, 1942)).

DEFINITION CHECKPOINT

Where the employee's act is wholly unconnected to the job for which he is employed, he is said to be "on a frolic of his own" and the employer is not liable.

- In *Beard v London General Omnibus Co* (CA, 1900), the employer of a bus conductor who, in the absence of the driver, negligently drove the bus himself was held not liable.
- This may be contrasted with *Kay v ITW Ltd* (CA, 1968) where the employee attempted to move a lorry belonging to another firm because it was blocking the entrance to his employer's warehouse to which he had been instructed to return a fork-lift truck. It was held that, since the attempted removal of the obstruction was done in order that the servant could complete his own task, the employer was vicariously liable.

On the other hand, it was held in *General Engineering Services Ltd v Kingston and St Andrew Corp* (PC, 1988) that firemen operating a "go-slow" policy who took five times as long as they normally would have done to drive to the scene of a fire (with the result that the plaintiff's premises were destroyed) were not within the course of employment. The courts have been faced with problems where the employee's act has been expressly prohibited. In principle, if the prohibition amounts to a restriction on the class of acts which the employee is employed to do, the employer is not liable; but he is liable if the prohibition relates merely to a mode of performing the employment. So an employee who, contrary to written instructions, raced his employer's bus with that of a rival company was held to be within the course of his employment (*Limpus v London General Omnibus Co* (HC, 1862)).

DEFINITION CHECKPOINT

Cases which have dealt with the problem of the giving of lifts to unauthorised passengers

- In *Twine v Bean's Express Ltd* (CA, 1946), it was held that such an act was outside the course of employment, though the view was expressed that, in so far as injury to persons other than the passenger was concerned, the driver would be within the course of his employment.
- Where a driver's foreman consented to the passenger's presence in the vehicle, however, the employer was held liable because the foreman, of whose lack of actual authority the passenger was unaware, was nonetheless acting within the scope of his apparent authority (*Young v Edward Box & Co Ltd* (CA, 1951)).
- The decision in *Twine's* case is not easy to reconcile with *Rose v*

> *Plenty* (CA, 1976) where a milkman, in allowing a young boy onto his float to help him with his milk round in contravention of his employer's instructions, was held to be within the course of his employment when the boy fell off and was injured. The majority of the court distinguished the earlier case on the ground that the engagement of the boy was done in furtherance of the master's business.

There are cases where the employee's act, although not part of his regular employment as such, is necessarily incidental to it. In *Staton v National Coal Board* (HC, 1957), for example, an employee cycling to the pay office on his employer's land to collect his pay after work had finished was held to be within the course of his employment. But whilst employment may start as soon as the employee enters his employer's premises, those travelling to or from work are not usually considered to be in the course of employment, unless, of course, they are travelling specifically on the employer's business or on some errand which is incidental to it. Thus, a driver who deviates from his route for the purpose of getting a meal may still be within the course of employment (*Harvey v R. G. O'Dell Ltd* (HC, 1958); cf. *Hilton v Thomas Burton (Rhodes) Ltd* (HC, 1961)). In *Smith v Stages* (HL, 1989), a worker travelling between home and a temporary workplace, and who was paid wages during that time, was held to be within the course of employment, notwithstanding that he might have a discretion as to the mode and time of travel.

An employer who uses force in the mistaken but honest belief that he is protecting his employer's property does an act incidental to his employment rendering the employer liable (*Poland v John Parr & Sons* (CA, 1927)). Clearly, though, punishment administered during the course of a private altercation which ensues after the need to protect the master's property no longer exists is not within the course of employment (*Warren v Henlys Ltd* (HC, 1948; (*Mattis v Pollock* (CA 2003).

Intentional wrongful acts—the "close connection" test

In *Lister v Hesley Hall Ltd* (HL, 2002), the House of Lords said the proper approach to the course of employment is no longer to ask the simplistic question of whether the acts were modes of doing authorised acts in the course of employment. A broad assessment should be adopted and the relevant question is whether the torts were so closely connected with the employment that it would be fair and just to hold the employers liable.

KEY CASE

A BROAD ASSESSMENT TO DETERMINE WHETHER THE ACTS WERE SO CLOSELY CONNECTED WITH THE EMPLOYMENT THAT IT WOULD BE FAIR AND JUST TO HOLD THE EMPLOYERS LIABLE.

Lister v Hesley Hall Ltd concerned a warden at the defendants' school for boys with emotional and behavioural difficulties who had subjected the claimants to systematic sexual abuse. It was held that the defendants had entrusted the care of the children to the warden and his torts had been so closely connected with his employment that it would be fair just to hold the defendants vicariously liable. An earlier case, *Trotman v North Yorkshire CC* (CA 1999), where an employer was found not to be vicariously liable for a teacher who used school trips to commit sexual assault on the ground he was not acting in the course of employment, was declared to be wrongly decided.

The broader approach in *Lister v Hesley Hall* was applied by the Court of Appeal in *Mattis v Pollock* (CA, 2003) where the owner of a nightclub was held vicariously liable to the claimant who suffered paraplegia following a stabbing by a doorman employed by the nightclub. The doorman, who had started a fight in the nightclub, went home to arm himself with a knife and returned to the vicinity of the club where he stabbed the claimant. The stabbing was found to be directly linked to the incident which had gone before and was so closely connected with what the doorman was expected to do that it fell within the scope of his employment. The "close connection" test was applied by the House of Lords in *Dubai Aluminium v Salaam* (2003) to include, not just intentional torts, but also breaches of equitable duty which were so closely connected with the acts that the employee was authorised to do in the course of the firm's business.

DEFINITION CHECKPOINT

The intense focus on the connection between the nature of employment and the tort committed was further emphasised in the following cases:

- In *Gravil v Carroll* (2008), where the wrongful act of a rugby player during a match was so "closely connected" with his employment that his club was vicariously liable.
- In *Ministry of Defence v Radclyffe* (2009), the *Ministry of Defence* was vicariously liable for the negligence of an officer who urged Radclyffe to jump from a bridge during an adventure training exercise in Germany. The connection between the nature of his

employment as an officer in the army and his breach of duty was held to be well within the *Lister* test.
- In *MAGA v The Trustees of the Birmingham Archdiocese of the Roman Catholic Church* (2010), the close connection test was considered in the case of a Catholic priest purporting to carry out his work as a priest when his true motive was to abuse the claimant (a non-Catholic boy who at no time had anything to do with the Church itself). Lord Neuberger in the Court of Appeal said there was no doubt that the claimant's case was weaker than that of the claimant in *Lister*—he concluded that the test laid down by Lord Steyn in *Lister was* satisfied.

The extent of an employer's liability for an employee who acts dishonestly for his own benefit had previously been considered in *Morris v C. W. Martin & Sons Ltd* (CA, 1966), where the defendants' employee stole a coat entrusted to him for cleaning. Whether, as was suggested, the defendants were in breach of their primary duty as bailees, they could equally have been regarded as vicariously liable for their employee's wrongful mode of performing that which he was employed to do, namely to keep the coat safe for its owner. A different problem emerges where the employee abuses his position for fraudulent purposes. In this case, if an employer makes it appear to third parties that the employee has authority to do acts of the type in question, he may be estopped from denying that the employee had any authority in fact. It is not enough that the employee's employment provides an opportunity for the commission of the wrong. The essential feature is that it is the position in which the employer places his employee that enables him to perpetrate the fraud whilst acting within the scope of the authority that he appears to have.

KEY CASES

THE ESSENTIAL FEATURE IS THAT IT IS THE POSITION IN WHICH THE EMPLOYER PLACES HIS EMPLOYEE THAT ENABLES HIM TO PERPETRATE THE FRAUD WHILST ACTING WITHIN THE SCOPE OF THE AUTHORITY THAT HE APPEARS TO HAVE.
- In *Lloyd v Grace Smith & Co* (HL, 1912), solicitors were held liable for the fraud of their managing clerk in inducing the plaintiff to execute documents which he falsely stated were necessary to effect a sale of her cottages, but which amounted to a conveyance of the property to himself.
- The House of Lords in *Dubai Aluminium v Salaam* (2003) held that the personal innocence of the other co-partners could not be taken

into account when determining their vicarious liability for the dishonest partner. According to Lord Millet, the mere fact that the employee was acting dishonestly or for his own benefit is seldom likely to be sufficient to show that an employee was not acting within the course of employment.

If the claimant is unaware that the fraudulent employee is the defendant's employee he cannot claim to have relied upon the employee's apparent authority and the defendant will not be liable unless, of course, the employee was within the scope of his actual authority (*Kooragang Investments Pty Ltd v Richardson & Wrench Ltd* (PC, 1982)).

Liability under Protection from Harassment Act 1997
Vicarious liability is not restricted to common law claims.

KEY CASE

VICARIOUS LIABILITY UNDER STATUTE
In *Majrowski v Guy's and St Thomas's NHS Trust* (2006), a former employee claimed that he had been bullied, intimidated and harassed by his departmental manager, acting in the course of her employment. He claimed for damages against the NHS Trust for breach of statutory duty under the Protection from Harassment Act 1997. The House of Lords dismissed the NHS Trust's appeal and held that an employer might be vicariously liable for a breach of statutory duty imposed on its employee, if in all the circumstances of the case, the test of fairness and justice was met and the connection between the employee's breach of duty and the nature of the employment was sufficient.

This means that an employer may be vicariously liable under the Act for breach of a statutory duty *imposed on the employee*, but not upon the employer directly, where it is fair and just to impose a duty and where there is a close connection between the acts of harassment and the nature of the employment. *Majrowski* was applied in *Green v DB Group Services Ltd* (2006) where a former employee claimed against her employer for damages arising from her psychiatric injury as the result of a campaign of workplace bullying and intimidation by her fellow employees. The conduct in question also constituted harassment within the meaning of the Protection from Harassment Act 1997 and, since the connection between the nature of the employment of the perpetrators and their acts of harassment was so close, it was just and reasonable to hold the employer liable for it.

Joint liability

Where an employee commits a tort in the course of his employment both he and his employer are liable as joint tortfeasors. This means that if the employer satisfies the judgment he may be able to claim contribution from his employee under the Civil Liability (Contribution) Act 1978.

▌DEFINITION CHECKPOINT

An employer may (at least in theory) be able to recover from his employee under the principle in *Lister v Romford Ice and Cold Storage Co Ltd* (HL, 1957)

Here, damages equivalent to an indemnity were awarded to an employer, who, having met the plaintiff's claim, sued his negligent employee for breach of an implied term of his employment contract that he would exercise reasonable care. In practice, however, the Lister principle is virtually defunct in view of an undertaking by employers' liability insurers that they would not seek to recover from an individual employee except where there was evidence of collusion or wilful misconduct.

. . . .

INDEPENDENT CONTRACTORS

In general, an employer is not vicariously liable for the negligence of an independent contractor in carrying out his work. He is of course liable if he authorises or ratifies the tort, as he is if he is personally negligent, for example by selecting an incompetent contractor or failing to give proper instructions or supervision. In addition, he may be under a non-delegable duty of care which cannot be discharged merely by entrusting performance to a contractor. It is worth noting that liability in all of these instances is not vicarious but arises as a result of a breach of a primary duty owed by the employer to the plaintiff. The remainder of this section deals with the employer's so-called non-delegable duties.

Common law

1. Withdrawal of support from neighbouring land

Where one of two adjoining landowners is entitled to support from the other and that other, either himself or through his contractor, undermines that support causing damage to his neighbour's land or building, he is liable (*Bower v Peate* (HC, 1876)). This principle was extended in *Alcock v Wraith* (CA, 1991) to impose a duty on the owner of a house who, in order to repair his roof, necessarily had to interfere with the integrity of his neighbour's roof.

2. Operations on the highway

Where a contractor is employed to do work on or adjoining the highway which creates a danger to users of the highway, the employer remains liable. So, in *Tarry v Ashton* (HC, 1876), where a contractor negligently fitted a lamp to the side of a house with the result that it fell and injured a passer-by, the employer was held liable. Although this principle applies to dangers created in any place along which the public may lawfully pass, no liability attaches to a person using the highway merely for the purposes of lawful passage. Thus, if a motor vehicle is negligently repaired by a contractor, the owner is not liable for an accident caused by the unroadworthy state of the vehicle (*Phillips v Britannia Hygienic Laundry Co Ltd* (HC, 1923)). Nor is there liability in respect of work carried out near the highway. In *Salsbury v Woodland* (CA, 1970), the employer was held not liable when his contractor negligently cut down a tree in his front garden and, in so doing, fouled some telephone wires which collapsed onto the highway and caused an accident.

3. Employer's duty to employee

The non-delegable nature of this common law duty is dealt with in Ch.7.

4. Extra-hazardous activities

Where the contractor's work, by its very nature, involves a special danger to others, it seems that the employer will be liable for the contractor's default.

KEY CASE

EXTRA-HAZARDOUS ACTIVITIES

In *Honeywill and Stein Ltd v Larkin Bros Ltd* (CA, 1934), the defendants were held liable where the contractors, whom they had employed to take photographs inside a theatre, negligently caused a fire in their use of magnesium flash powder. This principle probably applies only to acts involving the use of things regarded in law as "dangerous in themselves," of which fire and explosives are obvious examples. Since there is nothing inherently dangerous in the operation of felling a tree, *Salsbury v Woodland* (CA, 1970) was held not to come within this head of liability.

5. Nuisance, Rylands v Fletcher and fire

The extent of an employer's liability in these instances is dealt with in Chs 11 and 12.

6. Other cases

There seems to be no general principle which can be extracted from the examples discussed, and the courts may come to recognise new types of case giving rise to a non-delegable duty. An illustration is *Rogers v Night Riders* (CA, 1983), in which the plaintiff was injured when the door of a mini-cab flew open. Although the vehicle was owned and maintained by the driver, an independent contractor, the mini-cab firm was nevertheless held to be in breach of a primary duty owed to the plaintiff.

Statutory duties

Where a statute imposes an obligation upon a person to do a particular thing, he cannot escape liability by delegation to an independent contractor. If the statute empowers a person to do something which would otherwise be unlawful, that person will generally be liable for the negligence of his contractor (*Hardaker v Idle DC* (CA, 1896)). The precise nature of the duty depends, however, upon the construction of the Act.

Causal or collateral negligence

It is the nature of the work, and not merely the performance of it, which may cast upon the employer a non-delegable duty. He is therefore not liable for the causal or collateral negligence of his independent contractor because that does not involve him in any breach of duty. Collateral negligence is negligence purely incidental to the particular act the contractor was employed to do. Thus, in *Padbury v Holliday and Greenwood Ltd* (CA, 1912) the defendants were not liable when their sub-contractor, in fixing a casement, negligently left a tool on the window sill which the wind blew onto a passer-by below. By contrast, in *Holliday v National Telephone Co* (CA, 1899), the defendants employed a plumber to carry out work on the highway. The plumber negligently dipped his blowlamp into molten solder and the plaintiff was injured in the ensuing explosion. Reversing the decision of the Divisional Court, the Court of Appeal held the employer liable, though the distinction between this and the Padbury case is not easy to see.

VEHICLE OWNERS

A vehicle owner who allows another to drive it in his presence makes such a person his agent and is liable for his negligent driving. So too, if a person has authority to drive on behalf of, or for the purposes of, the owner, the latter is vicariously liable for his negligence even though not himself present in the vehicle (*Ormrod v Crosville Motor Services Ltd* (CA, 1953)).

KEY CASE

The leading case of **LAUNCHBURY V MORGANS** (HL, 1973) establishes that the owner is not liable simply for permitting another to use the vehicle for his own purposes. It must be shown that the driver was using it for the owner's purposes under delegation of some task or duty, and the mere fact that the owner has an interest in the safety of the vehicle's occupants is not sufficient.

According to *Norwood v Navan* (CA, 1981), a wife who uses her husband's car to go on a shopping expedition is not acting for his purposes under delegation of a task or duty so as to make him vicariously liable.

Revision Checklist

By the end of this chapter you should understand:

- the tests used to distinguish between an employer and an independent contractor;

- vicarious liability imposes liability on an employer for the tort of its employee without the need to prove fault on the part of the employer;

- the *Lister* test of whether an employee is acting in the course of employment and its application in subsequent cases;

- where an employee's acts of harassment in breach of a statutory duty imposed on the employee meets the "close connection" test, the employer could be vicariously liable (*Majrowski*).

QUESTION AND ANSWER

Question

Mediplus plc employs Andy as a medical sales representative and Elvira as an accountant. Although both Andy and Elvira have been repeatedly warned that Andy was not permitted to carry passengers in the company's car, he frequently gave Elvira a lift home from work. As Andy was about to leave Mediplus premises one evening, he was informed of an outbreak of a flu pandemic and instructed to deliver a supply of the anti-flu vaccine to the local hospital as a matter of urgency. He left work with the intention of delivering the anti-flu vaccine on his way home but Elvira was waiting by his car for a lift home that evening so he gave her a lift. As Andy drove at high speed through the town the car crashed into a wall. Elvira was so upset when she discovered that she had broken two of her teeth in the crash that she began to remonstrate with Andy and accused him of 'reckless' driving. Andy lost his temper and struck Elvira a severe blow to the head.

Discuss the liability (if any) of Mediplus in respect of the above incidents.

Elivra will seek to claim that Mediplus is vicariously liable for: (1) her broken teeth which resulted from Andy's negligent driving and (2) her head injuries which resulted from his criminal wrongdoing. We are told that Andy is an employee of Mediplus so the first of the conditions for vicarious liability has been met. The torts have also been committed, so the next question in determining whether Mediplus will be liable is whether the wrongs were committed in the course of Andy's employment. This will be the case where the employee does something authorised by the employer, or is an unauthorised way of doing that which he is employed to do. Where the employee's act is wholly unconnected to the job for which he is employed, he is said to be "on a frolic of his own" and the employer is not liable. In *Beard v London General Omnibus Co* (1900), the employer of a bus conductor who, in the absence of the driver, negligently drove the bus himself was held not liable. This may be contrasted with *Kay v ITW Ltd* (CA, 1968) where the employer was liable when the employee's tort was committed as he tried to remove an obstruction so that he could complete his own task.

Cases where the employee's act has been expressly prohibited (*Limpus v London General Omnibus Co* (1862); *Rose v Plenty* (CA, 1976)) and cases where giving of lifts to unauthorised passengers were at issue (*Twine v Bean's Express Ltd* (1946)) will need to be discussed. The question of whether Andy's deviation from his route takes him outside the course of employment will need to be considered (*Harvey v R. G. O'Dell Ltd* (1958) and *Hilton v Thomas Burton Ltd* (1961)).

In the context of Andy's criminal conduct, Mediplus will seek to establish that this behaviour took him outside the scope of employment and rely on *Lister v Hesley Hall Ltd* (2002). The House of Lords said the proper approach to the course of employment is no longer to ask the simplistic question of whether the acts were modes of doing authorised acts in the course of employment and the relevant question is whether the torts were so closely connected with the employment that it would be fair and just to hold the employers liable. *Lister v Hesley Hall* was applied by the Court of Appeal in *Mattis v Pollock* (2003), where the owner of a nightclub was held vicariously liable to the claimant who suffered paraplegia following a stabbing by a doorman employed by the nightclub. The stabbing was found to be directly linked to the incident which had gone before and was so closely connected with what the doorman was expected to do that it fell within the scope of his employment. On this basis, Mediplus will argue that Andy's conduct was not connected with what he is employed to do and they are not therefore vicariously liable.

Index

This index has been prepared using Sweet and Maxwell's Legal Taxonomy. Main index entries conform to keywords provided by the Legal Taxonomy except where references to specific documents or non-standard terms (denoted by quotation marks) have been included. These keywords provide a means of identifying similar concepts in other Sweet & Maxwell publications and online services to which keywords from the Legal Taxonomy have been applied. Readers may find some minor differences between terms used in the text and those which appear in the index.

(all references are to page numbers)